CHARLES DICKENS AND THE VICTORIAN CHILD

This book explores the ideas of children and childhood, and the construct of the 'ideal' Victorian child that rapidly develop over the Victorian era along with literacy and reading material for the emerging mass reading public. Children's Literature was one of the developing areas for publishers and readers alike, yet this did not stop the reading public from bringing home works not expressly intended for children and reading to their family. Within the idealized middle class family circle, authors such as Charles Dickens were read and appreciated by members of all ages. By examining some of Dickens's works that contain the imperfect child, and placing them alongside works by Kingsley, MacDonald, Stretton, Rossetti, and Nesbit, Malkovich considers the construction, romanticization, and socialization of the Victorian child within work read by and for children during the Victorian Era and early Edwardian period. These authors use elements of religion, death, irony, fairy worlds, gender, and class to illustrate the need for the ideal child and yet the impossibility of such a construct. Malkovich contends that we still long for the Victorian child within our literatures, and while debates rage over how to define children's literature, such children, though somewhat changed, can still be found in the most popular of literatures read by children contemporarily.

Amberyl Malkovich is Assistant Professor of British Literature, Children's and Young Adult Literature and Gender & Cultural Studies at Concord University, USA.

CHARLES DICKENS AND THE VICTORIAN CHILD

Romanticizing and Socializing the Imperfect Child

AMBERYL MALKOVICH

Routledge
Taylor & Francis Group

NEW YORK AND LONDON

First published 2013
by Routledge
711 Third Avenue, New York, NY 10017

Simultaneously published in the UK
by Routledge
2 Park Square, Milton Park, Abingdon, Oxfordshire OX14 4RN

First issued in paperback 2014

Routledge is an imprint of the Taylor & Francis Group, an informa business

Library of Congress Cataloging in Publication Data
Malkovich, Amberyl, 1974–
    Charles Dickens and the Victorian child : romanticizing and socializing the imperfect child / by Amberyl Malkovich.
        p. cm. — (Children's literature and culture)
    Includes bibliographical references and index.
    1.   Dickens, Charles, 1812–1870—Criticism and interpretation.   2.   Children in literature.   I. Title.
    PR4592.C46M35 2012
    823'.8—dc23
    2012032513

ISBN: 978-0-415-89908-6 (hbk)
ISBN: 978-1-138-85078-1 (pbk)

Typeset in Minion
by IBT Global.

*To the memory of my grandparents, father and uncle who guided
my days and inspired an unending love of learning and to my Uncle
Rick and his passion for family.*

For Zachary, with all my love.

Contents

Figures

Series Editor's Foreword

Dedicated to furthering original research in children's literature and culture, the Children's Literature and Culture series includes monographs on individual authors and illustrators, historical examinations of different periods, literary analyses of genres, and comparative studies on literature and the mass media. The series is international in scope and is intended to encourage innovative research in children's literature with a focus on interdisciplinary methodology.

Children's literature and culture are understood in the broadest sense of the term *children* to encompass the period of childhood up through adolescence. Owing to the fact that the notion of childhood has changed so much since the origination of children's literature, this Routledge series is particularly concerned with transformations in children's culture and how they have affected the representation and socialization of children. While the emphasis of the series is on children's literature, all types of studies that deal with children's radio, film, television, and art are included in an endeavor to grasp the aesthetics and values of children's culture. Not only have there been momentous changes in children's culture in the last fifty years, but there have been radical shifts in the scholarship that deals with these changes. In this regard, the goal of the Children's Literature and Culture series is to enhance research in this field and, at the same time, point to new directions that bring together the best scholarly work throughout the world.

Jack Zipes

Acknowledgments

The amount of time and effort that goes into the writing process cannot be properly qualified. Likewise, the writing process is never fully accomplished by the writer alone. To the valuable Routledge team, especially Jack Zipes, I am very grateful for all of your support and guidance through this experience. I would like to thank a wonderful teacher, scholar, and advisor, Dr. Jan Susina, for his suggestions and advice on this project. I would also like to thank Dr. Louisa Smith for her guidance, Bertram, and, most importantly, friendship. Equal thanks are owed to Dr. Nancy Tolson, who has been an inspirational teacher and colleague both in and out of the classroom. Likewise, I am indebted to Ms. Carmen Durrani for the endless hours of shared travel and wonderful companionship. Dr. Robert Niedringhaus deserves my express gratitude for all of his time and dedication. Your work and accomplishments never cease to amaze me. Thank you for everything you have done for all of your patients. To my two dear friends, Beryl Wagner and Russ Nelson, I'd like to extend an especial thank you for editing advice, road tripping, and for having a of love of literature that equals my own. I am also very thankful for the helpful suggestions NaToya Faughnder provided on the manuscript. Next time, the chowder is on me. I will ever be grateful to my friends, colleagues and students who have enriched this experience.

Many members of The Dickens Society have been helpful and encouraging throughout this process. I wish I had space to thank you all individually. I'd also like to express my gratitude to the many scholars, critics, and colleagues, some of whom I've known personally and others who have been equally inspiring along the way: Kathryn Graham, J. D. Stahl, Robin Carr, Bill Dyer, Donna Casella, Mary Poovey, Cynthia Huff, Ronald Fortune, James Kincaid, Stephen Prickett, Ruth Richardson, Kenneth Kidd, Richard Flynn, Judith Butler, Julia Briggs, and Richard Altick. Most importantly, my greatest thanks are to Zachary for treading this road with me, getting to know Dickens, and supporting each and every keystroke.

Extract of "The Fairy School," published in Thomas Keightley's *The World Guide to Gnomes, Fairies, Elves, and Other Little People* (1880). Rpt. in *Harper's*

Introduction

As Oliver Twist flees from a crime he has not committed, the words "Stop thief!" echo down a Victorian London street. By trying to escape the screaming mob, Oliver becomes labeled as a common criminal. Yet, as is presented in both George Cruikshank's 1837 illustration "Oliver amazed at the Dodger's Mode of 'going to work,' " and Roman Polanski's 2005 film version of the beloved Charles Dickens's (1812–1870) classic *Oliver Twist* (1837), in this scene Oliver is being severed from his life of poverty for the first time as he tries to escape not only the robbery victim, Mr. Brownlow, but also the mob of onlookers that gather to claim him. While Dickens indicates the true thieves of Mr. Brownlow's handkerchief, Artful Dodger and Charley Bates, have simply left the scene of the crime (*Oliver Twist* 117), Polanski depicts them in flight from it altogether. As Oliver tries to explain to a policeman, "It wasn't me indeed, sir. Indeed, it was two other boys" (*Oliver Twist* 117), Artful Dodger and Charley Bates " . . . filed off down the first convenient court they came to" (*Oliver Twist* 117). In both cases, his new friends abandon Oliver to his fate. A carriage, Polanski's representation of the separation of Oliver's dual existence, comes between them and Oliver is then pursued by the crowd, which includes his soon-to-be savior Mr. Brownlow. The carriage, indicative of movement in Oliver's life, also provides the momentary barrier that allows his escape.

Oliver is often thought of as the idyllic Victorian sentimental child, and as Dickens writes of his protagonist in the preface to the 1838 edition of *Oliver Twist*, his purpose is to show " . . . the principle of Good surviving through every adverse circumstance, and triumphing at last . . ." (33). Yet he also notes, "I have yet to learn that a lesson of the purest good may not be drawn from the vilest evil" (33). For Dickens, Oliver is not symbolic of the purest *of* good, but rather practices it when faced with situations he knows are right or wrong. Stories like Oliver Twist's have come to be associated with contemporary conceptions of Victorian childhood. Though many have read such literary constructions of the Victorian child as good or evil, critics and scholars have largely overlooked the idea of the imperfect child. Such

1

children are not constrained by gender or socioeconomic status nor do they simply accept their fates. Rather, the imperfect child is participatory in the development of their agency. As such, imperfect children depict the potential impact of reality upon culture and society and the way one may challenge such conventions for the betterment of everyone. These children are not limited by a binary construct of good/evil; Romantic[1] child vs. street waif. Through a transitory, blended space, such as occurs between the transition from the "real" to fantastic world and back again, their agency is strengthened and solidified. Ultimately, the imperfect child, though often looked upon as a nuisance by society and culture, develops a plan and path for their life in the face of adversity and rejects or accepts mores as they deem fit, thus becoming a self-advocate. They often care for others and take charge of difficult situations even when adults fail to enact change. The imperfect child is neither the Romantic child nor a street urchin but rather an individual who is comprised of both innocence and experience; who's "good" comes from their knowledge of the "vilest of evil."

Depictions of the imperfect Victorian child can be found in the works of Charles Dickens, Charles Kingsley (1819–1875), George MacDonald (1824–1905), Hesba Stretton (1832–1911), Christina Rossetti (1839–1894), and E. Nesbit (1858–1924), as well as many other nineteenth-century authors. Dickens did not write specifically for a child audience but rather for the general public, which included children. Inadvertently, he practiced what has come to be termed cross writing[2] because adults as well as children had access to his texts. Dickens has come to be known as one of, if not *the*, most popular authors of Victorian England, and the term "Dickensian" has become synonymous with not only the Victorian period but elements of it when we speak of things being sinister, ominous, or enigmatically ironic. As has been well established,[3] Dickens drew upon Victorian culture and society to help inform his work and this can readily be seen from the way he constructed his stories. His publications were and continue to be influential for authors. Kingsley, MacDonald, Stretton, Rossetti, and Nesbit are only a handful of writers Dickens's work helped inspire. Yet these authors, who also wrote for adults as well as children, are most often remembered as authors of children's texts rather than remembered for their adult material. Kingsley, MacDonald, Stretton, Rossetti, and Nesbit construct the Dickensian child in their children's texts and bring the imperfect child to younger audiences. Although Dickens is taught to child and young adult audiences in middle and high schools across the globe, he is not considered a children's author. His popularity and literary status remain constant and his fiction is often considered "classic" and "timeless," both of which are problematic terms. Consequently, his texts are largely used for college preparation. The works of Kingsley, MacDonald, Stretton, Rossetti and Nesbit are not as widely used in classroom settings, but are still popular for younger children or those searching for moral, spiritual, and/or religious literature. The construction, definition, production, education, and desire for the imperfect child, and the implications of its use in the classroom, form the focus of Chapter 1.

One of the most popular modes of constructing the Victorian child in nineteenth-century literature was to give the child character a spiritual crisis and pilgrimage along their troubled social and cultural journey. In this fashion, the child could be "saved." This is especially true of the imperfect child. In *Oliver Twist*, for example, Oliver has been raised in an orphanage run by the church system that was impacted by the Poor Law of 1834. Yet Dickens satirizes this system as one that "farms" children and says of poor Oliver, "If he could have known that he was an orphan, left to the tender mercies of churchwardens and overseers, perhaps he would have cried the louder" (47). Though many of Dickens's child characters resemble Oliver and his plight, Oliver, Tiny Tim from *A Christmas Carol* (1841), Paul Dombey of *Dombey and Son* (1846), Nelly Trent from *The Old Curiosity Shop* (1843), Amy Dorrit of *Little Dorrit* (1855), and Esther Summerson from *Bleak House* (1853) remain some of Dickens's most popular fictional children, exemplifying the construct of the imperfect child. These characters are not alone among Victorian imperfect child characters. Kingsley's Tom from *The Water Babies* (1863), MacDonald's Diamond of *At the Back of the North Wind* (1871) and Princess Irene and Curdie from *The Princess and the Goblin* (1872) and *The Princess and Curdie* (1882) series also follow the patterns of Dickens's imperfect children and childhoods in their construction and development culturally and spiritually. Stretton's most popular work, *Jessica's First Prayer* (1867), illustrates the life of Jessica, an orphan, a condition even most of Dickens's protagonists were able to avoid, and also illustrates the imperfect child, as do Rossetti's Flora, Edith, and Maggie from *Speaking Likenesses* (1874). The characterization of the imperfect child also carries over into E. Nesbit's Edwardian, yet very Victorian, children Edred and Elfrida of *The House of Arden* (1908) and Dickie Harding from *Harding's Luck* (1909).[5]

It is important to consider their differences and similarities, and thus the variety, in order to show the development of the imperfect child across the Victorian period. As evident in Nesbit's work, for example, continues to be a presence in post-Victorian literature and has become a standard literary representation of the child. As Ginger Frost asserts in *Victorian Childhoods* (2009), " . . . the Victorian child has a special appeal because of both the dramatic changes over the course of the nineteenth century and the popularity of many child characters in Victorian literature. In part because of the fictional accounts, modern readers often have contradictory views of childhood in the nineteenth century" (5). It is also significant how long this child has been overlooked even when it has been presented numerous times in mainstream literature, as is discussed in Chapter 5, such as in Lemony Snicket's *A Series of Unfortunate Events* (1999–2006) or J. K. Rowling's *Harry Potter* (1997–2007) series. However, the additional complexity nineteenth-century female authors faced was in their fight for recognition in Victorian society alongside their characters.

Gender construction and performance are equally significant to the development of the imperfect child because while sex does not determine if a child will be imperfect, such children often cross gender norms prescribed by society and culture. The ways in which the Victorian female child was and is both romanticized and socialized differs from that of the male child and this extends to class ideologies. Though Oliver and Jessica undergo similar crises, they are viewed and treated differently. In *Erotic Innocence: The Culture of Child Molesting* (1998) James Kincaid discusses the concept of child loving and how this has become not only accepted but also commercialized in both Victorian and contemporary culture and suggests:

> It is worth noting that these hollow child images [characters like Betty Boop without any "real" context] not only focus and allow desire but also erase various social and political complications, performing essential cultural work that is not simply erotic. By formulating the image of the alluring child as bleached, bourgeois, and androgynous, these stories mystify material reality and render nearly invisible—certainly irrelevant—questions we might raise about race, class and even gender. Such categories are scrubbed away in the idealized child, laved and snuggled into Grade-A homogeneity. (20)

Poor characters, like Oliver and Jessica, however, also fit Kincaid's depiction, for they are eroticized through their economic and familial plights and are often as alluring, if not more so, than bourgeois children, through their dirt, grime, and daily struggles. Kincaid finds, "When poor children are allowed to play this part, as they sometimes are, they are helped into the class above them; boys and girls leave difference behind and meld together . . ." (20). Oliver and Jessica exemplify such positions, as do many other Victorian child characters. Poor children and an impoverished childhood were popular narrative techniques used in Victorian writing. Such characters' bodies were often "othered" and such children became erotic creatures for the middle-class reading public for which Dickens, Kingsley, MacDonald, Stretton, Rossetti, and Nesbit were writing. As characters such as Oliver and Jessica achieve new positions and find faith, they become part of the collective "whole," and when this occurs their stories cease as they have been accepted and are no longer "interesting" and "erotic" to the reader's gaze.

Often the romanticized Victorian child is thought of as innocent and perfect. Perfection, or the "ideal" Victorian child, is often what readers look for in characters such as Oliver and Jessica. While the bourgeois child in literature does not typically face the same struggles as the working class child, he/she must often undergo a transformation into some semblance of societal and cultural perfection by the conclusion of his/her journey. In Lewis Carroll's *Alice's Adventures in Wonderland* (1865) and *Through the Looking-Glass and What Alice Found There* (1871), Alice, for example, undergoes many transformations. Yet these challenges occur in a fairylike world that parallels Alice's upper-class background rather than the discordant streets of London that working class Oliver and Jessica must navigate. However Alice, like Oliver and Jessica, does not *become* the idyllic Victorian child. The transformation that children like Alice, Oliver, Jessica, and similar child depictions undergo shifts their position to that of the ideologically imperfect child.

The romanticization of the child is overtly present in many works. It is through gender and class socialization in their works that Dickens, MacDonald, Kingsley, Stretton, Rossetti, and Nesbit illustrate the difficulty of attaining the culturally ideal child and childhood. The elements of the fairy tale and fairy world, which form the basis of the discussion in Chapter 2, are also important in the construction of the imperfect child and childhood. These fantastical spheres are venues and elements of a fantasy world where life is idyllic and perfect. The fairy tale was at the heart of Victorian writing, art, and the romanticized idea of life. Authors writing for both children and adults, including Dickens, used it as a tool in their writing. For many Victorians, the fairy world and all that it contained became a religion. Many noted personalities of the Victorian period, such as Charles Dickens and Arthur Conan Doyle, delved into expanding fields like occultism and mesmerism. As occultism spread throughout the nineteenth century and the sciences became more concrete, so too did the desire to believe in something tangible. The world of fairies could be found right outside one's backdoor. The fairy world was accessible yet belief in the imagination was also needed for it to be real. Authors capitalized on these emerging belief systems and incorporated them into writing, as can be seen in the works of Dickens, MacDonald, Kingsley, Stretton, Rossetti, and Nesbit.

Fantasy and fantastic worlds become central to the imperfect child's journey and experiences throughout these texts. Fantastic spaces offer alternative areas where protagonists, much in the vein of Shakespeare's dual plots of reality/fantasy in plays like *A Midsummer Night's Dream* (1594), may be free from social and romantic constructs of the "child" and "childhood." Fantasy, according to U. C. Knoepflmacher in *Ventures into Childhood: Victorians, Fairy Tales, and Femininity* (1998), for adults might " . . . embody a shared childhood preoccupation with loss and recovery" when shared with children (4). These authors brought childhood preoccupations into their own writing from incidents in their own childhoods. The imperfect child offers such writers a way to express social and cultural concerns and yet points out ways in which society and culture simultaneously "norm" both child and childhood. Writers such as Dickens, Kingsley, MacDonald, Stretton, Rossetti, and Nesbit also use fantasy to separate the child and childhood from social "norming" and the cultural gaze that seeks to "other" them until their own norming takes place. Knoepflmacher believes " . . . an adult reader is drawn into fantasy that remains essentially anti-adult in its regressive hostility to growth and sexual deviation" (5) as this, in essence, will allow the "child" and text to retain their innocence.

The imperfect child is not wholly innocent and therefore the use of fantasy allows for not only the character to undergo social norming, though the imperfect child might resist this for a time, but also for the adult to find the protagonist "purified." Thus the adult reader is also cleansed as the narrative comes to a close. Fantasy blends both "reality" and supernatural elements that allow and challenge characters and readers to use their imagination, which aids in obtaining redemption as characters and readers have an understanding of both areas. Both characters and readers are able to draw upon *what was* and *what is* and are left with hope for *what might be* through the journey to these places. The fantasy worlds and fairy tale themes used by these authors are not always straightforward in their construction. Dickens and Stretton only draw upon such ideas and weave them sporadically throughout their work, while Kingsley and Nesbit are straightforward in their use of fantastic worlds that parallel reality. Rossetti and MacDonald incorporate antifantasy worlds where grotesque monsters and freakish humanoids illustrate the ills of resisting socialization. All the while, social satire is embedded in all of their works. Knoepflmacher states this differs according to the gender of the author, for " . . . male ironists . . . remain far more sentimentally attached to childhood and children than female ironists. . . . For, unlike female authors who could look back at generations of maternal storytellers and identify themselves with an adult female authority, Victorian male writers turned to the child to find compensations for a middle-class culture's division of the sexes into separate spheres" (9). Male authors could look back to writers such as the Brothers Grimm and Hans Christian Andersen, among countless others. The storytelling tradition has historically been credited to women and is thus thought to be organic in nature whilst male authors have largely been credited with pen-and-ink composition. The use of the fantasy world was equally important to writers of both genders.

One of the primary ways Dickens, MacDonald, Kingsley, Stretton, Rossetti, and Nesbit illustrate the "othered" nature of the imperfect child is through the language associated with such characters, as will be considered in Chapter 3. Many critics have questioned Dickens's use of the language of the middle and upper classes for his working class characters, such as Oliver, Nell, and Amy. Such characters, it has been widely argued, would not be able to acquire such language because of their social and cultural positions. However, these children have some genetic predisposition, Dickens seemingly suggests, with such language acquisition because they come from such backgrounds through their fallen bloodlines. Dickens further attests to the education of many of his protagonists, regardless of gender, which has been attained in various ways. However, he shows that education and drive are necessary if one is to speak and function within Victorian society and culture. The same society and culture that is deemed to be an age of progress belittles many of its citizens. Naming, in this vein, becomes significant, for Dickens uses naming to paint vivid pictures of characters and settings in his works. Often such names establish a tone and persona for characters. Naming can provide not only humor, in some cases, but also project the socioeconomic status and cultural value associated with characters and settings in a story. Like Dickens, MacDonald, Kingsley, Stretton, Rossetti, and Nesbit also use language and naming to further illustrate the position of their characters. Already comprised of many dualities, the imperfect child rarely has a single name but often one or many assigned to them by society and culture. They often resist such labels, though they may later embrace or establish a new name, and thus identity, for themselves. This further speaks to the complex nature of the imperfect child who resists social norming but, in order to exist within society and culture, comes to terms with some elements of it by the close of the text. Such characters find their own place within a society and culture that often reject them due to uncontrollable circumstances.

Though the romanticizing and socializing of characters like Oliver Twist, Tiny Tim, Nelly Trent, Tom, Jessica, Edith, and Laura may occur differently according to the various approaches Dickens, MacDonald, Kingsley, Stretton, Rossetti, and Nesbit take in constructing their texts, the imperfect child is at the center. Predominantly innocent at heart, the imperfect child remains, however, exposed to the harsh realities of Victorian life whether he/she exists in a fantasy world primarily or coexists in a dual realm of fantasy and reality. Not to be confused with the idyllic sentimental child, the imperfect child usually attains atonement and lives or dies very peacefully at the conclusion of the respective tale. The use of death and disease in the tale of the imperfect character will be more fully examined in Chapter 4. Interestingly, such children also must journey from country to city or vice versa in order to achieve an imperfect status. The country is commonly thought of as idyllic, peaceful, and pure, and a natural, historic time and cities are associated with death, pollution, and disease, an illustration of an uncertain future. As Raymond Williams explains in *The Country and The City* (1973):

> It is significant, for example, that the common image of the country is now an image of the past, and the common image of the city an image of the future. That leaves, if we isolate them, an undefined present. The pull of the idea of the country is towards old ways, human ways, natural ways. The pull of the idea of the city is towards progress, modernization and development. In what is then a tension, a present experienced as tension, we use the contrast of country and city to ratify an unresolved division and conflict of impulses. . . . (297)

Such child protagonists do not always, however, do what is socially deemed "correct," and selfishness may override cultural mores for behavior that may also cross gender lines appropriate not only to sex but also class. Such hegemonic ideals can be challenged in the fantasy worlds created by these authors, but ultimately romanticizing these characters is nullified by their socialization into the larger cultural whole.

Though Dickens's work is aimed at a broad audience and he is not widely considered a children's author, as are MacDonald, Kingsley, Stretton, Rossetti, and Nesbit, he is still being taught, and in some cases enjoyed, by children and young adults while these children's authors have not been as fondly remembered by the mass reading public. Yet these authors did write for adults as well, though this is often forgotten and dismissed, as is Dickens's work especially aimed at a child audience. Pedagogical approaches to teaching these texts, if they are to remain in classrooms for children and young adults, must allow students not only reading and discussion time, but access to the text and cultural ideologies of Victorian England. Allowing children to devour what they read is what instructors encourage, but without access early in childhood "classic" books and stories may overwhelm readers. The construction of the imperfect child compels many readers to continue reading as we both enjoy watching imperfect children struggle and succeed and, as we continue to devour such books, look to be begging with Oliver for "some more."

Chapter One
Please Sir, I Want Some More
Learning . . . at Any Cost

As Oliver asks for more food, so do readers ask for more imperfect children in literature. Both Victorian and contemporary readers enjoy and desire stories of the imperfect child; a child whose construction is largely dependent on the learning it experiences. Learning here is not limited to traditional schooling, which would have been highly unusual for characters like Oliver or Little Nell to obtain. While elements of traditional classroom education do occur for some of Dickens's imperfect children, this usually happens in the outside world, such as on the harsh streets of London or the enclosed rooms of a dismal country estate. While the philosophy of Jean-Jacques Rousseau's *Emile or On Education* (1762) was still popular during the Victorian period, Dickens does not suggest children should be left to learn from nature alone and without benefit of a formal social education. The education received by children taught from Rousseau's perspective is realistic and only enhances the natural nature of the imperfect child.

This is not to say such a character is naturalistic in the literary sense, for the imperfect child is a creature more bound to literary realism in that he/she frequently has the freedom of choice. The imperfect child will often later learn from such experiences, for good or ill. As children of nature they are often associated with fairy creatures and/or coming from natural elements. Their circumstances are drawn from reality and Dickens depicts them undergoing such events through socioeconomic and familial struggles. Though some educators might find presenting the work of Victorian authors daunting, through using such texts in a classroom with discussion illustrating the ways in which such works speak to contemporary subjects, students may be better equipped to make literary choices of works outside of contemporary publication. The characterization of the imperfect child is also crucial to the development of such characters. Writers that use the imperfect child figure in their work emphasize the importance of learning, through a variety of methodologies, that such children must undergo in order to function within their various cultural landscapes.

Conceptions of the Child and Childhood

The development of the imperfect child grew out of the realistic portrayal of literary characters, a form Dickens[1] readily utilized, but also out of changes in the ways in which children were socially viewed. Children had been considered "little adults," in relation to Augustinian philosophies of childhood and therefore it was believed they were to be reared and treated as such. During the seventeenth century the work of the Educationalist movement, through philosophers like John Locke, constructed children as "tabula rasas,"[2] but the Victorian period saw drastic changes in the value of children emotionally and economically. Viviana A. Zelizer suggests, in *Pricing the Priceless Child: The Changing Social Value of Children* (1994), " . . . the expulsion of children from the 'cash nexus' at the turn of the past century, although clearly shaped by profound changes in the economic occupational, and family structures, was also a part of a cultural process of 'sacralization' of children's lives" (11) and "While in the nineteenth century, the market value of children was culturally acceptable, later the new normative ideal of the child as an exclusively emotional and affective asset precluded instrumental or fiscal considerations" (11). In characters like Oliver and Jessica we can see how child labor and suffering were "acceptable" but numerous Victorians, like Dickens and Stretton, did preach against the "acceptable" conditions of many children. Conditions, such as Oliver's "farming" or the abuse Jessica receives, were not necessarily overtly sanctioned or encouraged. However, by ignoring the problems children faced culturally and socially, Victorian society was accepting, condoning, and thus promoting such treatment. Though the imperfect child is a representation of the ills Victorian society and culture propagated, and authors like Dickens and Stretton were socially commenting on what was occurring around them, they too ultimately objectify this child, for they make money from the very issues they are purportedly speaking against.

While the concepts of suffering, begging, longing, starvation, death, loss, and innocence are all requirements nineteenth-century readers clamored for in the "ideal," sentimental, or pathetic Victorian child, contemporary audiences still seem to hunger for versions of the imperfect child. These characteristics are found in many famous children's texts, but it is not only children and young adults who are reading books with such imperfect characters as the Baudelaire orphans, Harry Potter, Cinderella, Charlie Bucket, or Oliver Twist. While we may question if children want to have or acquire characteristics or the lives of such children, it is through the romanticization of characters like the Baudelaire orphans and Oliver Twist that readers often find they can relate to such characters. Readers appreciate seeing these protagonists overcome tremendous odds and sacrifices in order to attain imperfection. This is something readers can better relate to than the idyllic child because those characteristics are often too difficult to attain.

We may question how a character such as Oliver Twist fits in with the genre of literature for children. Indeed, there is literature written especially *for* children and literature *about* children and the problem arises as to how one defines children's literature.[3] The imperfect child is found in both children's literature and literature marketed towards adults. If one were to mark children's literature as that which is written specifically for children, then we must question how novels like *Jane Eyre, Oliver Twist,* and even much of what we term fairy tales and folklore came to be read by children. However, literature about children does not completely fulfill such a definition either.

The exact definition of children's literature has been debated among parents, schools, publishers, and children's literature critics. Jack Zipes insists, in *Sticks and Stones: The Troublesome Success of Children's Literature from Slovenly Peter to Harry Potter* (2001), that children's literature does not exist because "There has never been a literature conceived *by* children *for* children, a literature that belongs to children, and there never will be" (40). Yet Zipes acknowledges children do have a culture of their own, but " . . . the institution of children's literature is not of their making, nor is the literature they are encouraged to read" (40). Karin Lesnik-Oberstein, in "Essentials: What Is Children's Literature? What Is Childhood?" (1999), contends:

> The definition of children's literature lies at the heart of its endeavor: it is a category of books the existence of which absolutely depends on supposed relationships with a particular audience: children. The definition of 'children's literature' therefore is underpinned by purpose: it wants to be something in particular, because this is supposed to connect it with that reading audience—'children'. . . . (15)

What parents, schools, publishers, and scholars generally agree on is that children and childhood are somehow inexplicitly entwined and what these social constructions develop is a culture of childhood in which "their" literature exists.

Just as contemporary ideologies of what the mass reading audience is, so too have notions of the child and childhood changed since the Victorian Era. What the Victorians considered as the reading public differs from the reading public of the twenty-first century. Richard D. Altick, in *Victorian People and Ideas* (1973), suggests that it was the growth in popularity of the "reading circle" (193), which I believe the family audience used, that produced a massive effect on Victorian literature (193). Altick reflects upon the " . . . familiar institution of the middle-class Victorian household, the reading circle, in which most members of the family, children and adults alike, joined to hear one of their number, usually the father, read aloud from a book or magazine" (192–93). According to Altick, in both their home reading and at school, Victorians taught the language and stories of the Bible (192) and this became a core component in many Victorian lives. Children were a central element in the development of literature and this group became more important to the reading public as the century progressed. While the argument as *to whom* was the writer scribbling is ongoing, we must focus on the makeup of an audience during a particular time period, as this denotes for whom the author may have intended the work.

While many of Dickens's stories are still contemporarily applicable, they might be considered hard for children to read due to Victorian language and social contexts. Length is also a consideration, for contemporary readers are presented with "classic" works with 700 plus pages and children are encouraged to read them or noted "abridged" versions of roughly 400 plus pages with little social or historical context provided. The *Harry Potter* novels become more accessible even with their seemingly daunting lengths because children are more readily accustomed to their social and cultural element.[4] The family would realistically be the target audience for Dickens as well as many other Victorian authors. Children who heard and read these works would grow with the publication of the text, which often would span a year or two because of installment or serial publication. In reading such works today in their ready-made 700-plus-page format, a counterfeit reading occurs, for this was not the original intent of their authors or publishers, even when such work was produced in the three-volume version allotted to lending libraries. Though not considered an author for children by contemporary standards, Dickens nonetheless is found in many children's anthologies, single texts on children's bookshelves, and is often mentioned in critical essays and books on children's literature. This may lead us to question where Dickens exactly fits in children's literature. Charles Dickens filled many occupational roles throughout his career, including working as a novelist, journalist, philanthropist, court reporter, editor, actor, and speaker. Yet the question as to his position as an author of children's literature is complex, as is the very definition of children's literature itself.

Dickens did write for children and his best-known work which fits this category is *The Life of Our Lord: Written for His Children During the Years 1846 to 1849* (1934). This work was written only for his children and not published until after his last living child was deceased. Dickens published *A Child's History of England* (1851–1853) in *Household Words* for two years and its audience is directed towards children and possibly the working classes. That can easily be detected in the tone of the piece. Dickens remarks in his introduction, entitled "A Preliminary Word," in the opening edition of *Household Words*[5] in March of 1850: "We aspire to live in the Household affections, and to be numbered among the Household thoughts, of our readers. We hope to be the comrade and friend of many thousands of people, of both sexes, and of all ages and conditions, on whose faces we may never look" (1). Dickens saw his journal in the hands of the mass reading public, regardless of class, gender, or age. While this speaks to Dickens's marketing abilities, it also illustrates what the content of *Household Words* would be and how he established it as a family-friendly text. Jay Clayton notes, in *Charles Dickens in Cyberspace: The Afterlife of the Nineteenth Century in Postmodern Culture* (2003), "His ambition was to reach every English-speaking reader on the globe, to saturate every communications market, to rig every *household* so that it could receive his *words*. He wanted his publications to be the gateway for all Victorian consumers of art and infotainment" (200). Dickens marketed, packaged, and delivered his material to a wide audience throughout the year and any new means of reaching his audience was met with interest—as long as he retained control over the way his work was disseminated.

During Dickens's life it was commonplace for his work to be copied and adapted. Dickens became a proponent for national and international copyright laws. While many parodies of Dickens's work existed, some of them were geared toward children to bring Dickens to younger audiences. In such cases the protagonist child characters' story was often excerpted, such as the story of Little Nell, and the primary focus was on the protagonists' development and role in the story. In this way child audiences may have better related to the story as they grew. As an additional marketing strategy, they would already have familiarity with the work of Dickens. One series that was produced during Dickens's lifetime was published in twelve small volumes by Clark, Austin, Maynard & Co. in New York and titled *Dickens' Little Folks* (1860).[6] According to the publishers in a note before the preface to each text, the series was published so that children could enjoy the works Dickens had written and also because of the " . . . well known excellence of his portrayal of children, and the interests connected with children—qualities which have given his volumes their strongest hold on the hearts of parents" (x); and in taking the child characters from their respective books, "We have brought down these famous stories from the library to the nursery—the parlor table to the child's hands . . ." (x). While they might have thought they were bringing it "down" to the hands of children, publishers such as Clark, Austin, Maynard & Co. were also capitalizing on Dickens's work and keeping it accessible to a wide audience. Through works such as this we can account for the idea that Dickens was not viewed primarily as an author for adults during his lifetime. Dickens's work for children was, however, undervalued in Victorian society and culture.

Contemporarily, Dickens's works are still popular, especially his most widely known text, *A Christmas Carol* (1843). Every Christmas adaptations of this classic Dickens novella can be found in theatres, bookstores, and movie houses and the original text is still widely read. The themes present in *A Christmas Carol* have also spilled into the rest of the Georgian Calendar year and inspired such texts as David Levithan's *Marley's Ghost* (2006), where Levithan draws from the original the theme of regret and applies it to Valentine's Day. The story of Scrooge has been retold for both children and adults and still remains a Christmas tradition for kids of all ages, as with Disney's *Mickey's Christmas Carol* (2010). Likewise, the recent popularity of zombie fiction has given way to revisions of the famous text through works like Jim McCann's *Zombies Christmas Carol* (2011) and Rebecca Brock's *A Christmas Carol of the Living Dead* (2010). Through Dickens's Scrooge does not set out to save London from an onslaught of zombies, such retellings keep the story contemporary and indicate its timelessness. *A Christmas Carol* possibly keeps Dickens popular with modern readers, but his stories like *A Child's History of England* and *The Life of Our Lord* are not always readily available. This is not uncommon among "classics"[7] for children. In *Inventing Wonderland: Victorian Childhood as Seen through the Lives and Fantasies of Lewis Carroll, Edward Lear, J.M. Barrie, Kenneth Graham, and A.A. Milne* (1995), Jackie Wullschläger notes that the most popular stories of the authors she uses in her text, such as Lewis Carroll, J. M. Barrie and Kenneth Graham, did not write their fantastical stories either for publication or a mass reading audience of the time; nor did they set out to be considered children's authors (4–5).

This argument may extend to Dickens's *The Life of Our Lord,* for the focus is overtly on the life of Jesus Christ and there is no fantasy world of pixies and queens in its covers. Moreover, it did not see publication until long after the author's death. Wullschläger's point is that writers often constructed texts for children without intent of publication. Though Dickens, MacDonald, Kingsley, Stretton, Rossetti, and Nesbit were celebrated as writers for adults before their children's books came into being, these authors are long remembered for these works and little else. What becomes problematic in Wullschläger's interpretation is her insistence that these writers were those who " . . . began and defined the course of our [Western] children's literature" (3) and their works " . . . form a rich and distinct genre which barely existed before Lewis Carroll wrote the Alice books and has not been matched since A.A. Milne finished the Winnie-the-Pooh series" (3). She finds *Alice's Adventures in Wonderland* to be the " . . . first English children's classic . . . (3)." Wullschläger dismisses many Victorian children's authors, does not discuss the idea of gender, and rarely touches upon the class from which these authors came. Nonetheless, she brings Dickens into her discussion. It is as if many authors want to use him as examples in their work but never claim him under the banner of children's literature.

The resistance of students to reading "classic" texts like Nesbit's *Arden* series and also from teachers to using them are evident in many high-school, junior-high, and collegiate children's literature courses. Teachers and parents have a huge impact on what is placed on classroom shelves and what is sold in area bookstores. Instructors may have a tendency to favor more contemporary texts, such as J. K. Rowling's *Harry Potter* series, while placing one or two texts that may be deemed "classic" on a syllabus. Arguably, contemporary works are more accessible to readers as child audiences readily know cultural nuances and modern language. Such arguments are disturbing because many college students enrolled in introductory literature courses have constructed views that "classic" texts are too dense for their reading level. Many students have never been exposed to "classic" texts. Such books may only be read if assigned. As often pointed out by educators, critics, and even parents, the largest barrier such students have is the language of these texts because they are not used to the culture, society, and language of such works. A "classic" text is typically thought of as old and may be kept around because it has "stood the test of time." Such clichéd terms are thrown about with little sense of definition or context. Here I will use "classic" to discuss books that are socially and culturally applicable to audiences across cultures and time periods and thus not place time or local constraints on such works. A "classic" in this sense is ultimately defined better by the reader than by a social or academic context because readers better understand their interests, knowledge, and limitations. However, such books are marginalized on bookshelf stores by being placed in their own corner sections and are often only picked up and read *to* children rather than *with* them in both classrooms and at home. By placing these texts in their own sections in classrooms, libraries, and at home, they are disconnected from other reading material. Through separating these "classics," this suggests that both a different level of thought and knowledge base is required to read them. This separation only reinforces their "untouchable" status.

In *Reading Otherways,* Lissa Paul explores why we should still read "classic" books and questions if books such as *Little Women* are still "worth reading" (50). She finds "Scholarly articles on *Little Women* were few and far between . . ." (52) until the rise of Second Wave feminist movements. What is important to note is that *Little Women* was originally intended for a child audience and books like Charles Dickens's *Oliver Twist* and *A Christmas Carol* and Charlotte Brontë's *Jane Eyre* were for both an adult and a family audience during the Victorian Era. The child audience of the Victorian Era was still a developing concept and a middle class family would typically read books like *Oliver Twist.* Children's literature existed primarily for middle and upper class children in the Victorian period because these families could afford such luxuries. Such literature was often filled with important moral lessons, as in *Little Women,* fantasy and adventure like that used by C. S. Lewis in his Narnia series, or images of the problematic romantic child, as Lewis Carroll depicts in *Alice's Adventures in Wonderland* and *Through the Looking-Glass.* While the field of children's literature is still growing and becoming recognized as a scholarly field of its own, texts such as *Little Women* are joining the ranks of texts taught in children's-literature courses. Dickens's works and even texts by writers who are known as children's authors, like MacDonald, Kingsley, Stretton, Rossetti and Nesbit, are largely kept at arm's length even though they have been assimilated onto the shelves of a child audience by librarians, publishers, educators, and parents.

In *Uncommon Sense: Theoretical Practice in Language Education* (1990), John Mayher challenges the typical pedagogical approaches, such as that of the banking method, English teachers have used for decades. These approaches, which he terms "common sense" methods, have long been in place and are ineffective, for they suggest an "I teach, therefore you learn" pedagogy. Teachers may believe they are making an investment in students and they, in turn, make a like investment as they study and participate in the academic environment. If there is little return on this interaction, either or both parties may see these dealings as futile and cease to participate to the best of their ability. In practice, the teacher, according to Mayher, teaches literature and has students write about it (14). The instructor then corrects the essays, teaches grammar and speech, and may serve as an advisor for a school newspaper or yearbook (14). Such traditional pedagogy is common when presenting "classic" texts in the classroom. Middle and high school teachers are often called upon to serve in more than one capacity and this commonly extends to activities outside of their concentrated discipline. Instead, Mayher believes instructors need to teach through an "uncommon sense" model in which they have reconceptualized who they are as teachers (3) and teach by understanding their own pedagogical methodologies. They must first question why they teach in the way they do rather than just instruct. In the uncommon model, there is more room for student engagement and not just transmission of information, which is essential when teaching the "classics." Presenting the construction of the imperfect child in the classroom, teachers may begin to use the "uncommon sense" model as instructors can use this character to develop new approaches to helping students understand "classic" texts. New models of teaching and exercises can develop out of presenting the imperfect child in the classroom and the discussion can extend to examining ways this character is found in contemporary ideologies of the child and childhood.

While *Little Women* is taught in children's literature courses, only excerpts of the text may be discussed. The introduction of "classic" literature, such as *Oliver Twist*, in the children's literature classroom is not uncommon. This "classic," which was initially written for the middle-class family audience, has somehow become associated with a children's audience. *Oliver Twist* stands among other works by Dickens as "children's literature," such as with *Great Expectations* and *A Tale of Two Cities*. Introducing all of the Dickens cannon has not, however, extended to lengthier texts such as *The Old Curiosity Shop*, *Little Dorrit*, or *Bleak House*. However, Little Nell, Esther Summerson, and Amy Dorrit can be found in many children's collections of short excerpts of Dickens's work, but these characters' entire story is rarely tackled in children's texts. This practice was typical of publishers during the early twentieth century so that not only more books could be sold but also exposure to these characters could include children as well as adults.

Determining the definition of a "classic" and pinpointing student resistance to reading such works may begin with examining why many of Dickens's texts (and those like them) have become associated with a children's audience. This examination should also investigate what may help make such texts more accessible to contemporary audiences. The imperfect child character of such "classic" works may allow educators to explore this further because as such these stories are read by both adults and children today. While length might hinder many of Dickens's novels from being read, fourth-grade children readily pick up novels in the lengthy *Harry Potter* series. There are also many abridged versions of such stories aimed at child audiences, but their impact and value are highly contested among scholars and educators alike. Unfortunately, such adaptations may "dumb down" the literature if adapters and publishers are not careful and much of the original story may be lost in translation. Many of Dickens's texts have become abridged for younger audiences and this is not only done through print versions but also visual media, such as Disney's version of *A Christmas Carol* (1983) in which Mickey Mouse is cast as Bob Cratchit and Scrooge McDuck is Ebenezer Scrooge. Because many Victorian works are now readily available as free downloads from various Internet sites, such texts may become more accessible to those who possess e-readers and the desire to seek out such material. While abridged and adapted versions may be entertaining, many adaptations are problematic because they are stripped of a portion of their original cultural and social nuances, such as inequality and prejudice.

The inequality that surrounds individuals in current Western culture is not unlike that found in the Victorian Era. Contemporary feminist-teaching approaches may help encourage reading of "classics" by not only connecting social concern for minorities and women with feminist theory but also by illuminating what has been done (and what might be accomplished) to make the plight of the position of women and minorities more widely known and understood. If labels such as "classic" are changed or removed altogether and texts like *Oliver Twist, The Water-Babies, At the Back of the North Wind*, and *Jessica's First Prayer* are placed beside contemporary works, social concerns may draw more readers to their covers. However, educators and parents need to be attentive, especially to public-school classrooms. The overt religious tone found in these stories may be problematic for some students and parents since this is not always found in mainstream children's literature. By linking our contemporary social, racial, economic, gender, and sexual orientation concerns with those of previous time periods and other cultures we may better understand our present ideologies and practices. This can help students understand literature and how it reconciles current issues. Feminist pedagogical practices offer some of the necessary tools that will allow instructors not only to instruct but also help build strong communities in the classroom that may eventually extend outside the classroom environment. In *No Angel in the Classroom: Teaching Through Feminist Discourse*, Berenice Fisher discusses the practice of consciousness raising in the classroom and in doing so she finds, "It promotes awareness of gender injustice and cultivates women's capacity to make their own decisions about how to respond to that injustice, even when these decisions differ" (39–40). While looking at "classics" through a feminist lens we must, of course, tread carefully so as not to impose a contemporary feminist view upon such literature.

The imperfect child learns through nature and formal education, whether it is at a formal schoolhouse or from a governess or tutor. Formal education during the early and middle Victorian period was rare, especially for the working classes and female children. As Altick explains, for the upper and upper middle classes formal " . . . schooling for the nobility and gentry was, in the main, what it had been since Tudor times. After home instruction or attendance at a private elementary school, the boys . . . were sent to one or another of the nine ancient public schools . . ." (252). Oliver is, perhaps by luck, educated both informally and formally but he also possesses an innate ability to learn from his environment. Yet for the lower middle and working classes formal education was wholly different because these children only had a few years of schooling (Altick 250), Dickens would illustrate this repeatedly in his work. Oliver, for example, after being "farmed" out and brought up by hand at the beginning of his story, is taken by Mr. Bumble for an appearance before the Board, a group of men associated with the parish in which Oliver has been raised.

Oliver has had no formal education at this point, except that found at the back of Mrs. Mann's hand. The Board declares to Oliver, "You have come here to be educated, and taught a useful trade. . . ." (54) and Oliver is assigned to pick oakum at six in the morning. As Dickens notes, "For the combination of both these blessings [education and being taught a trade] in the one simple process of picking oakum, Oliver bowed low by the direction of the beadle, and was then hurried away to a large ward, where, on a rough hard bed, he sobbed himself to sleep" (54). Oliver does not have a choice between learning a trade and obtaining a liberal education. The education he is supposed to have at the hands of the Board is thrust upon him and limiting rather than allowing for freedom of learning. This is a methodological approach more grounded in nature, and espoused by philosophers such as Locke. Oliver will eventually return to this pastoral paradise and take up liberal studies. Amazingly, Oliver has lived through being farmed, and Dickens finds that only two children out of ten make it through this system (48–49). Oliver's ninth birthday finds him " . . . a pale, thin child, somewhat diminutive in stature, and decidedly small in circumference. But *nature or inheritance* [genetics] [my emphasis] had implanted a good sturdy spirit in Oliver's breast" (49). Oliver has not only lived through such an inhumane system, but has come through it without loss of hope, though what type of hope he is left with readers are not told.

The imperfect child is not limited by socioeconomic status as Dickens illustrates with a range of characters from Oliver to those like Paul Dombey, a sickly upper class child. Paul's birth is his father's fixation and even the death of his wife in childbirth is not important. The father's only concern is that the child is a son and his family name will not die out. Paul's older sister, Florence, becomes less of a concern to her father while his son becomes an obsession. Paul is a sickly child whose death destroys his father's hopes that his family name and business will carry on after his own demise. Even though Paul is educated to take up his father's business, his sickness complicates his schooling so that he becomes more fairy-like than human. His nurse, Mrs. Pipchin, grows frightened of the boy and his inquisitive and analytical nature unnerves her. During one exchange Paul ponders Mrs. Pipchin's age and she inquires as to what he is thinking and scolds him that he must never say such things. Paul suggests she is not polite to " . . . eat all the mutton-chops and toast . . ." as she has done, and she believes him to be wicked as he talks back to his elders (123). She considers Paul a "little infidel" (123) and Paul " . . . sat turning over [their argument] in his mind, with such an obvious intention of fixing Mrs. Pipchin presently, that even the hardy old lady deemed it prudent to retreat until he should have forgotten the subject" (123). This incident begins an odd connection between the two and Paul and Mrs. Pipchin become odd soulmates. Mrs. Pipchin begins to stay up during the night with Paul out of fear of him and they are noted as being of the same nature. "The good old lady might have been—not to record it disrespectfully—a witch, and Paul and the cat her two familiars, as they all sat by the fire together. It would have been quite in keeping with the appearance of the party if they had all sprung up the chimney in a high wind one night, and never been heard of any more" (124). Mrs. Pipchin believes the spirit of his dead mother has possessed Paul, for he does not behave like "normal" children (125–26). From both the harsh formal education Paul receives and his father's obsession, Paul's death becomes tragic, though his life and death scene, much like that of Little Nell's, is sentimentally heart wrenching.

Pathos and Plight

Dickens's writing appeals to readers of all socioeconomic backgrounds as he tries to realistically display the life and times of Victorian culture and society. His work contributed to the rise in literacy throughout the nineteenth century. Dickens suggests hope for all socioeconomic classes as even Oliver has, somewhere, though we are not told how, learned to read in his nine years of being farmed and time in the workhouse. It is difficult to not forget, however, that while individuals like Mrs. Mann made money off of the plight of orphans, so too did Dickens in sales of his texts with the orphan character at the center of the story. Dickens was a philanthropist and gave monetarily and physically to many causes, but he was still making his living off the backs, so to speak, of children such as Oliver and Jessica. If this child type was to socially disappear or conditions surrounding the treatment of such children change, so too would much of Dickens's income. While he did speak against issues such as farming, economically he also relied upon society's continued disregard. The imperfect child held economic and emotional value for society as a whole and this is not something that has changed. All we have to do now is to see a "Save the Children" commercial or a Jerry Lewis telethon to see the ways in which children and their circumstances are exploited for the economic and emotional satisfaction of society. The largest change, however, is that we have come to romanticize such a child, especially in so-called "First World" countries, rather than draw upon this image of the child for economic value through manual labor, as in many "Third World" countries. We continuously create the imperfect child by denying things like health care and schooling and sentimentalize the imperfect child to fulfill our economic and emotional desires. The suffering of Oliver and the Baudelaire orphans allows us to "do good" and thus feel better about ourselves.

Though Oliver does not have an ideal upbringing, Dickens outlines the plight of imperfect street children, like Artful Dodger from *Oliver Twist* or the crossing sweep Jo in *Bleak House*. For children like Jo, who had few friends and no known relations, life was made from the little work that could be found in the rough streets of Victorian London. Education occurred there not in the country lanes and meadows with a single tutor as Rousseau prescribed but in the filth-ridden back alleyways and dark stairwells of the capital city. For the majority of these street children there was little social movement. Handouts were commonly begged for or pinched from passersby, and, though some children did manage to make their way out of slums like Tom-all-Alone's, most ended up like Jo and died from disease and want.[8] An education in such circumstances meant something other than words on a page or sums making sense. In Jo's case it meant life and death. Dickens makes it clear that through formal social education,[9] Jo might stand a better chance to make a living and be a productive member of society. He notes in *Bleak House*:

> It must be a strange state to be like Jo! To shuffle through the streets, unfamiliar with the shapes, and in utter darkness as to the meaning, of those mysterious symbols, so abundant over the shops, and at the corners of streets, and on the doors, and in the windows! To see people read, and to see people write, and to see the postman deliver letters, and not to have the least idea of all that language—to be,to every scrap of it, stone blind and dumb! It must be very puzzling to see the good company going to the churches on Sundays, with their books in their hands, and to think (for perhaps Jo *does* think, at odd times) what does it all mean, and if it means anything to anybody, how comes it that it means nothing to me? . . . It must be a strange state, not merely to be told that I am scarcely human (as in the case of my offering myself for a witness), but to feel it of my own knowledge all my life! (257–58)

Jo's deplorable condition, satirized by Dickens to illustrate how society and culture have created Jo and his situation yet ignore his status, does not allow him to learn through the traditional model offered through schooling. Jo,

Dickens suggests, has the capacity to think, even if sporadically. Jo remains, however, socially constructed and situated as less-than, as a subspecies of animal. Jo's death is his only release from his misery. Yet Jo is among friends when he dies, which is better than many children in his situation might have hoped for on the seedy streets of London. Oliver has it much "better" than Jo.

Oliver's schooling, like that of many working class children, has been inadequate, whereas the education of the poor and female children of the working classes was barely existent. The formal education for a child like Esther Summerson would have come from governesses and tutors and " . . . was devoid of intellectual content, let alone intellectual challenge" (Altick 54). Yet working class female children would have a very different experience. Altick finds that when educated, the working class was expected to produce rather than think and in educating them society " . . . did not aim to create a nation of readers, concertgoers, or gallery visitors" (250) but rather they were to manufacture " . . . a steady flow of productive, sober, and docile recruits into the labor force" (250). Esther, who could have become one such recruit, is kept by her godmother and attends a " . . . neighboring school where [she] is a day boarder . . ." (*Bleak House* 29); yet because of her place in society, she is kept from making friends among her peers. She has been taught, among other things, how to read and walks daily from home to school and back with " . . . books and portfolio . . ." (31) in hand. While Esther does not find herself particularly "clever" (29), we know she has been trained to take care of a household, as she later does for Mr. Jarndyce, and as a governess with the Miss Donnys at Greenleaf for six years. Esther's education greatly surpasses that of Little Nell, who struggles on the London streets to obtain any education. Yet even she knows how to read and write. Interestingly, Amy Dorrit, whose education we hear more of than Little Nell's, is left to acquire her own formal education as well as that of her siblings. Dickens notes of Amy in *Little Dorrit*:

> At thirteen, she could read and keep accounts—that is, could put down words and figures how much the bare necessities that they wanted would cost, and how much less they had to buy them with. She had been, by snatches of a few weeks at a time, to an evening school outside, and got her sister and brother sent to day-schools by desultory starts, during three or four years. There was no instruction for any of them at home; but she knew well—no one better—that a man so broken as to be the Father of the Marshalsea, could be no father to his own children. (81)

Girls had a more difficult time obtaining an education, as Dickens illustrates, than their male counterparts. Yet ultimately Dickens indicates that education, in any form, is both necessary and ideal for the imperfect child as it contributes to one of their greatest assets, the ability to critically think. While this is important for all children, according to Dickens, the imperfect child is often caught between two worlds and thus the educational experiences occur in a blended space. The imperfect child's knowledge is arguably a product of this environment. This occurs regardless of gender.

The education the imperfect child receives through their everyday interactions with society and culture illustrates the way they learn to negotiate difficult circumstances. Dickens does not neglect to emphasize the importance of formal schooling and points out the problematic system in place in Victorian society, as he does in *Hard Times* (1854). As Oliver learns to pickpocket, a skill that could be profitable, though deadly, from Fagin's gang or Amy Dorrit learns how to receive an education and work for her lot in life, Dickens suggests that such skills are, while not always encouraged, much more realistic for children than the formal education of a Victorian classroom. This combination of naturalistic learning and formal education, Dickens suggests, is essential in the development of the imperfect child. Later authors would also illustrate the importance of utilizing both types of education, as George Mac-Donald does with Diamond and Nanny in *At the Back of the North Wind*.

Spirituality and Education

MacDonald, a well-educated Congregational minister, was a freelance writer and author of many stories for children. The construction of Diamond's story is perhaps one of the most conflicted yet fantastic, for Diamond seemingly exists in a dual universe. Readers are left wondering if he has existed in reality/fantasy, reality/delusion, or a combination thereof. He is seemingly a "perfect" child, for he is industrious, does not complain about his station, is loyal to his family, and loves everyone around him.

Yet Diamond questions, not necessarily society literally, but rather Nanny and North Wind, those he has the most contact with throughout the text. Diamond is a creature of nature, one that interacts with and lives (and dies) through his contact with it. Nancy Springer describes Diamond's personality in her foreword to the 1998 Tor edition of *At the Back of the North Wind* as:

> Quite literally perfect! First of all, he has the perfect name. . . . The name sets him apart, makes him special, as befits one who is also perfect in goodness: Diamond speaks truth, loves his horse and his mother, soothes babies, takes over the family business when his father is sick, impresses important people, inspires improved behavior in those around him—he is just too cute to shoot. (xi)

Diamond becomes a construction of the "ideal" child with just a surface read, but Diamond is aware of the turmoil life can offer and he, much like Oliver, looks past it to embrace the positive. However, Diamond faces death much more literally than Oliver, who knows fear that Diamond more readily embraces.

Diamond is, for all intents and purposes, close to the "ideal" child Victorians had been taught to romanticize. Through the Romantic period, artists like William Blake considered the urban child, but artists such as the Pre-Raphaelites illustrated the perfect child late in the Victorian period. This angelic image of a child as an untouched, innocent soul was largely unrealistic in nineteenth-century London, much as it is today. It is still an ideal, though audiences have come to more readily seek out the "imperfect" child. Readers clamor for the imperfect child because he/she is a more pragmatic example of everyday children who face the struggles of Victorian life and are successful, whether through death or life, in reaching a happy ending. Springer concedes:

> Diamond is, I think, a peculiarly Victorian superhero, Little Child as Godlike Being. . . . Usually, in these stories, the perfect little child humbles and enlightens those around him/her, then dies. . . . MacDonald plays on this familiar theme—but with important variations. You might say that, consciously or not, he uses the expectations of his readership to pull them in, and then when he has them where he wants them—facing the North Wind. (xi)

Diamond suffers, but he does not often complain. His concern is more with what occurs around him and he is fully aware, almost as a grown individual might be, of the plight of society. Through his eyes, MacDonald constructs a social consciousness. Diamond's childhood allows him both knowledge and naïveté. This is illustrated through his many discussions with North Wind and Nanny. Nanny notes she has had an encounter with North Wind and yet believes it was only a dream. Diamond explains, "I don't know that . . . I believe North Wind can get into our dreams—yes, and blow in them. Sometimes she has blown me out of a dream altogether" (271). To which Nanny states, "I don't know what you mean, Diamond" (271), and Diamond answers, "Never mind. . . . Two people can't always understand each other. They'd both be at the back of the north wind directly, and what would become of the other places without them?" (*At the Back of the North Wind* 271). Nanny, and the majority of the characters in the text, find Diamond "touched," but when Nanny explains to Diamond that they call him "God's baby" (272), Diamond exclaims: "How kind of them! But I knew that" (272). Diamond is well aware of his difference and the world around him yet he learns about it and embraces those close to him.

Diamond's formal education really begins with his association with the writer, Mr. Raymond, a Mr. Brownlow figure,[10] who takes in and cares for Diamond's ever-growing family, related and unrelated. As Oliver comes to live with Mr. Brownlow, Mr. Raymond takes a liking to Diamond and is readily intrigued by the boy and challenges him through "work" to read books and discuss the stories with him. Late in the text, Diamond is reading " . . .

the story of the Little Lady and the Goblin Prince" (314) and he explains, " . . . Any story always tells me itself and what I'm to think about it. Mr. Raymond doesn't want me to say whether it is a clever story or not, but whether I like it, and why I like it. I never can tell what they call clever from what they call silly, but I always know whether I like a story or not" (314). When questioned if he always knows *why* he likes a story, he notes, "No. Very often I can't at all. Sometimes I can. I always know, but I can't always tell why" (315). Challenging Diamond's analytical skills, Mr. Raymond also uses Diamond as a sounding board for his stories, thus using him, as Zelizer explains, as social capital. Diamond develops his critical thinking ability though he is unable to fully articulate what he thinks of the stories he reads for Mr. Raymond, who in turn cares for all of the children in the text he can, though he does not engage them in the way he does Diamond.

Nanny is a working class crossing sweep in the same vein as Jo from Dickens's *Bleak House*. She has a home and someone who takes care of her, though wretchedly, as does Dickie Harding of Nesbit's *Harding's Luck*. Nanny and Dickie are taken in by women who are not genetically related to them and treat them poorly, though they do supply meager housing and food for these children of the street. On first meeting Nanny, Diamond is aware that the wind may " . . . perhaps kill her" (45) and Nanny explains her situation to Diamond and states that she lives with Old Sal and has no parents (47). Interestingly, Diamond shows his awareness of the situations children like Nanny face and asks her, "But old Sal doesn't beat you, does she?" (47), to which Nanny claims, "I wish she would" (47). Diamond has learned of circumstances that a child like Nanny might face through both his interaction with the North Wind and possibly everyday observations around London. Nanny finds she would prefer Old Sal to beat her because, in Nanny's estimation, that would mean Old Sal cared about her. As Nanny feels her own mother would beat her, this is a sign of affection and attention (47). Nanny learns the harshness of life from an early age and her surprise at Diamond having both mother and father illustrates how this is unique to children in her position.

Though Nanny has no formal social classroom education, she engages in many philosophical discussions with Diamond. Through Diamond, Nanny, and eventually her friend Jim, find work and housing with Mr. Raymond. Such pairings are not uncommon in MacDonald's writing and even in more fantastical stories like *The Princess and the Goblin* (1872) and *The Princess and Curdie* (1873), where the imperfect child is readily apparent. The imperfect child MacDonald constructs in Diamond loses some of the naïveté in the Princess and Curdie. The Princess is fully aware of her station. In *The Princess and the Goblin* she has promised Curdie a kiss and insists to her nurse, who does not think she should kiss such a lowly boy, "Nurse, a princess must *not* break her word" (43). It is largely through her interactions with her grandmother that Princess Irene is able to develop her sense of self and of those around her both socially and culturally. There is little mention in either of her stories of any formal education. Through her position as a member of the aristocracy it is illustrated that while she wishes to challenge the rules, she is bound to act socially appropriate. Additionally, Curdie learns from the Mistress of the Silver Moon in *The Princess and Curdie*. In his initial meeting with her she suggests to him, "Remember, then, that whoever does not mean good is always in danger of harm. . . . It is very dangerous to do things you don't know about" (25). MacDonald indicates that learning for the imperfect child, children who come from and interact with nature, is more organic than formal.

Eco-Learning—The Power of Nature

Kingsley, much like MacDonald, illustrates the life of a working class imperfect child in *The Water-Babies* through Tom, a chimney sweep who falls into a fairy-like world that teaches him many things through connectivity with nature and its inhabitants. It is readily apparent that the treatment of the imperfect child in Victorian culture and society was terrible. Children such as Oliver and Tom were largely seen as "things" rather than the children Victorians were supposed to revere. An illustration of this hypocrisy, Tom, actually lives the life Oliver might have faced if he had not begged his way out of the situation. While the working class child is perhaps the most common character used when illustrating the imperfect child, class standing is not the most significant issue. Kingsley explains that Tom, who has no other name:

> . . . lived in a great town in the North country, where there were plenty of chimneys to sweep, and plenty of money for Tom to earn and his master to spend. He could not read nor write, and did not care to do either; and he never washed himself, for there was not water up the court where he lived. He had never been taught to say his prayers. He never had heard of God, or of Christ, except in words which you never have heard, and which it would have been well if he had never heard. He cried half his time, and laughed the other half. (2–3)

Tom readily accepts his way of life and waits to grow up so that he can be in charge as is his master. "As for chimney-sweeping, and being hungry, and being beaten, he took all that for the way of the world, like the rain and the snow and the thunder. . . ." (2). Tom knows no other life and only sees his own as improving as he gets older—if he gets older. After his adventure underwater, Tom goes home with Ellie and becomes " . . . a great man of science, and can plan railroads, and steam engines, and electric telegraphs, and rifled guns, and so forth; and knows everything about everything. . . . And all this from what he learnt when he was a water-baby, underneath the sea" (327). Kingsley, however, does not reward Tom with marriage to Ellie, an upper class child, as

MacDonald does with Princess Irene and Curdie. This suggests one may only, even through education, advance so far socially and culturally. The moral Kingsley, who was involved in Christian Socialism and believed educating the working class was a way to improve their lot and that of society, offers is " . . . do learn your lessons, and thank God that you have plenty of cold water to wash in; and wash in it too, like a true Englishman. And then, if my story is not true, something better is; and if I am not quite right, still you will be, as long as you stick to hard work and cold water" (329). Though Kingsley finds education important, he more readily emphasizes that, when one learns through natural as well as formal means, more learning can occur. Still, education must be a social responsibility, as Tom learns through his education with Mrs. Bedonebyasyoudid.

Though not all working class children, like Nanny, face beatings, the majority of working class children, like Jo, Tom, and Jessica, do undergo physical abuse, yet these children seem open to learning and embracing hope. The fates of the majority of Victorian working class children would more than likely resemble Jo's. Jessica, in *Jessica's First Prayer*, faces the wrath of her alcoholic mother daily and has learned to fend for herself. Stretton describes Jessica as a child with:

> . . . a pair of very bright dark eyes being fastened upon him [the coffee stall owner] and the slices of bread and butter on his board, with a gaze as hungry as that of a mouse which has been driven by famine into a trap. A thin and meager face belonged to the eyes, which was half hidden by a mass of matted hair hanging over the forehead, and down the neck; the only covering which the head or neck had, for a tattered frock, scarcely fastened together with broken strings, was slipping down the shoulders of the little girl. (7–8)

Jessica's initial education comes in the form of abuse not only from her mother but also from the desolate court in which she resides. Stretton indicates that Jessica's mother had not taken care of her daughter for she did not " . . . provide her with food or clothing, and the girl had to earn or beg for herself the meat which kept a scanty life in her. Jess was the drudge and errand-girl of the court; and what with being cuffed and beaten by her mother, and overworked and ill-used by her numerous employers, her life was a hard one" (22). Jessica's only real pleasure is to meet Daniel, who later schools her along with the Chaplin on Wednesdays. This becomes her secret. Stretton's association with Sunday-school moralism is littered throughout Jessica's tale and evangelicalism is evident in most of her work. Jessica's story is not all sentimental. Stretton emphasizes that one must work to overcome life's hardships and that Jessica cannot fall much below her bedraggled social status. Jessica, much like Tom, accepts her position and the way she is treated. She does not look to or think of a future. When Daniel takes an interest in her and she befriends the

Minister's children, her chances in life are improved. This occurs through education and finding religion, something also important in the construction of the imperfect Victorian child. This is one element that the contemporary construction of the imperfect child has lost, as will be explored later.

Rossetti, like Stretton, uses religion as an important element in the construction of the imperfect child in her text *Speaking Likenesses* (1874). She constructs fantasy worlds through which her protagonists learn a variety of lessons, yet her frame is that of the older woman telling tales to a group of young girls in a formal educational setting. The majority of the children in her tale are upper and middle class, indicating that such children are not bound by class constraints. Rossetti opens her story of Flora on her birthday when Flora receives educational materials like a " . . . story-book full of pictures from her father, a writing-case from her mother . . ." (326). Flora is unhappy and though she has everything she could want on her birthday such as friends and presents, she sulks until she goes through a fantastical world in which she learns that she cannot have everything her way. When given most of what she wants, she learns to " . . . bear a few trifling disappointments, or how to be obliging and good-humored under slight annoyances" (342). Rossetti teaches young women that they should not necessarily speak out about feelings but think of others first. As the girls cry out for another story in the series of three, Aunt speaks of Edith, another well-off young lady who, like Little Red Riding Hood, strays from her path and does not follow orders from her elders. When she attempts to boil a kettle of water, Edith is surrounded by natural elements like trees and animals. As her tale progresses, she learns that she is to listen to her elders and follow directions. Another Little Red Riding Hood tale follows that of Edith. In this story, Maggie, a working class girl, tries to make her way through a forest and encounters a variety of creatures and people who try to take her goods. Here the audience learns the duty expected of young women to both country and family to avoid temptation, and that nature can be one of the best teachers.

Playful Pedagogy

A reader of Rossetti's work, Nesbit is well known for her construction of fantasy worlds. Her illustration of these follows the tradition of MacDonald, Kingsley, and Rossetti in that the protagonists of *The House of Arden* (1908) and *Harding's Luck* (1909) only enter fantasy worlds from the real world most readers can relate to on a daily basis. Though writing these tales during the Edwardian era, Nesbit was raised and began writing during the nineteenth century, so much of her work bridges the two periods. A supporter of education more readily learned through experience than in the classroom as she outlines in *Wings and the Child or the Building of Magic Cities* (1913), Nesbit introduces Edred and Elfrida's schooling in *The House of Arden* as tedious and routine for they " . . . went to school every day and learned reading, writing, arithmetic, geography, history, spelling, and useful knowledge, all of which they hated quite impractically, which means they hated the whole lot—one thing as much as another" (4). Though Nesbit does recognize that what the children are learning is "useful knowledge," she strongly suggests this scheduled methodological approach to learning is problematic. And she points out, "The only part of lessons they liked was the home-work, when, if Aunt Edith, had time to help them, geography became like adventures, history like story-books, and even arithmetic suddenly seemed to mean something" (*The House of Arden* 4). It is through story and experience, Nesbit believes, that learning becomes not tedious but interesting. The classroom is a place to gain knowledge but through application of what is learned in the classroom knowledge occurs.

Edith was Nesbit's first name and she becomes Aunt Edith to her readers and markets her own work through *The House of Arden* much as MacDonald does in *At the Back of the North Wind*. Thus, she envisions herself as teacher to children reading her text. "I wish you could teach us always . . . it does seem so silly trying to learn things that are only words in books," notes Edred; and Aunt Edith explains, "I wish I could . . . but I can't do twenty-nine thousand and seventeen things all at once, and . . ." (*The House of Arden* 4). Here she stops in mid-sentence and moves on to discuss other matters. For Dickie Harding, in *Harding's Luck*, his ability to learn allows him to progress in the world, for Nesbit explains that the majority of children know two languages (7) and "Dickie, however, had learned his second language from books. The teacher at his school had given him six . . . all paper-backed. They made a new world for Dickie. And since the people in the books talked in this nice, if odd, way, he saw no reason why he should not—to a friend whom he could trust" (7). Dickie is a boy fallen on hard times, yet heir to a fortune much like Oliver. Readers may sense, if properly taught, children will flourish but they need to have an interest taken in them, as Dickie's teacher does. Still, the learning Dickie cultivates occurs not in the classroom but outside of it when he reads books he can access and thus understand. This learning gets him through the difficult situations he faces. Repeatedly, in *The House of Arden* and *Harding's Luck*, as in much of her other work, Nesbit displays, like Dickens and other authors, her dissatisfaction with current philosophical ideologies towards education and prescribes a different way for children to learn—through both formal social education and the experience of the imperfect child.

Though the construction of the imperfect child has not been investigated critically, it is a character audiences still enjoy reading about. Not bound by class constraints, the imperfect child develops from and in nature challenges many social ideologies and cultural mores, undergoes tremendous hardships, experiences magic through everyday occurrences, learns through both formal social methods and experience, and is often exposed to religion. Such a child, a Dickensian child I would argue, is not wholly sentimental, as characters such as Oliver and Jessica often are labeled, but rather imperfect, for they have knowledge of the world an actual Victorian child could have experienced. They do lead and are often thrust into horrendous circumstances. Often naïveté leads them out of such situations but it is also their ability to analyze their situations that enables them to negotiate their circumstances. Imperfect children do not sit mutely by and let the world happen to them. Rather, they take part in it, as does Diamond when seeking out work for his friends. Pedagogically, students must be taught to contextualize or historicize the Victorian and early Edwardian periods if they are to fully understand the circumstances such characters find themselves in. It is important to extend our understanding of the imperfect child because this character is a complex creation and product of the Victorian era and more realistic than other constructions of the child, such as the sentimental child. Contemporary constructions of the imperfect child, like those of the Baudelaire orphans, do not draw children to religion but to more faith in themselves. Readers still hearken for the imperfect child, however, as they can relate more readily to their struggles and experiences. It is not gruel we are given through such stories, but the development of imperfection, which is perfection unto itself, which we all possess and hopefully understand.

Chapter Two

I Believe, I Believe!
Fairies, Their World,
and Authorial Preservation

"The English are, so far as I know, the hardest-worked people on whom the sun shines. Be content if, in their wretched intervals of pleasure, they read for amusement, and do no worse. They are born at the oar, and they live and die by it. Good God, what would we have of them!"
—Charles Dickens in a letter to Mr. Charles Knight, 17 March, 1854.

Entwined in the leaves of many Victorian novels is the fairy tale motif that has long been popular with writers. During the Victorian period, people became almost obsessed with the fairy world and fairy tale as scientific progress challenged deeply held religious beliefs and ideologies. While the fairy world and fairy tale are interesting to people across the world, the Victorian Era widely marked, especially in written form, the societal and cultural curiosity Western culture held for the fairy realm and story. As Carol G. Silver points out in *Strange and Secret Peoples: Fairies and Victorian Consciousness* (1999), "The Victorians' enthrallment is vividly revealed in the fairy tales and fantasies, written for both children and adults, that surface to create the 'Golden Age of Children's Literature' and to begin the passion of the twentieth century for fantasies for grown-ups" (4). Fairy worlds and stories about them engage both children and adult readers. During the Victorian period, both children and adults were interested in the activities and environments of the fairy realm and this is still true, as can be seen in media such as movies targeted towards both audiences. This is evident in watered-down Disney[1] film versions of fairy tales, such as *Cinderella*

(1950), and the recent release of Guiller del Toro's *Pan's Labyrinth* (2007), which is reminiscent of the original fairy tales where fairies interacted with and preyed on their human brethren. Likewise, many contemporary works, such as Cassandra Clare's *Infernal Devices* (2010–2012) series or the *Wicked Lovely* (2007–2012) collection by Melissa Marr, draw on traditional tales of the realm of faery and illustrate how the dark side of pixie dust can be found in brimstone and ash. The imperfect child was found, fostered, and developed out of interaction in fairy tales and the fairy world of Victorian society. Although interest in the fairy world and stories has never waned, they have continuously been adapted to fit the needs of ever-changing audiences and ideologies of childhood.

As scientific progress began to "explain" the world in which they lived, the Victorians, as Silver suggests, believed in a fairy world separate from their own because of both religious and scientific philosophies (7). Many textual studies like Thomas Keightley's *The World Guide to Gnomes, Fairies, Elves, and Other Little People: A Compendium of International Folklore* (1850), later reprinted as *The Fairy Mythology: Illustrative of the Romance and Superstition of Various Countries,* and Robert Kirk's earlier *The Secret Commonwealth: An Essay on the Nature and Actions of the Subterranean (and for the Most Part) Invisible People, Heretofore Going Under the Name of Elves, Fauns, and Fairies* (1815), existed as scientific, folkloric, and religious research into the realm and stories of fairy creatures. Keightley rightly notes:

> The legends will probably fade fast away from the popular memory; it is not likely that any one will relate those which I have given over again ... For human nature will ever remain unchanged; the love of gain and of material enjoyments, omnipotent as it appears to be at present, will never totally extinguish the higher and purer aspirations of mind; and there will always be those, however limited in number, who will desire to know how the former dwellers of earth thought, felt, and acted. For these mythology, as connected with religion and history, will always have attractions. (vi)

Modern culture tends to divorce the scientific and religious approaches to the study of the fairy realm. Fairy tale and folklore studies and scholars keep many of the "original"[2] tales in the public eye. In addition, film versions of fairy tales, most notably by Disney, have been impressed upon the general public for consumption while stories of long ago are fading from memory culturally and socially.

Twisting Wonderlands

Among those who loved the fairy world and tale during the Victorian period was Dickens. In the majority of his works he utilizes fairy tale motifs. This can be taken quite literally from Dickens's famous quote from his tale "A Christmas Tree" (1850), which he published in the December 21, 1850 edition of *Household Words*, "Little Red Riding Hood was my first love. I have the impression that if I had been able to marry her, I would have known perfect happiness" (qtd. in Kotzin's *Dickens and the Fairy Tale* [1972], 44). This expresses both his early knowledge of fairy tales and the impression they left upon him and his writing. Dickens did not believe that fairy tales should be adapted and when George Cruikshank, one of Dickens's most famous illustrators and longtime collaborator, rewrote some of the more popular fairy tales, such as "Cinderella" (1853) and "Jack and The Bean-Stalk" (1853), Dickens quickly responded in his October 1, 1853 *Household Words* article "Frauds on the Fairies." In "Frauds on the Fairies," he accuses Cruikshank of rewriting and tampering with the stories and especially took offense because Cruikshank uses the fairy tales to promote his own beliefs, including " . . . Total Abstinence, Prohibition of the sale of such spirituous liquors, Free Trade, and Popular Entertainment" (98). Dickens suggests in "Frauds on the Fairies":

> . . . Fairy tales should be respected . . . , but every one who has considered the subject knows full well that a nation without fancy, without some romance, never did, never can, and never will, hold a great place under the sun. And while the theatre has done something to preserve these stories, it becomes doubly important that the little books themselves, nurseries of fancy they are, should be preserved. To preserve them in their usefulness, they must be as much preserved in their simplicity, and purity, and innocent extravagance, as if they were actual fact. Whosoever alters them to suit his own opinions, whatever they are, is guilty, to our thinking, of an act of presumption, and appropriates to himself what does not belong to him. (97–98)

Dickens believes that Cruikshank has stolen that which belongs to all and thus tarnished the tales.

Dickens had written to W. H. Wills, his assistant editor of *Household Words*, on July 27, 1853 regarding the intention of writing "Frauds on the Fairies." Dickens explains to Willis in his letter that in this essay, "Half playfully and half seriously, I mean to protest most strongly against such alteration—for any purpose of the beautiful little stories . . ." (qtd. in Kotzin 38). Later in a letter on September 18, 1853 to Angela Burdett Coutts, Dickens kept his intention for his response clear. He explains to Coutts, "Frauds on the Fairies," "I think will amuse you, and enlist on my side—which is for a little more fancy among children and a little less fact" (qtd. in Kotzin 38–39). In regard to Dickens's response to Cruikshank's changes, Fred Kaplan states in *Dickens: A Biography* (1988), "Sensitive to the denigration of imagination, Dickens attacked Cruikshank's exploitation of traditional fairy tales. . . . He felt strongly that the primacy of the imagination and its pleasures were being threatened by politics, by rational and irrational ideologies, by the dry-as-dust social scientists and utilitarians" (275). "Frauds on the Fairies," while "half playfully" written, helps establish Dickens's thoughts on the hegemonic contemporary conditions of education, propagation of social issues, use and belief in fairy tales and the fairy world, and the preservation of fancy for English society and culture.

Dickens's belief in the importance of the imagination is evident in the lives his characters lead, which are often grounded between reality and fantasy worlds. It was a place Dickens himself often inhabited thorough his writing. Dickens also suggested that only a formal approach to learning and education would, as he explores in much of his own work, leave society barren. As Kaplan indicates, Dickens believed educational reformers were taking " . . . the 'fairy' out of 'tale,' the fanciful out of literature and life. . . . The imagination was treated as a poor second cousin of reason, logic, and science" (305). Through his characterization of the imperfect child, Dickens illustrates that both fancy and reality are equally important in developing socially and culturally grounded individuals.

Associations with the fairy world and fairy tale were important elements in the development of the imperfect child for Dickens, MacDonald, Kingsley, Stretton, Rossetti, and Nesbit. Here imperfect children gain experience and knowledge of the world around them and contextualize how society and culture impact their growth. The concept of the fairy world falls between scientific and religious philosophies that were undergoing severe changes during the Victorian period. Imperfect children need to pass through some sort of fairy realm in order to develop as characters. The imperfect child has an innocent soul, but seems to have an innate knowledge of the ills of Victorian society and culture. The Romantic child is an innocent born with experience to yet be writ upon its slate and a creation of the " . . . central conflict between Reason and Feeling . . ." (1), as Peter Coveney outlines in *Poor Monkey: The Child in Literature* (1957). The Romantic child grew out of philosophies by writers such as Rousseau, a believer in reason and intellect, and Blake, who encouraged feeling as a positive element in the education attained by the "natural" child. Rousseau and Blake occupied two different camps in their ideological approaches to childhood and education. "The cult of the child," Coveney suggests, " . . . informed the romantic literature of childhood [and] lay with the opposing school, with the 'cult of sensibility' associated with Rousseau" (4). Sense and sensibility dueled for a place of significance and importance in Victorian culture and society and thus in its literature.

Religious and scientific ideologies offer us different ways to view the world, but the history surrounding these belief systems is complex. When these philosophies collide, societal confusion may only be the beginning of the chaos that can take place when trying to decipher one's spiritually. Though these two ideologies may be those taught earliest in life, there exists yet another system of belief, the fairy tale, which most of us can also recall learning about early in childhood. Yet this is seemingly abandoned as we "mature" and is replaced by the binary of science and religion. While science and religion have become the two predominant ways in which to view the world politically, socially, and culturally, many individuals still love to "believe" in the fairy world we learned of as children. Religion and science are often used interchangeably with faith and reason. When we begin to examine these as systems of belief we can see where the existence of one may threaten the other. To the Victorians, the fairy tale was both entertaining and offered them a different way of "seeing" the world. Here the imperfect child inhabits, explores, and dreams in and about, even if for a time, the fairy tale world. Existence in such a space shapes children's ideologies and perspectives of their Victorian world and circumstances. The fairy realm is a place the imperfect child needs to encounter, often on both a tangible and aesthetic level, in order to remain hopeful their lives will positively change.

Victorian authors often drew upon fairy tale plots in their own work, as does Dickens. Two such fairy tale plots Victorian authors used are the "lost heir to a fortune," as is the case for Oliver Twist, or the common plotline of "finding the idyllic marriage partner," as Amy Dorrit does. These plots not only illustrate the parallels of these stories with everyday lives but also assure readers' familiarity with such story elements and this, in turn, ensures sales. In *Dickens and the Invisible World: Fairy Tales, Fantasy and Novel-Making* (1979), Harry Stone finds, "The fairy story was an emblem, at once rudimentary and pure, of what contemporary society needed and what it increasingly lacked. The fairy story was also inextricably associated with childhood; it shaped the very character of future generations" (4). Victorians developed the literary fairy tale from traditional fairy tales into morally acceptable, cultivated literary stories that made them appropriate for children. In his own writing, Dickens follows such a pattern, and while he avoids overtly projecting religious dogma, he does assert the moral ideologies present in the newly developing Victorian fairy tale.

In nineteenth-century Britain, science was beginning to anchor itself as a concrete, plausible approach to explaining the physical world. This world was foreign to Victorian society, but could help people view the world in ways they had only imagined. A threat to the already fragile religious philosophies of the time, science was rejected by some and embraced by others. Some critics, such as A. O. J. Cockshut in "Faith and Doubt in the Victorian Age" (1993) feel " . . . the destructive influence of Darwin is largely mythical. . . . For some, certainly, the new evidence that the earth and human race were both unimaginably older than had been previously supposed was disturbing, but it was a disturbance more of feelings than of intellect" (48). While there were many religious groups who did feel the "new science" was a threat, there were many others who embraced its theories and possibilities. Likewise many individuals found a common ground between the two ideologies. Such people as Frank Miller Turner suggests in *Between Science and Religion: The Reaction to Scientific Naturalism in Late Victorian England* (1974):

> ... found [that] the Christianity in which they had been reared [was] too limited for their intellects and the scientific naturalism that bid for their allegiance too restrictive for the range of their ideals and aspirations. Consequently, in terms of their contemporary intellectual and social environment, they came to dwell between the science that beckoned them and the religion they had forsaken. (1).

Dickens was among these individuals. In his construction of the imperfect child, Dickens draws upon the fairy tale and character in order to parallel the authentic world with the fairy world. This world becomes a transitory space where characters like Oliver and Little Nell might undergo their lessons in order to realize their societal and cultural place.

At the Prize-Giving of the Institutional Association of Lancashire and Cheshire: Manchester in December of 1858, Dickens noted:

> ... let me say one word out of my own personal heart, which is always very dear to it in this connexion. Do not let us, in the midst of the visible objects of nature, whose workings we can tell off in figures, surrounded by machines that can be made to the thousandth part of an inch, acquiring every day knowledge which can be proved upon a slate or demonstrated by a microscope—do not let us, in the laudable pursuit of the facts that surround us, neglect the fancy and the imagination which equally surround us as part of the great scheme. Let the child have its fables; let the man or woman into which it changes, always remember these fables tenderly. Let numerous graces and ornaments that cannot be weighed and measured, and that seem at first sight idle enough, continue to have their places about us, be we never so wise. The hardest head may co-exist with the softest heart. The union and just balance of these two is always a blessing to the possessor, and always a blessing to mankind. The Divine Teacher was as gentle and considerate as He was powerful and wise. . . . As the utmost results of the wisdom of men can only be at last to help to raise the earth to that condition to which His doctrine, untainted by the blindness and passions of men, would have exalted it long ago; so let us always remember that He set us the example of blending the understanding and the imagination, and that, following it ourselves, we tread in His steps. . . . Knowledge, as all followers of it must know, has a very limited power indeed when it informs the head alone; but when it informs the head and heart too, it has the power over life and death, the body and the soul, and dominates the universe. (qtd. in *Speeches* 284–5)

Dickens is speaking of something more than just religion and science; he is discussing belief as of the utmost importance in helping mankind. The fable or fairy tale, according to Dickens, does this. In neglecting the imagination we remove a vital part of what it means to be human. The fairy tale was also seen as a threat to Christianity. During the Victorian period, many religious groups, including the Evangelicals,[4] discouraged the reading of fairy tales. Such stories were deemed unnecessary and, in many ways, dangerous to a child's development. The romantic idea of the child and childhood was important during the Victorian Era, and as the divisions in religious sects increased, children and their welfare became a crucial point of argument for many of these religious groups. Many Evangelicals, for example, felt the threat to their authority and little in the way of entertainment was allowed adults and children alike. Cockshut, among other critics, believes, "By doing away with all religious authority except the Bible, parental authority became, in practice, absolute. It was the parents who awed the children into restraining their natural inclination to play or even read" (31).

Figure 2.1 "The Fairy School." Illustration from Thomas Keightley's *The World Guide to Gnomes, Fairies, Elves, and Other Little People* (1880). Rpt. in Harper's Bazaar, 30 January 1896. © Culver Pictures Inc., and Reprinted with permission from Culver Pictures, Inc.

It was such "threats" fairy tales posed because they were full of "vice" and, though morally structured, led a reader to fanciful beliefs.

Dickens believed children should be exposed to fantasy and to a rich fantasy life and he carries this out in the development of his own novels. In *Social Dreaming: Dickens and the Fairy Tale* (2002), Elaine Ostry finds " . . . to fancy is not just an escape for Dickens, but essential to societal betterment, and even survival: it is the keynote of his utopian vision. Dickens's social agenda is opposed to utilitarianism, but his embrace of fancy is not a nostalgic reaction against the modern industrial society. . . . On the contrary, he wants to use fancy to draw from new technology . . ." (110). Fairy tales formed another lens through which Victorians were able to view the world and led many to the realm of the supernatural. The occult and the supernatural world became topics of everyday conversation and Dickens took part in this as he even believed in mesmerism and amateurishly practiced it later in his life. Fairy tales and fairy tale characters were often thought to be a part of not only their own realm, but also of the physical world. Fairy tale characters might be depicted taking part in everyday activities humans engaged in as in the illustration of "The Fairy School" (Figure 2.1). The realm of the supernatural stood in stark contrast to scientific and religious ideologies as it bridged both the seen and unseen. On one

Figure 2.2 "Gnomes Terrifying a Miner." Illustration from Thomas Keightley's *The World Guide to Gnomes, Fairies, Elves, and Other Little People* (1880). © Culver Pictures Inc., and Reprinted with permission from Culver Pictures, Inc.

hand, a person must believe in what they cannot tangibly "see," as in traditional Christian faith, but on the other, they could seek out facts of the fantasy world that are described in fairy tales and fables.

Dickens uses conventional fairy tale components in his work, but he also develops fables and allegories from traditional fairy stories in order to augment the "possible" other world. This is a Victorian world that might look gloomy with a smoggy sky, but could have the promise of fresh air and riches. A fascination with the supernatural world, one that could not be proven or unproven by religion or science but might possibly exist, enhanced Dickens's work. This newly developing faith was the crossroads between the worlds of religion and science. It was a world people could rarely inhabit, as with heaven, but it was tangible and one might catch a glimpse of it or its occupants. In some cases, it was also a place where fairy characters and humans could interact with one another as illustrated in "Gnomes Terrifying a Miner" (Figure 2.2) that is reminiscent of Curdie's encounters with such creatures in MacDonald's *The Princess and the Goblin* and *The Princess and Curdie*. An important state when this might occur was during daydreaming, dreams, or right before a person falls asleep. During such stages Dickens uses fairy tales and stories in his work for adults as a "way of seeing" in the worlds of *Oliver Twist*, *The Old Curiosity Shop*, *A Christmas Carol*, *Dombey and Son*, *Bleak House*, and *Little Dorrit*.

Dickens's Fair(l)y Children

Reminiscent of the abandoned child in many fairy tales, Oliver's squalling from his first breath gives him credibility as Dickens's first imperfect child. As Rumpelstiltskin makes the mother guess his name or he will steal away her child, Oliver's mother inversely passes away without leaving her child a name. In the form of the workhouse, society must then step in and guess what to do with him. They determine raising him by hand will be best for all parties concerned. Oliver is swept into being farmed and lost among the cupidity of Victorian church bureaucracy. Logic suggests no child in Oliver's situation would remain "pure" and "innocent." Yet Dickens writes in his preface to *Oliver Twist*:

> . . . I wished to show, in little Oliver, the principle of Good surviving through every adverse circumstance, and triumphing at last; and when I considered among what companions I could try him best, having regard to that kind of men into whose hands he would most naturally fall; I bethought myself of those who figure in these volumes. (33)

Oliver is not meant to be "pure" and "innocent," but rather to retain the "principle of Good" and survive to better himself. Oliver does this by immersing himself in the fairy world of London, a world he knows nothing of initially.

Dickens overtly omits any sense of fancy from his preface to *Oliver Twist*. He illustrates the harsh truth of reality, as the romance many found in the lives of thieves would be omitted from the pages of *Oliver Twist* (34–35). Dickens further indicates his knowledge of societal romantic notions of crime in his discussion of Nancy and he calls upon readers' hypocrisy and argues that Nancy deserves a place among all other such characters. Her life, poverty aside, represents the middle and upper classes (*Oliver Twist* 35). Though Oliver becomes a part of this world for some time, he is not raised in London's streets and dank corridors. Dickens extends his belief: "I have yet to learn that a lesson of the purest good may not be drawn from the vilest evil" (*Oliver Twist* 33). Certainly Oliver indicates this throughout his travels from the workhouse to his adoption by Mr. Brownlow.

Oliver's natural goodness is rarely questioned, but in order to be good, one must also know the evils of the world and what to avoid. Oliver's journey leads him through such earthly evils, though he is depicted as good in word and illustration. Cruikshank, after Dickens's death, notes in a letter to *The Times* on 30 December of 1871 that he suggested to Dickens the plot and characters that comprise *Oliver Twist*. This has been widely discussed, but interestingly Oliver's appearance does eventually change, for, as John Harvey points out in *Victorian Novelists and Their Illustrators*, Dickens had wanted Oliver to appear as a "queer sort of chap" while Cruikshank, as he indicates in his letter to *The Times*, thought he should appear more comely (202). Oliver's appearance does change from the first two plates in the text to the third and those that follow. What is important is that Dickens did not intend for Oliver to be purely "good" and untainted from the world around him, but rather that he learn from both his mistakes and those made by others to determine what was "good."

Born to a woman who merely asks, "Let me see the child, and die" (*Oliver Twist* 46), Oliver becomes the ward of the church immediately. His mother's only discourse indicates what is to become of her. Regarding Oliver's fate, "Oliver cried lustily. If he could have known that he was an orphan, left to the tender mercies of churchwardens and overseers, perhaps he would have cried the louder" (*Oliver Twist* 47). While Dickens's sarcasm is readily evident to readers, at birth Oliver is unknowingly thrown into a world of chaos and greed.

Oliver's value as a commodity is clearly evident from the onset. After being raised for nine years by hand from Mrs. Mann, Oliver is given over to Mr. Bumble, the parish beadle. Oliver's ninth year finds him " . . . a pale thin child, somewhat diminutive in stature, and decidedly small in circumference. But nature or inheritance had implanted a good sturdy spirit in Oliver's breast: . . ." and he is kept in a coal cellar, in a fairy tale fashion, before he is released to the beadle (*Oliver Twist* 49). Though he is sold into labor and escapes to London, Oliver is thought to be a thief by everyone except Mrs. Bedwin, Mr. Brownlow's housekeeper. The beadle manages to taint Oliver's reputation, but

Mrs. Bedwin will not believe it. Mr. Grimwig, Mr. Brownlow's friend, admonishes her, "You old women will never believe anything but quack-doctors and lying story-books" (*Oliver Twist* 176). Yet it is such storybooks that help construct her system of faith and belief in a very unlikely boy.

Dickens's use of overt fairy tale language is not as prominent in *Oliver Twist* as it is in many of his subsequent novels, but the motifs are readily apparent. Oliver's journey from a small country town to London and back to the pastoral country is evident in the text as a parallel to his own development. In moving from one phase to another, Oliver both develops his knowledge of "goodness" and overcomes what might have happened to him had he remained in the care of Fagin, the noted Jew and criminal, into whose hands he falls when he first enters London. While the country is pastoral and "good" for Oliver later in the text, the small town he has left and the city he enters are not necessarily so respectable. In *The Country and the City*, Raymond Williams rightly suggests, "Dickens's ultimate vision of London is then not to be illustrated by topography or local instance. It lies in the form of his novels: . . . It does not matter which way we put it: the experience of the city is a fictional method; or the fictional method is the experience of the city" (154). The backdrop of London, much like a fairyland, helps construct the imperfect child Oliver is to become. He must pass through this before he can fully appreciate the reality of both "good" and "bad" around him.

Fagin's[5] den is where his gang of young boys can experience the "bad" aspects of life. It becomes not only their safe haven from the dark streets of London, but much like Peter Pan's tree house for the Lost Boys in J. M. Barrie's *Peter and Wendy* (1911), it is also a free space where they imbibe all the vices they would not be allowed to taste if they were under the supervision of caring parents. The hideout is described as:

> The walls and ceiling of the room were perfectly black with age and dirt. There was a deal table before the fire, upon which were a candle, stuck in a ginger-beer bottle, two or three pewter pots, and a loaf and butter, and a plate. In a frying-pan, which was on the fire, and which was secured to the mantelshelf by a string, some sausages were cooking; and standing over them, with a toasting fork in his hand, was a very old shriveled Jew, whose villainous looking and repulsive face was obscured by a quantity of matted red hair. . . . Several rough beds made of old sacks, were huddled side by side on the floor. (*Oliver Twist* 105)

Fagin provides this home for his gang as long as they produce at "work." Depicted as vile, and as widely noted by critics such as Dennis Walder in *Dickens and Religion* (2007), Fagin takes on the visage of a devil that is corrupting the minds and lives of those who come into contact with him. Fagin serves as an illustration of the Antichrist who leads small children, and thus society, astray. Like the Pied Piper, Fagin gathers his small band who are no longer "seen" by society as individuals but rather fairylike beings that exist on the fringes of society. Much in the way Sunday School Moralists[6] were gathering and tending the poor, so too were people like Fagin preying on the innocent and unknowing. The children, most notably Dodger and Charley Bates, have been assimilated into Fagin's lifestyle and Oliver is representative of someone who lurks on the outskirts, who has not been tainted, by an ultimate commitment to Fagin. As Oliver eventually reads of the exploits of criminals in *The Newgate Calendar*, Fagin, in storyteller fashion, " . . . obviously hopes to inspire his young charge with the lives of criminals" (151) as Monica Flegel notes in *Conceptualizing Cruelty to Children in Nineteenth-Century England: Literature, Representation and the NSPCC* (2009). Oliver's shifting from one reality to another through his dream states is indicative of the transitory nature of the lifestyle Oliver could choose. He is groomed for Fagin's trade in thievery, though he ultimately rejects it, which helps illustrate a sense of agency in the young orphan.

Pickpocketing, not an uncommon employment for young boys in Victorian London, is how Artful Dodger and his gang make their way in London's dirty streets. This is the trade Fagin teaches his young protégés. In a description that might be taken out of *Oliver Twist*, Henry Mayhew[7] notes in the fourth installment of his *London Labour and the London Poor: A Cyclopaedia of the Conditions and Earnings of Those That Will Work, Those That Cannot Work, and Those That Will Not Work* (1851) series, "Many of these ragged urchins are taught to steal by their companions, others are taught by trainers of thieves, young men and women, and some middle-aged convicts" (304). The convict and his clan were often fantastical creatures themselves, hiding in dark dens of iniquity, under bridges, or simply wandering the local causeways trying to pose as pedestrians.

Training such as Oliver undergoes was often done through play that would teach children the proper way to relieve potential marks of their possessions. Handkerchiefs and other linens were commonly lost in such exchanges. Mayhew depicts one such training lesson where " . . . the trainer—if a man—walks up and down the room with a handkerchief in the tail of his coat, and the ragged boys amuse themselves abstracting it until they learn to do it in an adroit manner" (304). Through play and the use of imagination, the child's reflexes and eye-hand coordination are supposedly bettered so that their touch becomes light and quick. Oliver is trained in such a way to pick pockets by Fagin (*Oliver Twist* 110–11) so that he too might help bring in capital for the thieving band. Though thievery is central to Oliver's education with Fagin, he is actually being primed for darker burgle work with Bill Sikes, a much more violent criminal than Fagin.

Characters such as Sikes were not uncommon among Victorian criminals and their stories became fantastical stories for the public, who read about them in magazines and various texts published for the reading public. As audiences around the world become fixated on sensational stories, the Victorians read avidly about their own celebrities who were just as fantastical as stars are to us today. The O. J. Simpson trial or Charles Manson prove that criminality can cause celebrity status, as was the case for many Victorian villains. After being forced to return to Fagin and his gang, Oliver is thrust into an attic and Fagin gives him a book to read. Popular during the Victorian period and consumed like fairy tales, texts like penny dreadfuls[8] and *The Newgate Calendar*[9] would outline the lives of villains who were often imprisoned and eventually hanged in Newgate Prison. Fagin wants to scare Oliver into imagining what he might face if he leaves the safety of the gang. It also serves as a warning to Oliver of what he does not want to become. While some of the Newgate stories play fast and loose with the truth, the replacement of fairy stories with Newgate tales suggests Oliver's innocence is tainted by societal problems, such as murder. Oliver has a very real dose of reality thrust upon him. As he reads the Newgate collection, Oliver:

> . . . read of dreadful crimes that made the blood run cold; of secret murders that had been committed by the lonely wayside; of bodies hidden from the eye of man in deep pits and wells: which would not keep them down, deep as they were, but had yielded them up at last, after many years. . . . Here, too, he read of men who, lying in their beds at dead of night, had been tempted (so they said) and led on, by their own bad thoughts, to such dreadful bloodshed as it made the flesh creep, and the limbs quail, to think of. The terrible descriptions were so real and vivid, that the sallow pages seemed to turn red with gore; and the words upon them, to be sounded in his ears, as if they were whispered, in hollow murmurs, by the spirits of the dead. (*Oliver Twist* 196–97)

While Oliver grows afraid of the book, it is such a work, perhaps the very one Nancy later reads (409), that frightens her right before her death.

Though a very tainted fairy godmother figure, Nancy saves Oliver though she cannot save herself. Dickens makes no apologies for Nancy to his audience and states he wishes to depict her in all her truth, misery, and sorrow. Through Nancy's actions Dickens's message reverberates most loudly: "I have yet to learn that a lesson of the purest good may not be drawn from the vilest evil" (*Oliver Twist* 33). In all of Oliver's imperfection, Nancy still believes in him, as does Mrs. Bedwin. While Dickens does not relate much of Nancy's background, a reader understands she is a product of Fagin's training and both a thief and prostitute. Mayhew outlines such characters as dressing:

> . . . in a light cotton or merino gown, and ill-suited crinoline, with light grey, or brown cloak or mantle. Some with pork-pie hat, and waving feather-white, blue or red; others with a slouched straw-hat. Some of them walk with a timid look, others with effrontery. Some have a look of artless innocence and ingenuousness, others very pert, callous and artful. (*LLLP IV* 358–59)

Mayhew suggests, "Many of these unfortunate girls have redeeming traits in their character. Some are kind-hearted and honest, and not a few are even generous and self-denying" (*LLLP IV* 360). Nancy does not want Oliver to become like Dodger or Charley Bates, and in saving Oliver redeems herself, even though she dies. She becomes a fairy godmother for Oliver and allows for his transition from one world to another. Dickens indicates such passages are not always simple, for city people can invade the pastoral countryside thus polluting the environment, as Fagin tracks Oliver down in the country. As Fagin is jailed and Oliver begins his new life, Dickens's illustration of the city converging into the country is marked and left in the narrative. The pastoral, in this sense, becomes the ultimate place for a "good" life, one where Oliver, like Little Nell, finds peace.

In *The Old Curiosity Shop*, Dickens provides readers with a fairy tale from the beginning of the text. Master Humphrey thinks of Little Nell after meeting her: "I sat down in my easy-chair, and falling back upon its ample cushions, pictured to myself the child in her bed: alone, unwatched, uncared for, (save by angels), yet sleeping peacefully. So very young, so spiritual, so slight and fairy-like . . ." (20). *The Old Curiosity Shop* contains all of the elements of traditional fairy tales. The figure of Little Nell is Sleeping Beauty, while Quilp, who is on numerous occasions referred to as a "dwarf," resembles the evil dwarf found in many fairy tales. The powers Quilp possesses are both human and supernatural in nature and he often appears as a devil or demon that delights in tormenting those around him. In fact this is his only enjoyment in life. In tormenting others, Quilp asserts his power and control usually through surprise. As Stone states, "This sadistic demon has other supernatural powers. He can appear out of nowhere, and he can vanish in a trice" (110). Kit is the heroic prince who sets out to save Little Nell. According to Michael Kotzin:

> The typical fairy tale has a central character, usually an isolated, virtuous young man or woman who is often a youngest child. The hero confronts a villain, such as a cruel stepmother or a supernatural figure such as a giant, ogre, or witch. He may receive help from a supernatural being, such as some sort of good fairy. He usually is victorious over his adversary, achieves comfort and happiness, and sometimes gets married. (8)

Dickens believes that the traditional fairy tale should not be altered and he does not do so in the case of *The Old Curiosity Shop*. Just as Hans Christian Andersen's Little Match Girl dies happily, so does Little Nell. Traditional fairy tales must remain untouched in Dickens's eyes, but literary fairy tales are different, as is the case with Dickens's work *The Magic Fishbone* (1867). The world Little Nell must inhabit forces her to take action, for neither religious faith nor facts can aid her. She exists in both the "real" and "Fairie" worlds. "Particular qualities of the world of 'Fairie' include the presence of magician acts, the animation of non-living things, the transformation of one thing or person into another, and an unnaturally quick or unnaturally slow passage of time" (Kotzin 8). The world of "Fairie" allows Little Nell to escape London with her grandfather and offers her hope where she has none in the streets of London.

The fairy world of London that Little Nell escapes Dickens recaptures in grotesque fashion in *A Christmas Carol*. The imperfect child Little Nell becomes less apparent in Tiny Tim. For contemporary readers, Tiny Tim has become a much more significant character than the space Dickens allots him. Students' first recollection of *A Christmas Carol* is often of Tiny Tim and his famous statement, "God bless us, every one." Dickens's popularity, many people feel, is due to the staying power of *A Christmas Carol*. Tiny Tim tells us we should be happy, no matter what our lot in life brings. Yet Tiny Tim is, like many of Dickens's characters, an imperfect child. It is the fairylike quality of his nature that makes him memorable to us, even if it is sweeter than sugarplums at Christmas. Readers first see Tiny Tim on his father's shoulder, but Dickens points out, "Alas for Tiny Tim, he bore a little crutch, and had his limbs supported by an iron frame!" (*A Christmas Carol* 79). While there is a semblance of helplessness in Tiny Tim's physical frame, he is like a family Jiminy Cricket who ultimately keeps up the family's spirits in the face of their poverty and helps melt Scrooge's icy, miserly heart.

Tiny Tim's good nature is evident in all he says and does but his sickly nature and brooding countenance make him an early construction of Paul Dombey. In church, Tiny Tim's father recollects, he is "As good as gold ... and better. Somehow he gets thoughtful sitting by himself so much, and thinks the strangest things you ever heard. He told me, coming home, that he hoped the people saw him in the church, because he was a cripple, and it might be pleasant to them to remember upon Christmas Day, who made lame beggars walk and blind men see" (*A Christmas Carol* 80). Tiny Tim, much like Diamond in George MacDonald's *At the Back of the North Wind*, is not unselfish in his declaration, for he wants to become a symbol that suggests Jesus Christ. He does not believe he is Jesus Christ, but rather wishes for people to see his affliction and thus draw a connection with what the holiday is supposed to reflect: kindness and charity.

Tiny Tim remembers Christian charity while still living the life of a pauper. He becomes a model of kindness for Scrooge, who is an ogre bested by this Tom Thumb parallel. Dickens notes, "Scrooge was the Ogre of the family" (*A Christmas Carol* 83). Tiny Tim knows enough of the cruelty of the world around him to realize that only through social unity can conditions be better for "everyone." *A Christmas Carol* is a fairy tale Dickens makes applicable all the year round, and its continuing popularity assures Dickens's place at the Christmas hearth as a staple of the holiday. Yet it is Tiny Tim's one proclamation, "God bless us, every one," that we most recall. His significance as a Dickensian imperfect child lies in the fact that he lives and does not die, like Little Nell or Paul Dombey. This makes his a fairy story because a child facing his experiences in Victorian society would likely die. After the deaths of two characters in his works, Dickens constructs Tiny Tim to live. His counterpart, Paul Dombey, does not meet with such a fairy tale happy ending.

Child death occurs in much of Dickens's early work, such as Dick in *Oliver Twist* and Little Nell in *The Old Curiosity Shop*. This continues into *Dombey and Son* with the passing of Paul Dombey. The title offers an ironic commentary on the status of parent/child relationships and the social view of female children and expresses the satirical association between Mr. Dombey and his daughter. Paul Dombey, the much-wanted son of Mr. Dombey, occupies a very small space in the text. But his status as an imperfect child is readily established. Paul's birth is reminiscent of the fairy tale motif of the dying mother, like Snow White's, dying upon the birth of her child, and this parallels Oliver's birth and Little Nell's loss of her own mother. Harry Stone believes, in *Dickens and the Invisible World: Fairy Tales, Fantasy, and Novel-Making*, Paul " . . . has a child's frankness and freshness of vision, but also a child's naiveté. . . . His psychology is right, too. He shows jealousy, and hostility as well as gratitude, irrational fear as well as sensitive insight" (160). Paul, often considered "old" by critics, is born with his insightful and quizzical nature, as is common among imperfect children, who are often part of reality and fantasy worlds. Traded, like a changeling for a human infant, between Richards, his wet-nurse, and her sister for Richards's own child, Paul becomes a creature caught between socioeconomic and environmental class issues. Stone suggests, "Paul is born with the tokens of time on him. . . . He also has a childlike percipience, and almost otherworldly wisdom. He is, in fact, the changeling that his father feared he might be . . ." (161). As Paul's character develops, time itself becomes disjointed and chaotic.

Shifted from one "school" to another, Paul sinks into poorer health until he dies a melodramatic death typical of Dickens's writing. Paul is a fairylike child, an angel too good for this world. His caretakers, Mrs. Wickam, for example, believe that if Paul grows too fond of someone he comes into contact with, that person might die due to Paul's supernatural nature (126–27). This is reminiscent of the dying children in Christina Rossetti's poems in *Sing-Song: A Nursery Rhyme Book* (1872). Such belief follows Paul throughout his short life as he lives for both his sister and the moment. Paul's interaction with his father is not often detailed as the boy is thought of as just a part of Mr. Dombey's greater plan for his business lineage. Depicted as almost being five, Paul had:

> . . . a strange, old-fashioned, thoughtful way, at other times, of sitting brooding in his miniature arm-chair, when he looked (and talked) like one of those terrible little Beings in the Fairy tales, who, at a hundred and fifty or two hundred years of age, fantastically represent the children for whom they have been substituted. He would frequently be stricken with the precocious mood upstairs in the nursery; and would sometimes lapse into it suddenly, exclaiming he was tired . . . (*Dombey and Son* 109)

In his dreamlike states, which are similar to Oliver's fainting spells, Paul is able to shift from reality to a fairy realm where his precious waves crash upon shores, something outside of his confining quarters.

Dickens suggests Paul is not "normal" even in his contact with others, for "Consistent with his odd tastes, the child set aside a ruddy-faced lad, who was proposed as the drawer of this carriage [Paul's wheelchair], and selected, instead, his grandfather—a weazen, old, crab-faced man, in a suit of battered oilskin, who had got tough and stringy from long pickling in salt-water, and who smelt like a weedy sea-beach . . ." (*Dombey and Son* 127). This grandfather, like Paul, is closer to nature, whereas his biological grandson, who has been touched by society with his "ruddy-face," is not. Being closer to nature and part of a widely unknown and separate part of society and reality, Paul feels closer to people like this grandfather, who is part of nature and he more is comfortable having them around. Dickens further notes that Paul was " . . . never so distressed as by the company of children—Florence alone excepted—always" (*Dombey and Son* 127). Paul is constantly noted as being "odd" or, as Mrs. Wickam suggests, "changed" (*Dombey and Son* 125). Paul Dombey, unlike his stronger sister, is not meant to live.

Florence Dombey, Floy, as Paul calls her, is a constant companion to her brother and becomes the one person he especially looks up to and loves. Yet Florence is also a creature caught between the fairy world and Victorian society. Readers' first glimpse of Floy is after the birth of her brother when she is huddled in a corner of her mother's dying room. Florence is, in her father's estimation, " . . . not worth mentioning. [But she had] stolen into the chamber unobserved, [and] was now crouching timidly, in a corner whence she could see her mother's face. . . . such a child was merely a piece of base coin that couldn't be invested—a bad Boy—nothing more" (*Dombey and Son* 13). Though Mr. Dombey does his social duty in taking care of his offspring, Florence is nothing to him because she cannot contribute to his business. Florence is distraught and yet ignorant of death, so the way Richards helps her understand is through story. Using a fairy tale, Richards explains that while there was once a beautiful mother and daughter, whom her mother loved very much, the lady died and went to heaven, where she prayed her daughter would be good and remember she was loved (*Dombey and Son* 36–37). The use of this story encourages Florence to remember her mother and grow up to be a good daughter. She believes that she can be with her mother again. Florence's inquisitive and insightful manner helps her develop far beyond the ideal Victorian daughter.

Florence is a child much like her brother. She glances "keenly" (13) at her father as her mother passes away and later he begins to fear the child that did not interest him before the birth of his son. His feelings changed into " . . . uneasiness of an extraordinary kind. He almost felt as if she watched and distrusted him. As if she held the clue to something secret in his breast, of the nature of which he was hardly informed himself. As if she had an innate knowledge of one jarring and discordant string in him, and her very breath could sound it" (*Dombey and Son* 42). Mr. Dombey also finds he is "ill at ease about her. She troubled his peace" (*Dombey and Son* 42), for Florence is witness to his treatment of her mother's death and has insight into his character. Though a dutiful daughter and sister outwardly, Florence challenges social norms. Like many of Dickens's heroines, Florence leaves her father altogether only to reunite with him later on her own terms.

Just as Little Nell becomes lost in the London streets, so does Florence. However, unlike Little Nell, who is a child of London, Florence is unable to traverse her way in its labyrinth. After losing her clothing by being tricked by an old woman, Florence, like Jack and Jill in a wild forest, has to find her way out of the maze of streets and buildings that make up a poor section of London. As if sprung from a fairy tale, Walter, her future husband, comes to her rescue when she is stranded on a wharf with only one shoe on. He " . . . picked up the shoe, and put it on the little foot as the Prince in the story might have fitted Cinderella's slipper on. [Walter] felt . . . like Saint George of England, with the dragon lying before him" (*Dombey and Son* 92–93). Florence has been transformed by a wicked witch in London's forest into a poor waif rescued by a prince and through Walter's help, the princess is able to return to her familial castle. Resembling the imperfect child Cinderella, Florence also knows no love at home but makes her way between the worlds of the poor and wealthy. Likewise, Stone suggests Florence is " . . . both lost babe in the wood and outcast Cinderella" (171) and she must travel on one path, that of her haunted reality, to reach a contented life and sense of agency with Walter at the end of her journey. Esther Summerson, much like Florence, ends up happily married, although Esther does not grow up knowing who her parents really are because an evil aunt straight out of a fairy tale raises her.

Bleak House opens with a fairy tale monster, the Megalosaurus, which would be " . . . forty feet long or so, waddling like an elephantine lizard up Holborn Hill" (13). This helps illustrate the premise that even those living in London are lost in its ancient labyrinth of muck, mire, and murkiness. Though this mythological creature is reminiscent of the rise in popularity of the dinosaur during the Victorian Era, it also indicates Dickens's use of simile to illustrate the London in which characters such as Esther existed. Dickens suggests everyone is oblivious to what surrounds him or her as if Victorian society was lost in one large foglike fairy world. In *Victorian Fantasy* (2005) Stephen Prickett notes, " . . . this kind of reference, with its vivid sense of the humorous grotesque, nevertheless only serves to illustrate how far Dickens is in mood from those who came to find in the dinosaurs and other prehistoric creatures the true image of the monsters of the mind" (80). Those images that Dickens finds to be all too real in the very people surrounding the imperfect child are created in Esther.

From the beginning of her tale Esther notes she was raised " . . . from my earliest remembrance—like some of the princesses in the fairy stories, only I was not charming—by my godmother" (*Bleak House* 28). Though Esther is educated and cared for, she is not loved nor does she have any living parent known to her. An aunt, posing as her godmother, raises Esther with the help of a housekeeper, Mrs. Rachael. When Esther inquires after her mother, her aunt exclaims, "Submission, self-denial, diligent work, are the preparations for a life begun with such a shadow on it. You are different from other children, Esther, because you were not born, like them, in common sinfulness and wrath. You are set apart" (*Bleak House* 30–31). Crushing as this is to Esther, she does not want her aunt to try to explain and she finds "Imperfect as my understanding of my sorrow was, I knew that I had brought no joy, at any time, to anybody's heart, and that I was to no one upon earth what Dolly was to me" (*Bleak House* 31). Dolly, Esther's doll, becomes her best friend and she explains to Dolly the source of her sorrow. Not only is Esther living a fairy tale existence, but she is also at the center of a princess tale where she plays the part of the overlooked princess.

Esther becomes dutiful and educated, but as her life continues and her aunt dies, she is shipped off to a school where she learns to be a governess much as Charlotte Brontë's Jane Eyre. When Esther leaves Mrs. Rachael, who has inherited all of her aunt's belongings, Esther looks at a rug that has roses on it and says " . . . which always seemed to me the first thing in the world I had ever seen, was hanging outside in the frost and snow" (*Bleak House* 36). The parallel to Snow White's conception is evident. Esther's mother "dies" upon her birth and she is raised by a wicked, cold stepmother, as is Snow White. Though Snow White was a wanted birth, Esther's mother never says Esther was not desired. Socially her mother must abandon Esther or they could both face shame. Dickens was writing *Bleak House* as Cruickshank's revisions of traditional fairy tales began to be published. Dickens wrote his article "Frauds on Fairies" immediately after finishing *Bleak House*, though the idea had been on his mind and contributed to the novel's development, Esther's included. Being in the world through an "uncommon" sin, Esther's mother traded in her progeny, her own blood, for a better life and Esther must pay for it with a life set in "shadow." Esther is not unlucky in life. Rather, this "shadow" indicates the ignorance she has about her lineage.

Though looked after by Mr. Jarndyce, Esther undergoes a transformation, both physically and mentally, after she contracts smallpox. Esther finds her world transformed as well, for when she awakens she finds herself in new surroundings that look as "If a good fairy had built the house for me with a wave of her wand, and I had been a princess and her favored godchild . . ." (*Bleak House* 571). Esther, unlike Snow White, is able to meet her mother but it is through her own strength and perseverance and old-fashioned coincidence that this comes about. Though self-deprecating at times, Esther's staying power is an asset. Dickens does not draw her, as many critics have suggested, as a weakling. Rather, Esther is someone like Oliver who must overcome great odds in order to achieve a sense of identity and validity in Victorian culture.

The fairy tale pattern can be found among most of Dickens's texts and an overt example of this can be found in *Little Dorrit*. Often noted as among his later or "dark" novels, *Little Dorrit* is perhaps one of Dickens's most realistic texts. The emphasis of the fairy tale world in its pages is hard to miss. The Marshalsea Prison serves as the "castle" and this structure keeps debtors in and the rest of the world out on a daily basis. Amy Dorrit, also known as Little Dorrit, has been born and raised in the prison walls, and still becomes a resourceful young woman as she takes care of her family when they seemingly do not wish to acknowledge their social position. While Amy cares for her family and others around her, she dreams of a life beyond the prison walls. During her storytelling to Maggy, an adopted "daughter," we see Amy strongly believes in the fairy tale. Amy and those around her understand through her stories, not riches. As Dickens later indicates when the newfound family fortune is unwisely invested, wealth may be fleeting, but one must make one's own happiness in life.

As the novel opens, the beating and glaring of the sun are everywhere. This is not to be confused with the stare or glare of religion or science, for Dickens calls it in *Little Dorrit* a " . . . universal stare [which] made the eyes ache" (15). It is as if nature is staring and people begin to take refuge. In *Dickens and the Broken Scripture* (1985), Janet Larson believes that Dickens uses the books of Revelation and Ecclesiastes to illustrate competing interpretations of experience in *Little Dorrit*. Janet Larson suggests in *Dickens and the Broken Scripture,* in the opening chapter, "Sun and Shadow," Dickens " . . . presents a paradigm of this contention and its partial resolution, engaging in dialectical interplay two Theorems of the Universe, both biblical, that contend for mastery" (179). Dickens begins his story and the fairy tale atmosphere in the local gaol, the Marseilles Prison, where readers are first introduced to the prisoners, or "birds." Rigaud and John Baptist are both dressed like pirates, one being "A sunburnt, quick, lithe, little man, though rather thickset. Earrings in his brown ears, white teeth lighting up his grotesque brown face, intensely black hair clustering about his brown throat, a ragged red shirt open at his brown breast. Loose, seamanlike trousers, decent shoes, a long red cap, a red sash around his waist and a knife in it" (*Little Dorrit* 19). The daughter of the warden is described as having a " . . . fair little face, touched with diving compassion, as it peeped shrinkingly through the grate, was like an angel's in the prison" (*Little Dorrit* 19). Dickens incorporates nature, faith, and fairy tale elements in his story. This takes place throughout the text, but most striking are the fairy tale elements Dickens uses that strengthen the frame of the story. Silver attests to the importance of fairy beings and their world to Victorian society and finds:

> For the study of the fairies appealed to those in the new disciplines emerging as the "social sciences," to a rising group of folklore theorists . . . to cultural anthropologists . . . and even to archaeologists. . . . The theories that folklorists . . . postulated to rationalize the irrational, to explain the

supernatural and belief in it simultaneously explain the culture itself—
exposing fears and fantasies close to the Victorian unconscious. Looking
at the ways Victorians looked at fairies provides an insight into the under-
lying attitudes of a society. (4)

Dickens weaves the importance of the fairy tale and the fairy world throughout
the pages of *Little Dorrit* in not only setting and tone, but also with characters.

These characteristics are not limited to villains or secondary personalities,
but can be found in the heroine of the story. Amy Dorrit appears to be a fairy
creature as she appears to sit in shadow and industriously works and leaves

THE STORY OF THE PRINCESS

Figure 2.3   "The Story of the Princess." Illustration from Charles Dickens's Little Dorrit (1857), illustration by H.K. Browne. Rpt. in *Little Dorrit*, (New York:
Books, Inc., 1867) Frontispiece.

the Clennam house with little notice. Seeing her for the first time, Arthur Clennam, the male protagonist of the story, finds her " . . . diminutive figure, small features, and slight spare dress . . ." out of place as she appears older than a child; however, " . . . she was so little and light, so noiseless and shy, and appeared so conscious of being out of place . . . that she had all the manner and much of the appearance of a subdued child" (*Little Dorrit* 63). Amy's fairylike qualities are what draw Arthur to learn more about her and the mysterious life she leads. It is not only Arthur who views Amy as mysterious and subdued, for on her nineteenth birthday Young John Chivery, a young man in love with Amy, declares her to be a " . . . sweet nursling of the Fairies" (*Little Dorrit* 211). This imagery is associated with Amy throughout the text. Not only does Dickens use fairy tale elements in *Little Dorrit*, but also religion and science. Dickens employs fairy tale elements in *Little Dorrit* to illustrate societal fascination with such ideologies and to present an alternative way of viewing the world as did many Victorians.

Though there are many instances of Dickens's use of fairy tale elements as ways of viewing the world in *Little Dorrit*, the most important and telling scene of the fairy tale takes place in Chapter 24 of Book 1 entitled "Fortune Telling." In this chapter Amy tells Maggy a fairy tale to help her understand her situation, much like Richards does for Florence Dombey. Ironically, Larson uses the picture illustrating this very scene, "The Story of the Princess" (Figure 2.3), on the front cover of her text, *Dickens and the Broken Scripture*, but barely mentions the event. When she does there is little reference to the telling of a fairy tale.

Looking longingly out her window, Amy weaves the fairy tale for Maggy that she requests; it has a princess and that should be " . . . a reg'lar one. Beyond all belief, you know!" (*Little Dorrit* 286). In the story the princess has everything she could desire and "When she was a child, she understood all her lessons before her masters taught them to her, and when she was grown up, she was the wonder of the world" (*Little Dorrit* 286). Amy relates that near the castle of this princess is a cottage, which is owned by a poor young spinning woman to whom the princess pays a visit. The princess is allowed to see the secret shadow the spinning woman keeps in a hiding place and the shadow goes to the grave with the death of the young spinning woman. The mysterious shadow is of "Some one who had gone by long before: of Some one who had gone on far away quite out of reach, never, never to come back" (*Little Dorrit* 288). Larson believes " . . . Amy sees herself in her confessional fairytale as the 'tiny woman' forever spinning in vain at her wheel of fate and hiding love: an image that implies Ecclesiastes' most dismaying theorem of existence" (221). While Amy hides her love for Clennam and is a dutiful daughter and sibling, she also desires her own future and can be viewed as the princess character of her story. Amy also becomes the princess who looks longingly out of her carriage daily at the little cottage where the "tiny woman" has love and she does not. As Amy dreamily stares out her bedroom window she feels she can never possess Arthur's love. Amy's story is more than a tale of romantic love, however. As Kotzin notes, Amy's tale is " . . . an allegory about herself [which] has an unhappy ending. In the [late] novels, optimism is reduced to, at best, a modest hope. Joy is reduced to a sense of duty" (72). The fairy tale Amy relates to Maggy reflects hope, but also her duty to her family, and as the Princess must ride in her carriage daily so too must Amy look after her relatives.

Although writers before Dickens used fairy tale elements in their work, Dickens consistently uses fairy tale elements in the composition of *Oliver Twist*, *The Old Curiosity Shop*, *A Christmas Carol*, *Dombey and Son*, *Bleak House*, and *Little Dorrit*. Dickens not only sees the world through the lens of fairy tale, but also incorporates religion and science in his stories. In this way he illustrates the importance of these ways of looking at the world for Victorian society. While many critics have posited that science was one of the primary reasons the Victorians questioned religion and the church, this argument has shifted, as other societal issues such as gender, class, and race have come under closer critical examination. Indeed, in his "Frauds on the Fairies," Dickens, in the midst of decrying Cruikshank's fairy tale revisions, calls for the preservation of the "original" fairy tales. His argument is more than this, however, for Dickens suffered through the many unauthorized retellings of his own work. While preservation was important for the stories, Dickens's chief concern was the meaning these tales had for British people.

Later Use of the Imperfect Fair(l)y Child

Much like Dickens, George MacDonald was also concerned with the need for fancy in Victorian society. MacDonald entwines reality alongside the fairy world in much of his writing and this is very evident in *At the Back of the North Wind*. Diamond's journey with North Wind brings him, readers come to understand, to his death. Much like Little Nell, he traverses this path alongside many other characters, often leading them rather than being led. Curiously, his name suggests he is rare, precious, transparent, and yet strong. As Lisa Hermine Makman explains in "Child's Work Is Child's Play: The Value of George MacDonald's Diamond" (1999), it would not indicate such things to a Victorian audience (119). Rather, Makman believes, "In England at the time MacDonald wrote his story, the slang expression 'diamond cracking' referred to work in coal mines and that coal was dubbed 'black diamond' " (119), which offers a connection to his later works, *The Princess and The Goblin* and *The Princess and Curdie*, which followed Diamond's story. The concept of coal as "black diamond" would be familiar to Victorian audiences, as would diamonds.

Yet Diamond means something more. Makman also notes, "Diamond's name thus contains divergent images of children in circulation at the time: the idealized toy-child, inherently valuable, necessarily good, and the piteous child-slave, toiling to produce value, potentially corrupt, and in dire need of rescue" (119). Representative of the idealized child, Diamond is, however, imperfect, for he is both ill and his innocence is tainted by a very harsh Victorian reality. Diamonds when initially found are neither perfect nor valuable. Through the processing of the gem the value becomes evident. Diamond's value is economic, as when he takes over for his father when he is ill, and as an imperfect construction of a working class child. In both cases, Diamond produces value for readers as children like him did for society. Diamond is rescued not only by North Wind, but also by himself through the use of his fairylike prowess.

Though Diamond exists as a creature of a fairy world, he is caught between a fairy world and Victorian England. Both of these existences are hard, but Diamond traverses them with the help of North Wind. As he interacts with her more continuously, Diamond grows weaker physically but stronger in spirit. MacDonald connects spirituality and religion with fairy tale-like components to both entertain and teach, much like Charles Kingsley does in *The Water Babies*. MacDonald states in his essay "The Fantastic Imagination" (1893), "For my part, I do not write for children, but for the childlike, whether of five, or fifty, or seventy-five" (7). Like Dickens, MacDonald writes for all readers, but wishes to challenge readers to use their imaginations and does not want to give them definitions or rules of how to read or think. MacDonald explains in "The Fantastic Imagination":

> The natural world has its laws, and no man must interfere with them in the way of presentment any more than in the way of use; but they themselves may suggest laws of other kinds, and man may, if he pleases, invent a little world of his own, with its own laws . . . which is the nearest, perhaps, he can come to creation. (5–6)

Diamond exists in such a world, a blending of natural and fantastical spaces. Diamond tends to see in dreams that explain where he has traveled and where he will be going, though this is confusing to him initially. While trying to explain this to Nanny, Diamond states, "I believe North Wind can get into our dreams—yes, and blow in them. Sometimes she has blown me out of a dream altogether" (*At the Back of the North Wind* 271). He realizes that the fantasy world North Wind exists in allows her access to everyone, if they will only listen. Like Paul Dombey, Diamond has keen insight into the world around him. Yet while Paul sails out of life on the water, Diamond rides out on the wind.

Fantastical worlds are also prevalent in MacDonald's *The Princess and the Goblin* and *The Princess and Curdie* and, as the titles suggest, they provide a more overt use of a fairy tale structure and world than does *At the Back of the North Wind*. The primary characters in *The Princess and the Goblin* and *The Princess and Curdie*, Princess Irene and Curdie, end up happily married, as one would assume a fairy tale and nineteenth-century novel ends. Their story also overtly ends as they do not have any children. The fairy tale plot MacDonald uses enhances the constructions of these characters as imperfect children. They exist in a kingdom, as one has come to expect in literary fairy tales, and both know their socioeconomic and physical places. In *The Princess and the Goblin*, Princess Irene is sequestered at birth to a house in the country that is " . . . half castle, half farmhouse, on the side of another mountain, about halfway between its base and its peak" (1). She literally lives a half-existence, as MacDonald does not hesitate to point out. In *The Princess and the Goblin*, Irene is a child of nature. As MacDonald notes, "Her face was fair and pretty, with eyes like two bits of night sky, each with a star dissolved in the blue. Those eyes you would have thought must have known they came from there, so often were they turned up in that direction" (2). Much like the goblin king living in the mountains, Princess Irene must exist as both a human and child of nature as does Curdie, a miner's son. Curdie mines daily and he is not afraid of the goblins inhabiting the mines because he knows the tricks to avoid them. Princess Irene's first encounter with Curdie in *The Princess and the Goblin* shows him to be:

> . . . dressed in miner's dress, with a curious cap on his head. He was a very nice-looking boy, with eyes as dark as the mines in which he worked and as sparkling as the crystals in their rocks. . . . His face was almost too pale for beauty, which came of his being so little in the open air and the sunlight . . . but he looked happy, merry indeed. . . . (36)

While Princess Irene lives in the "top" half, literally, of her town, Curdie inhabits and works in the lower portion. They are brought together in a natural environment by realistic events and, through these experiences, their status as imperfect children becomes more salient because of the blended space they have traveled through.

The mingling of reality and the fairy world, a space Princess Irene and Curdie occupy, offers a similar position to that of many Dickens characters in that these characters develop sensibilities and ideologies due to their exposure to both elements. While MacDonald's characters are more readily found in a traditional fairy tale realm, their day-to-day activities are those of Victorian citizens. Curdie, for example, is a miner's son. Princess Irene, named after one of MacDonald's daughters, exists as a princess. For Curdie, a member of the working class, to climb and defy social hierarchical ladders would be nearly impossible. In *Secret Gardens: The Golden Age of Children's Literature from Alice's Adventures in Wonderland to Winnie-The-Pooh* (1985), Humphrey Carpenter finds *The Princess and The Goblin* to be a " . . . story redolent of Grimm and Perrault. . . . Really, *The Princess and the Goblin* is as powerful a piece of religious teaching as ever came the way of a Sunday School child" (83). Yet MacDonald illustrates the imperfection both children must possess in order to believe in a higher power. Through his use of the fairy tale motif,

MacDonald was " . . . creating an alternative religious landscape which a child's mind could explore and which could offer spiritual nourishment" (Carpenter 83). This is important because they do not live in a space where only dragons and princes lurk, but where everyday activities such as mining, cooking, and sewing happen as they also do in traditional fairy tales. The goblins are a part of this world, and continue to be in *The Princess and Curdie*, but are not the primary focus of either story.

MacDonald continues the story of Princess Irene and Curdie in *The Princess and Curdie*. This text illustrates their connection to both fairy realms and reality; areas that contribute to their status as imperfect children. The tale of *The Princess and Curdie* occurs about a year after their story begins in *The Princess and the Goblin*. Though titled *The Princess and Curdie*, the story is more about Curdie than Princess Irene. The more mythical beings, such as the Uglies, are introduced in this extension of the story. Curdie, now thirteen, is mining with his father at the beginning of the text when he happens upon Princess Irene's great-great-grandmother, who is a magical being representative of the universe and all that it creates. In *The Princess and Curdie* she relates a secret to Peter, Curdie's father, " . . . you, Peter, and your wife both have the blood of the royal family in your veins. I have been trying to cultivate your family tree, every branch of which is known to me, and I expect Curdie to turn out a blossom on it. Therefore I have been training him for a work that must soon be done" (54). Curdie, readers come to find, is of royal lineage and related to Princess Irene's family.

Not only is a "branch" of the family mentioned, but also the great-great-grandmother notes they have "blood of *the* royal family," of "a" royal family. Being the Princess Irene's great-great-grandmother, they both possess her connection with nature though they must function in the "real" world. Curdie is also granted the special power of being able to " . . . know at once the hand of a man who is growing into a beast; nay, more—you will at once feel the foot of the beast he is growing . . ." (*The Princess and Curdie* 73). The power of being able to know the true nature of a man's soul further connects Curdie with natural intuition, but these are not meant to be magical powers to save mankind nor to change Curdie. They do, however, help him to "see" those that might have evil tendencies and bring him and those around him closer to nature. They give Curdie knowledge of a person's spirituality that is a key component to his imperfect character.

While MacDonald illustrates a world in which both fantasy and reality blend in *The Princess and the Goblin* and *The Princess and Curdie*, as does Shakespeare in *A Midsummer Night's Dream*, Kingsley separates these worlds in *The Water-Babies*. Tom literally falls into the realm of an underwater fantasy world and brings his knowledge as a Victorian chimney sweep with him. While many critics, such as Naomi Wood in her article "A (Sea) Green Victorian: Charles Kinglsey and *The Water-Babies*" (1995), find there are two distinct worlds where Tom exists, one the natural world, the other and harsh reality (233), there has been little discussion of the blending of these spaces. As Tom falls into the water world where he meets fairies and water nymphs, among other creatures, he is on his way to becoming a water baby. In this underwater world not only natural elements exist but also those of the fairy realm, which ultimately impact and educate Tom so that he becomes a productive member of society when he returns to the chaotic Victorian world. The Queen of the Fairies finds Tom and tells her children that she has brought them a brother, though they are not to play with him or let him see them until he is no longer a "savage" (*The Water-Babies* 58). Rather, they must protect him from things he may come into contact with that may harm him in the underwater realm (*The Water-Babies* 58). The Queen of the Fairies, Susan A. Walsh believes, in "Darling Mothers, Devilish Queens: The Divided Woman in Victorian Fantasy" (1987), are "These Earth-Mothers of Victorian fantasy [such as the Queen of the Fairies], Titanias in the root sense, are a direct outgrowth of Romantic longings for the in-dwelling spirit of nature in its succoring, maternal capacity" (32). The lack of a mother, or any parental figure except Mr. Grimes, for the orphaned Tom, robs Tom of innocence and a true childhood.

The fairies step in and help Tom to learn about the world around him and how to function in it. He is a changeling that has no replacement and is not really missed in the real world he leaves behind. The Queen of Fairies has planned from the beginning to educate him and thus hopefully save him. Kingsley notes:

> Some people think that there are no fairies. . . . But in the wide world . . . and plenty of room in it for fairies, without people seeing them; unless, of course, they look in the right place. The most wonderful and the strongest things in the world, you know, are just the things, which no one can see. . . . There must be fairies; for this is a fairy tale: and how can one have a fairy tale if there are no fairies? (59–60)

While Kingsley is largely concerned with investigating and promoting Christian spirituality, he draws upon nature, fairy tale characters, and themes in order to illustrate Tom as an imperfect child. The blending of his knowledge of Victorian London and its promises for him and the natural world and the fairy realm help Tom function in Victorian society after his rebirth.

Spirituality and rebirth, whether through a physical death like Little Nell's in *The Old Curiosity Shop* and Paul Dombey's in *Dombey and Son* or a metaphorical one such as Tom's in *The Water-Babies* or Jessica's of Hesba Stretton's *Jessica's First Prayer*, were primary focuses for many authors[10] in the very religious atmosphere of Victorian England. Yet these fairy tale elements become a part of the structure of texts, such as Stretton's *Jessica's First Prayer* and Edith Nesbit's *The House of Arden* and *Harding's Luck*, and they are entwined in the construction of new fairy tales, such as with Christina Rossetti's *Speaking Likenesses*. Stretton uses fairy tale elements in her story of a street orphan,

Jessica, who is an abused and neglected child and must roam and forage for her food and shelter. She "dies" after an illness, and is reborn through finding friends and faith. Jessica is more literally thrown into a religious setting than Tom, but her existence in Victorian society is fantastical to middle-class readers who might not have experienced or been exposed to such hardships. There are no Fairy Queens or great-great-grandmothers to save her, but much like a Mr. Brownlow, Jessica is "saved" with Daniel's help. Her own compunction saves her and draws Daniel's attention. Resembling the Little Match Girl, in *Jessica's First Prayer* Jessica makes a pact with Daniel that she will only come once a week to his coffee-stall and not tell anyone she is coming. In exchange he will give her a treat. This is a bargain she readily keeps (*Jessica's First Prayer* 12). She survives, fairylike, on the streets of London scrounging for food and shelter. Often abused, this Cinderella in the making undergoes more hardships.

Jessica is familiar with fairies and notes to the minister she " . . . used to be a fairy in the pantomime, till I grew too tall and ugly" (40). Later she explains to Daniel that she " . . . used to like reckoning days when I was a fairy" (50), and though she takes it to mean a payday, this is a reference she uses in the text to indicate positive events. Stretton titles chapter four "Peeps into Fairyland" and Jessica discovers the world of the church with its singing and finely dressed congregation. No mention is given to actual fairy creatures or such an environment, but Jessica, Stretton wishes to stress, finds this a place of fantasy and wonder in the Victorian hell she inhabits outside of the church walls.

While Jessica's contact with the fairy realm is through imagination and spirituality, Christina Rossetti's Flora, Edith, and Maggie from *Speaking Likenesses*[11] are taught lessons through contact and immersion in fantastical realms that seem to come and leave in a short time frame. The stories, related to five little girls by their aunt, do not contain particularly happy endings, nor do they overtly teach moral lessons. Flora, Edith, and Maggie are rather cross and bullheaded young ladies that come into contact with fantastical creatures, their speaking likenesses, during their stints of misbehavior. As the children plead for more stories, the aunt continuously denies them the pleasurable tales one would commonly expect such a group of young women would be told. It seems as if the aunt takes perverse pleasure in such a denial. The aunt is tyrannical and controls the stories, a contrast Rossetti makes with the way middle and upper class young women are taught. In *Ventures into Childland: Victorians, Fairy Tales, and Femininity* (1998), U. C. Knoepflmacher finds, "The children in *Speaking Likenesses*, however, can no more challenge their domineering aunt than the girl heroines in the aunt's three stories can usurp the power wielded by the adult women who are their indisputable superiors" (358). Yet the children she creates in her storytelling are not innocent creatures, for they encounter fairy creatures and environments much like another young girl, Lewis Carroll's Alice, and the parallels with *Alice's Adventures in Wonderland* and *Speaking Likenesses* have been critically made many times.

Flora's temper on her birthday worsens as everything, from the food to the play, does not go her way (*Speaking Likenesses* 327–28). Her party, later paralleled with a party in which all of the furniture and guests interact, and which turns horrifically nightmarish, sets the mood and backdrop for her tale. She is shuttled between her real party and the fairy realm, from which she meets her parallel, the Birthday Queen, who declares everything is "mine," much as Flora had during her own party. Flora sees many reflections of herself, due to all of the mirrors, in the Birthday Queen and struggles to leave the party, and after much abuse awakens to find it was only a "dream." Flora, "Before tea was over . . . had nestled close up to Anne, and whispered how sorry she was to have been so cross" (*Speaking Likenesses* 342). Through interaction with a parallel fairy universe Flora learns how to act and treat others. She thus encounters the very socialization the imperfect child undergoes after her interaction with the fairy realm.

Though Flora's tale is the longest of the three in *Speaking Likenesses*, Edith and Maggie also encounter a fairy world that challenges their ideologies about their social and cultural status and importance. For a family picnic Edith runs ahead to light a fire and begins brewing tea, but she is unable to do either and in the process becomes frustrated. With only six matches and four of them spent, Edith fears "Her relations, friends, and other natural enemies would be arriving, and would triumph over her . . ." (*Speaking Likenesses* 346) and she does not know what to do. Edith begins talking to animals that try to give her suggestions on how to start her fire. With their help, she might have succeeded, but she nastily tells them to do it themselves, as if she were speaking to those "relations, friends, and other natural enemies" and is unable to start her fire. Just as the adults enter the story, the animals scuttle away. While the fairy realm, through the personification of animals, welcomes and tries to assist Edith, she resists their knowledge and advice.

Maggie's tale is not as savage as Flora's nor as forlorn as Edith's, but in Little Red Riding Hood fashion, she is swept into a world of monsters and unaided by those that might help her. Unlike Flora or Edith, Maggie is a working class and an orphan living with her grandmother. She runs deliveries for her grandmother's store. After noticing some customers had left an item in the store, Maggie tries to deliver it to them only to enter a wood and be struck on the head. Afterwards, she sees fairies and begins to play among them. Maggie is challenged throughout her journey and ends up saving animals along the cold forest path. While the parallel Rossetti sets up with Red Riding Hood is obvious, as the illustrator Arthur Hughes draws Maggie with a cloak on her back, Maggie saves other creatures and finds warmth in hearth and home. This is something Flora and Edith have come to take for granted until their encounters with the fairy creatures and realms in their own tales.

In E. Nesbit's *The House of Arden* and *Harding's Luck*, the interaction of children, unlike Rossetti's Flora, with the fairy world is much more direct, for they are able to choose when they wish to have contact with the fairy creatures they have met, though those creatures do not always wish to have contact with Dickie, Elfrida, and Edred. Overtly, Elfrida's name speaks to her fairy nature of being elfish and she is cleverer than her brother. The countryside they live in is grounded in traditional ideas of fairies and fairy worlds, so the children are not able to escape this. They encounter a witch throughout their time travels and Old Beale, whom readers encounter in both books, speaks of " . . . fairies [that] churn butter for the bride so long as there's no cross words, They don't ever get too much to do, them fairies" (*House of Arden* 188). Elfrida and Edred, who ask Old Beale for a story, are warned through these stories not to fight and to keep occupied.

The children also reference fairy stories as they are searching for the lost treasure of their home. As they search among some doors for an entryway, Edred suggests that lying behind one door might be "Bluebeard's wives, I shouldn't wonder . . . with their heads," and his sister responds in a horrified tone (*House of Arden* 40). While the siblings, Elfrida and Edred, are able to move between time and space, they are more limited than their cousin Dickie. Dickie also comes into contact with the witch, who uses many guises in the texts, and time shifts much more readily than his relatives. Magic for these children, as it does in much of Nesbit's work, becomes a part of their everyday activities. The imperfection of their character resides in the blended space they occupy through the bit of magic they possess in nature, reality, and fairy space. All of these spaces were being redefined for Victorian society and would have been interesting to readers.

The fairy creatures' imperfect children encounter help them change personal ideologies about themselves and Victorian culture. As Altick points out in *Victorian People and Ideas*, the impact of emerging literacy among all classes helped further belief systems other than traditional religion and science (62–63). Dickens uses the fairy tale motif for many reasons but his primary impetus is to " . . . symbolize a beautiful world of the imagination which . . . is contrasted with the dull, ugly bourgeois world." (Kotzin 83). The use and cultivation of the imagination was important to Dickens and often writers such as MacDonald, Kingsley, Stretton, Rossetti, and Nesbit. Stone points out: "The literature of childhood nursed the imagination and softened dehumanizing toil. What Dickens most valued in that literature was its ability to nurture the imagination. Without imagination (or "fancy," as Dickens often called it), human beings could not truly be human (3). Dickens, MacDonald, Kingsley, Stretton, Rossetti, and Nesbit balance the need for imagination and faith alongside the harshness of Victorian reality. In this way the death of the imperfect child, like Paul Dombey, or the realistically happy endings of Amy and Arthur in *Little Dorrit* or Elfrida and Edred in *House of Arden*, are hopeful.

Chapter Three
Belittling and Being Little
Resisting Socially Imposed Physical and Gendered Limitations

"One of my aims has been to show that provided forbidding jargon is avoided, there need be no divorce between linguistics and the study of literature. I may perhaps be permitted to add that many of my students when exposed to a linguistic analysis of Dickens's prose have told me that they found this approach refreshing and rewarding. But let the reader judge for himself."

—**Knud Sørensen**, *Charles Dickens: Linguistic Innovator* (7)

Thoroughly covered, the Victorian body would have left much to the imagination alongside the fairies and fairy world Victorian fancy romanticized. Women and children were "othered" in this society so that they were often idealized through these romanticized conventions of the physical and mental characteristics attributed to them. These straightforward Victorian ideologies are important in the construction of the imperfect child who not only possesses a small physical form, which might often struggle with an illness, but also is thought of, and labeled, as being little. The physical constructions of the imperfect child, though small, are antithetical to their actual presence both culturally and socially. While authors such as Dickens, MacDonald, Kingsley, Stretton, Rossetti, and Nesbit might suggest the physical form is culturally and socially deemed inconsequential, the very naming of their characters, like Little Nell, Tiny Tim, and Elfrida, often indicates they are people of momentous importance in the construction and progression of the text. Often belittled by those around them and possessing minute forms, the imperfect child develops through employing linguistic, cultural, and social conventions of language and idealized characteristics. As Haig A. Bosmajian states in *The Language of Oppression* (1983),[1] "The power which comes from names and naming is related directly to the power to define them. . . . The names, labels, and phrases employed to 'identify' people may in the end determine their survival" (5). Dickens, MacDonald, Kingsley, Stretton, Rossetti, and Nesbit interchange the Victorian notions of "othering" and thus illustrate the importance of the tiniest Victorian citizens and how they are often overlooked.

Language and the Body

Using the form of the imperfect child, these authors are not simply trying to draw upon the sentimental nature of their audience, but rather utilizing it as a rhetorical tool to construct their respective characters. This becomes a thematic function in the plot driven by pathos, which is characteristic of many nineteenth-century texts and was popular among readers. Imperfect child characters often possess diminutive physical forms, as their names, cognomens, and labels of endearment often indicate. This form allows them to tread relatively unseen in Victorian culture and society as they blend into its background. The flitting ability these characters are endowed with, reminiscent of their fairy nature, is directly proportional to their size though not meaning, for they embody the clichéd phrase of being "larger than life." The very terminology often associated with characters like Elfrida or Tiny Tim is indicative of naming representative of physical characteristics; and such names are commonly drawn from fantastical terminology, such as one being called a dwarf or giant[2] if they are disproportionately above or below the average build for their society.

In *Victorian Childhood: Themes and Variations* (1987), Thomas E. Jordan notes, "From study of records in a variety of sources it appears that at age sixteen years nonfactory youths were 1.60 inches taller than those at work, a trend that persists in the data until, at age eighteen, the nonfactory lads were 6.47 inches taller than the factory boys' mean height of five feet three inches . . ." (4). Variants will exist, naturally, across age, gender, and class lines, but what is important about this examination is twofold in that it illustrates the effects working class life had on the physical body and how such children were labeled. While our ideals of nutrition and treatment have changed, the Victorians were only beginning to establish the impact of the conditions children such as Jo, in Dickens's *Bleak House*, were undergoing.

Children did not necessarily encounter physical problems through work alone, but the factors that accompanied such environments also established many of the problems children like Jo would face. Class lines are important as upper class children were not exposed to such horrendous conditions and would often not suffer from such maladies, but could become disabled or deformed through other means. After an examination of various studies on children's body formation during the Victorian era, Jordan suggests, " . . . Around the average—that is, across the full range of social classes—the distribution of heights was wide. The children of the poor and rich of the same age were several inches and several more pounds apart" (21). For working class boys, for example, Jordan outlines, "The Children's Employment Commission of 1843 was told that boys of fifteen to sixteen frequently looked like twelve-year-olds (Second Report 1843), and puberty was quite delayed" (21). Though these examples are restricted by gender and older adolescence, they indicate exactly how stunted such bodies could become. Many other contributing dynamics, such as disease and abuse, were also instrumental in stunting and scarring children, as is evident in the case of the imperfect child.

Crippled children were not uncommon during the Victorian period, but their treatment by society was harsh. Authors often drew upon such disabilities, as with E. Nesbit's illustration of Dickie Arden in her *House of Arden* and *Harding's Luck* or Dickens's creation of Tiny Tim in *A Christmas Carol*, both lamed boys who walk with assistance. Dickie was dropped as a child and Tiny Tim, though we are not overtly told, Jordan believes has " . . . poliomyelitis; [where] children like Tiny Tim in "A Christmas Carol" got around with the aid of a crutch" (43). Other common elements that could have contributed to crippling children were things not readily heard of in the Western world today, such as rickets or dysentery. Crippled children of the working class could beg, seek out shelter in churches, and, depending on the disability, do minor work. For the majority, however, they would be unable to find lucrative work, which was not uncommon for many members of the working class. Physical abuse[3] was also common and children like Dickie could be beaten and thus sustain injury that would effect them the rest of their lives. During his many journeys, which allow him to escape his crippled existence for a time, Dickie laments returning to his reality where he must walk with assistance and cannot play as other children do. By being branded a "cripple," "poor," "fallen," or "thief," such children were depicted as being of a particular class and commodity. These titles suggested that such children were not only uneducated but that they were unable to learn through formal schooling. In *Victorian Childhoods* (2009), Ginger S. Frost explains that children raised in government-run institutions, such as a workhouse, were always attached to a social disgrace, and "Poor children, in particular, had few ways to feel superior in life, but one way was to ridicule the pauper, illegitimate, or the disabled child" (140). By preying on one another, such children asserted their dominance in a world that readily regulated them to the side streets and alleyways of Victorian England. In labeling children as cripples or physically limited, their speech was also impacted and many of them seem older than we might think realistic today.

Speech used by the imperfect child is often dualistic. This becomes a linguistic function to illustrate their dual existence between realms of fairy and reality and the way they are culturally and socially constructed. The majority of imperfect children, however, speak very clearly and as someone who has had an education, such as Oliver Twist. Jessica's speech in Hesba Stretton's *Jessica's First Prayer* is a more realistic example of the impact of her environment than Oliver's. Dickens draws upon Oliver's genetic background to illustrate his separation from the environment he grows in. Readers know from the onset that Oliver is not a true street orphan, as Dickens constructs Little Nell and various other protagonists. Dickens often draws upon environmental conditions to show their impact on characters like Jo in *Bleak House*. Jo's destiny is relatively predetermined through there and he has nowhere to really turn for help and does not know how to help himself. Oliver and Nell draw upon hope and inner strength, whereas Jo sees his social condition clearly and accepts his fate. Raymond Chapman finds in *Forms of Speech in Victorian Fiction* (1994) that the populace:

> . . . at least in their public attitudes, regarded them [children] with ambivalence amounting to doublethink. The Romantic notion of childhood innocence and natural goodness was still strong, not yet challenged by Freud or by novelists in the century to come. At the same time, the Augustinian and Calvinist view of human depravity was not confined to extreme Evangelicals. Children were liable to lose their innocence very easily and needed to be protected against the world and against their own propensity towards evil. This was especially so for girls, for whom one false step could be social disaster as well as spiritual peril. (165–66)

Such changing ideologies surrounding the concept of the child and childhood indicate the difficulty in presenting only binary options of their existence. In believing children were born innocent, they are categorized as being limited, for a time, to one space from which they will undoubtedly fall and become sinners, thus losing their innocence. Innocence, in this view, can never really be retained but is something individuals always try to regain. In exploring the notion of the blended space, the space the imperfect child transitions through, however, realism becomes paramount. Children, like Oliver Twist, Jessica, and Tom, are able to remain "good," but have knowledge of the harshness of Victorian reality, which the Romantic notion of childhood neglects. The perfect childhood and children become unrealistic. The speech patterns of imperfect children only follow the blended space from which they emerge as they often interchange formal and informal speech patterns. These speech patterns are indicative of fantastical and realistic realms, but also illustrate the maturity of imperfect children. The imperfect child uses language forms and conventions that are often used by adults. This further indicates the imperfect child's cross nature, for they neither exist as children nor miniature adults in society and culture. This literary convention used by Dickens, MacDonald, Kingsley, Stretton, Rossetti, and Nesbit in their constructions of the imperfect child draws us back to a newly developing type and experience of the child and childhood where children lose innocence, but retain hope.

Names "Inwented," Character Confirmed

Naming is one of Dickens's most memorable devices. The clever name constructions he develops not only are humorous but also follow the long literary tradition of illustrating character types. Textual names for people and places were especially important during the Victorian period so that readers could establish mental images of who and/or where events would unfold. This technique is still widely used as we continue to establish ideas through the metaphors we construct socially, culturally, economically, and politically. Dickens was a master at painting images of people and places and tapping into metaphoric constructions. As George Lakoff and Mark Turner establish in *Metaphors We Live By* (2003), "Our ordinary conceptual system, in terms of which we both think and act, is fundamentally metaphorical in nature.... Our conceptual system thus plays a central role in defining our everyday realties" (3). The name of Charley Bates, often referred to as Master Bates in *Oliver Twist*, for example, establishes him metaphorically as a working class individual who might have a sense of humor about him due to the sexual connotation to his name: Charley Bates, or "Master Bates" (*Oliver Twist* 114) on several occasions, a small injection of crude humor on Dickens's behalf. Elsewhere, he is usually referred to as Charley Bates, but rarely Charley. In name alone, Charley and many of Dickens's other characters carry metaphorical concepts and their actions in the text support archetypical metaphors readers have inherently ingrained in their ideological systems. This naming system functions dually in that it is both humorous for readers and inherently provides social and cultural commentary for both readers and writers. In hearing the name of J. K. Rowling's Harry Potter, for example, readers do not immediately mentally construct the image of a blue-eyed, blond-haired, tall Adonis who will run fullback for the Dallas Cowboys. What springs to mind are images of a dumpy, sullen working class individual who might know a trade or possibly be a beggar. P. L. Travers's Mary Poppins is another character we might think of as being energetic, and always "popping" in, which she does. She is, however, not merry in the original text, so naming can also lead readers to establish some misconceptions about a character and/or place. When writers use this ironically, they are also allowed to continuously develop humor and pathos throughout their narratives and thus keep readers hooked. Through the use of metaphor and irony the names characters bear, such as Oliver Twist, challenge the archetypical metaphorical constructions we have conceived about their characteristics.

Socially, Oliver Twist is a misfit and has little hope of attaining an education, much less learning to speak Standard English. His orphan status allows for little social movement and his exposure to "proper" English culture is almost nonexistent. Yet, Oliver has one special gift bequeathed to him by his dead mother: his genealogy. Oliver's parentage, while questionable to those around him, is overtly that of at least a middle class background and readers can determine this by his speech alone. As Monica Flegel argues in *Conceptualizing Cruelty to Children in Nineteenth-Century England: Literature, Representation, and the NSPCC* (2009), " . . . though he is illegitimate, he nevertheless sustains a native virtue that is the result of heredity" (152). His background strengthens Oliver's character and while he chooses a path of virtue rather than one of vice, it is, nevertheless, a choice he makes. Through Oliver's middle class lineage and working class exposure, Dickens indicates that children deemed "fallen" by societal standards have value. However, if proper care is not given to them, as in Nancy's case, they may be forced into a life of vice, as she readily points out to Fagin, "I thieved for you when I was a child not half as old as this (pointing to Oliver). I have been in the same trade, and in the same service, for twelve years since; don't you know it? . . . It is my living, and the cold, wet, dirty streets are my home; and you're the wretch that drove me to them long ago, and that'll keep me there, day and night, day and night, till I die!" (167). Working class Nancy, a Fallen Woman[4] according to Victorian standards, confronts her oppressors knowing that she has few ways out of her situation. Oliver is granted a choice, as one may argue Nancy was, but without the care shown Oliver, her road to a "proper" Victorian life would have been much more difficult to tread.

Unnamed by his mother, Oliver is named by Mr. Bumble, the parish beadle. Oliver's naming is a process, as Mr. Bumble points out when Mrs. Mann questions, "How comes he to have any name at all, then? [and] the beadle drew himself up with great pride, and said, "I inwented it" (*Oliver Twist* 51). For in the naming process, Mr. Bumble explains, "We name our foundlings in alphabetical order. The last was a S,—Swubble, I named him. This was a T,—Twist, I named *him*. The next one as comes will be Unwin, and the next Vilkins. I have got names ready made to the end of the alphabet, and all the way through it again, when we come to Z" (*Oliver Twist* 51–52). Names created for the orphans of Mr. Bumble's parish are at his whim. There is really no practical or logical method to his naming practices. Mr. Bumble has defined who and what Oliver, and a host of other children are and will be, as Bosmajian suggests (5). Further, Mr. Bumble, as many oppressors have done historically, has resorted to a system of naming that produces little more than lists of people with names imposed upon them. Bosmajian rightly explains, "One of the first acts of an oppressor is to redefine the 'enemy' so they will be looked upon as creatures warranting separation, suppression, and even eradication" (6). Oliver is separated from middle-class society. The name "Oliver" itself is supposed to have multiple meanings, but the primary meaning is peace. Yet, there seems to be another meaning attributed to this name: elf army or host of elves. Oliver's conception, life, and experiences lead to the very twist in the plot that occurs, for his story is a twist on the existence such a child would experience in Victorian culture and society.

Oliver's notion of who he is as an individual and how he is seen socially shows as he begins his journey from Mrs. Mann's house. On his ninth birthday

Oliver, who is described as being "a pale thin child, somewhat diminutive in stature, and steadily small in circumference" (*Oliver Twist* 49), is led away by Mr. Bumble to begin his great expectations that will be assigned to him by the board. Prone to fits of crying, Oliver faces The Board,[5] who asks him what his name is; and Oliver, frightened and scared, is unable to answer (*Oliver Twist* 53–54). He cannot clearly say who he is in the face of those who have inundated him throughout his short life. Referred to as "boy" and a "fool" by the board, Oliver is further dehumanized. Oliver has no idea what an orphan is, and the board defines this for him (*Oliver Twist* 54). With *Oliver Twist*, Dickens illustrates the little acknowledged product of orphaned, working class children in Victorian England. Often, these children, as Dickens indicates in *Oliver Twist*, were not addressed by their given names, but rather nouns akin to their employment or socioeconomic status. For his initial employment, Oliver is sent to pick oakum, a tarlike substance, and then he is off to be apprenticed to Mr. Sowerberry, a casket maker. Because he can learn a trade and be sold off, Oliver is a monetary asset to the church. Through Oliver, Dickens is able to appeal to a public at large that was often sentimentalizing children and child death. Thus, Oliver becomes a commodity to Dickens. As Zelizer explains, " . . . the changing relationship between the economic and sentimental value of children resulted in a unique pattern of valuation in children in the United States" (15), and this was also true in England.

Oliver is only called by his first name by those who were deemed his "master," such as Mr. Bumble. Commonly called "boy" or by Noah Claypool, a charity boy kept by Mr. Sowerberry, "Work'us," Oliver shifts from being a miserable orphan to a more miserable orphan. He spends so much time being starved, beaten, and crying in the first few chapters that readers hardly know what to make of Oliver. Dickens also refers to Oliver as a "chance-child" (*Oliver Twist* 77) whose fates are left to "chance." He is a male version of Cinderella who also sneaks out of an abusive household to take her chances elsewhere. This is not surprising as Dickens's love for the fairy tale and incorporation of fairy tale elements in his work are widely known. At least Oliver is left with some hope of escape and the ability to strike out on his own, which ultimately takes him to London.

Oliver is called by a variety of names, and Dickens even writes of him as "Little Oliver Twist" (124). The term "little" is applied to many more of his future characters, such as Little Nell. Being a term of endearment, the word "little" functions to describe many of Dickens's characters' physical statures and characteristics, as well as the way in which society and culture treat and view such individuals. Oliver is born, as his half-brother Monks calls him, a "bastard" (*Oliver Twist* 457), but the narrator defends such individuals, as Mr. Brownlow notes, "The term you use . . . is a reproach to those who long since passed beyond the feeble censure of the world. It reflects disgrace on no one living, except you who use it. Let that pass. He was born in this town" (457). Oliver's name and social status are not as important in Dickens's eyes as are his personal actions. Little Nell, yet another orphan, is another Dickens construction of the innocent being viewed and treated as a mere trifle by society.

In *The Old Curiosity Shop*, Nelly Trent is regularly referred to as Little Nell due to her physical form and meek characteristics. Though Dickens paints Oliver Twist as weak, the strength and determination in Nell help define her as one of Dickens's strongest heroines. Many critics, such as Raymond Chapman, believe "Simplicity is a mark of some characters, but it seems to spring from their nature and position rather than their sex. Many of Dickens's heroines are simple and direct to the point of naivety, but similar discourse can be found in some of his male characters . . ." (146). But what Chapman sees as being "naïve" stems from directness because these characters do not necessarily hedge their actions or statements. They often are the ones to lead, as in the case of Little Nell, or strike out on their own, even covertly, as with Amy Dorrit. Readers and critics rarely credit such actions. From the onset of the text, Nell is described by all who meet her in phrases indicative of her size, such as a "little creature" and "a pretty little child" (*The Old Curiosity Shop* 4–5). As she plods on through the London night with Master Humphrey, he notes, "She put her hand in mine, as confidingly as if she had known me from her cradle, and we trudged away together: the little creature accommodating her pace to mine and rather seeming to lead and take care of me than I protecting her" (*The Old Curiosity Shop* 11–12). Nell engages discussion with Master Humphrey, a stranger, and ultimately leads the way through the labyrinth of London streets. Dickens illustrates that while she may be seen by society through the eyes of Master Humphrey as "little," she is not. Nell, being "little" and lost in the large labyrinth, indicates how she is seen by Victorian society and lost amongst them. However, as Nell is the one to help Master Humphrey regain interest in the world, one he commonly traverses only at night and in shadow, Dickens is pointing out her larger value. In *Metaphors We Live By*, Lakoff and Turner mention Michael Reedy's concept of the "conduit metaphor" where "The speaker [author] puts ideas (objects) into words (containers) and sends them (along a conduit) [written/heard text] to a hearer [reader] who takes the ideas/objects out of the word/containers" (10). Dickens does this when he uses the term "little" and like words in phrases to describe Nell.

Being physically little during the nineteenth century was not uncommon due to social conditions such as malnourishment, disease, and abuse inflicted upon "others." The majority of Dickens's child characters, like Tiny Tim, are physically small. Tiny Tim is both physically handicapped and socially a misfit because he comes from a working class family. The family is, however, the one thing Tiny Tim is blessed with, for the majority of Dickens's other child characters do not have a loving and supportive immediate family. This may later come in the form of adopted parents or a reconnection with family that is still living, such as Florence Dombey and her father. Tiny Tim is depicted, as I point out in Chapter 1, as he " . . . bore a little crutch, and had his limbs supported by an iron frame!" (*A Christmas Carol* 79). Due to the family's poor financial state, Tiny Tim and his siblings do not receive proper nourishment, but the love of the Cratchit family provides the stimulation the family needs to hope for a better life. Tiny Tim's view of the world is not pure and innocent, for he knows his situation and how he is viewed by Victorian society. Tiny Tim, however, remains optimistic even with the challenges he faces, and, after receiving economic help from Scrooge, who " . . . was better than his word. He did it all, and infinitely more; and to Tiny Tim, who did NOT die, he was a second father" (*A Christmas Carol* 116), he lives. Seeing Tiny Tim as a helpless, working class child and knowing one's own misery, readers are inspired to keep faith and hope through the viewpoint of a crippled and undernourished child. Tiny Tim's value lays ultimately in his size and condition as Dickens appeals to readers' sympathies and thus pocketbooks.

Scrooge's outlook on the conditions of the poor in *A Christmas Carol* is indicative of those Dickens saw as part of Victorian society and culture. The misery surrounding the populace was addressed in text and politics, but middle and upper class societies often ignored the working class and therefore constructed a societal barrier separating the "them" (the working classes) from the "us" (the middle and upper classes). At the beginning of *A Christmas Carol*, Scrooge finds that institutions in place to take care of the poor, which amount to prisons and Union workhouses, and laws such as the Poor Law[6] should be enough. If these are not and/or the poor do not wish to take advantage of them, he suggests, such people should die and " . . . decrease the surplus population" (39). This is the situation the Cratchit family faces. Even though Bob Cratchit has a job, it does not pay enough for his family to live decently. Tiny Tim speaks with relative clarity and uses educated diction, suggesting that the family might be a fallen middle-class family. Tiny Tim's death, shown to Scrooge by the Ghost of Christmas Future, however, shows the family's interest in education and religion as they are huddled around the fireplace reading the Bible (*A Christmas Carol* 105). The Bible, being the one book many families would own, would be the one text they all would have access to and might read; and as the family is huddled together reading, this suggests the importance of education for the Cratchits, whose breadwinner is employed as a clerk. Though the use of gaslight in homes began to grow around the 1840s for those who could afford it, the Cratchit family would have been too poor to use it, and having to read by candlelight would impact one's sight (*A Christmas Carol* 105). This illustrates hardships Tiny Tim, an early construction of Paul Dombey, would have known.

Dickens uses the depiction of the "old child" in the construction of imperfect child from *Oliver Twist* throughout his work. Class status is not a determiner of how being deemed an "old-fashioned" child impacts such children. His circumstances are not the only element that shapes Paul Dombey's psychological state, for he seems born with an old soul. Paul Dombey is also a commodity and he is seen as a Dombey from the beginning. Rarely is Paul viewed as a person, but rather an extension of the Dombey clan or a continuation of decaying family gentry. Mr. Dombey's sole reason for having a wife and family seems to be to continue his family lineage; and Paul is a commodity from the beginning of his small, sickly life, which he begins as "Son" and is " . . . tucked up warm in a little basket bedstead, carefully disposed on a low settee immediately in front of the fire and close to it, as if his constitution were analogous to that of a muffin, and it was essential to toast him brown while he was very new" (*Dombey and Son* 11). In continuing his family line, Mr. Dombey renews a family legacy and, as he produces goods, so does he produce an heir. Paul is seen as the long-awaited son, while his sister Florence is viewed as little more than a nuisance.

Where Paul attains his name from his father and his grandfather and the three words "Dombey and Son" " . . . conveyed the one idea of Mr. Dombey's life" (*Dombey and Son* 12), Florence is neatly tucked in the background as if she were discarded day-old bread, rather than a new muffin. Dickens notes that she was not worth notice for Mr. Dombey, but does explain during Paul's birth and their mother's death:

> There had been a girl some six years before, and the child, who had stolen into the chamber unobserved, was now crouching timidly, in a corner whence she could see her mother's face. But what was a girl to Dombey and Son! In the capital of the House's name and dignity, such a child was merely a piece of base coin that couldn't be invested—a bad Boy—nothing more. (*Dombey and Son* 13)

Florence as a female child would not carry on the family name or participate in the Dombey business. She is not an asset, but a hindrance on the Dombey economy. Mary Poovey points out, in *Uneven Developments: The Ideological Work of Gender in Mid-Victorian England* (1988), that during the Victorian period, "If women were governed not by reason (like men), but by something else, then they could hardly be expected (or allowed) to participate in the economic and political fray" (11). Florence would have little economic value for the House of Dombey, but as the vision of childhood changed so too would a female child's value socially. Written upon her body at birth, Florence's use as a commodity is a settled matter. Through marriage, Florence's last name will change and she will no longer be a Dombey, which is questioned in the text numerous times even before she has grown up. In *Gender Trouble: Feminism and the Subversion of Identity* (1999), Judith Butler rightly notes:

> . . . the naturalized knowledge of gender operates as a preemptive and violent circumscription of reality. To the extent the gender norms . . . establish what will and will not be intelligibly human, what will and will not be considered to be "real," they establish the ontological field in which bodies may be given legitimate expression. (xxiii)

Her father or society, simply because of her gender, do not treat Florence's birth as legitimate as Paul's is, although Victorian society was very clear about the distinction between legitimate and illegitimate births.

Paul and Florence are, much like Oliver, Nell, Tiny Tim, Esther, and Jo, called by names that belittle them, especially little Paul and little Florence. In keeping with this rhetorical device, Dickens illustrates continuously that the term is not only an expression of endearment but also the way society both sees and treats the imperfect child. In "The Portrayal of Death and 'Substance of Life': Aspects of the Modern Reader's Response to 'Victorianism' " (1980), W. L. G. James writes of Little Nell and her name and his sentiments can also be applied to Florence, "For under the intrusive sentimentality that surrounds Nell—even in her name and the diminutive 'Little'—there is a consistent and haunting awareness of the void that lies on the other side of surface reality" (231). These "little" children, who might be little in physical form, are belittled and often betrayed by the very society and culture that form their realities. The imperfect child, however, challenges his/her belittled status, whether overtly or on the sly.

Dickens does not just present characters with descriptive names based upon their physical forms or social standing, but creates characters and situations from everyday experiences. He addresses these characters with a different form of writing, a form he actually creates. In *Writing in Society* (1983), Raymond Williams finds, "The most important thing to say about Dickens, then, is not that he is writing in a new way, but that he is experiencing in a new way, and that this is the substance of his language" (91). Dickens's use of metaphor, irony, and satire can be found throughout the body of his work, but combining reality, fancy, fantasy, romance, sentimentality, and the grotesque keep his texts popular. Dickens's writing is not limited to one group of people. The construction of the imperfect child, a trope he could continuously draw upon, became a cornerstone of his writing. As Williams suggests in *Writing in Society*:

> We can then see more clearly what Dickens is doing [in his writing]: altering, transforming a whole way of writing, rather than putting an old style at a new experience. It is not the method of the more formal novelists, including the sounds of measured of occasional speech in a solid frame of analysis and settled exposition. Rather, it is a speaking, persuading, directing voice of a new kind, which has taken over the narrative, the exposition, the analysis, in a single operation . . . the prose, in fact, of a new order of experience; the prose of the city. (93–94)

Dickens's urban depictions are not his only accomplishments. It is Dickens's passion, which was already present in his speeches and written text, where his expansion of traditional textual elements such as characterization and dialogue, as Williams points out in *Writing and Society*, impacts his writing most poignantly. Dickens uses parallels between naming and metaphor to reflect his ideologies about Victorian society and culture. Often Dickens uses names as metaphors to reflect surroundings or circumstances, as with Esther Summerson, for with a last name that indicates growth and joy, readers may understand she will have a prosperous life. Her first name, Esther, most readily ties to the biblical Esther, who is largely credited for saving the Jewish people from death. Dickens's energy further sparked his development of his characters, for as Oliver Twist is hustled about London, so too is Esther Summerson pushed towards a new beginning to her life.

Esther Summerson's lineage is not questioned during her childhood, for her aunt/godmother knows how Esther came into being. Esther's curiosity about her parents, especially her mother, is unique in that readers hear this from her own testimony. Esther's first-person narrative, which begins in the third chapter of *Bleak House*, is interspersed with other forms of narrative. Readers are able to hear from Esther how the events of her life have unfolded. Esther's speech is indicative of her education and a mark of her breeding, and she is groomed to be a housekeeper and/or governess. She does not introduce herself, but rather speaks of her experiences self-deprecatingly as she does from the beginning of the third chapter when she claims not to be "clever" (*Bleak House* 29). Esther's acknowledgment of her writing also indicates self-awareness, for she notes, "It seems so curious to me to be obliged to write all this about myself! As if this narrative were the narrative of *my* life! But my little body will soon fall into the background now" (*Bleak House* 40). However, Esther seems to understand her social value. In feeling "obliged" she indicates she feels indebted to someone or something to write out her life. Her value, she seems to indicate, is bestowed upon her by those who have taken notice of her and given her, as an orphan, a chance at a decent life.

Esther's recollection of her interest in her parents as a child is subjective, but she notes her own prejudices and readers gain insight into how she views herself and how she understands the ways in which society sees her, for she is often called phrases such as Little Mother or Dame Durden, rather than her given name. As she begins her narrative, Esther suggests, "I have mentioned that, unless my vanity should deceive me (as I know it may, for I may be very vain, without suspecting it—though indeed I don't), my comprehension is quickened when my affection is. My disposition is very affectionate . . . (*Bleak House* 29). Readers are not just told how and why a character acts in a particular manner, as we are with Oliver Twist or Little Nell, but rather Dickens allows us insight into Esther's psyche by giving her version of the story, which is, of course, still Dickens's version of the tale.

Esther becomes, as she outlines, a companion and housekeeper and is seen as a spinster, a career for which she has been groomed. Mary Poovey discusses the role of women such as Esther in *Uneven Developments: The Ideological Work of Gender in Mid-Victorian England*[7] and notes how society saw them. As W. R. Greg outlines in his 1862 essay "Why Are Women Redundant?" these women:

... constituted the border between the normative (working) man and the normative (nonworking) woman. Not a mother, the governess (and those like her) nevertheless preformed the mother's tasks; not a prostitute, she was nevertheless suspiciously close to other sexualized women; not a lunatic, she was nevertheless deviant simply because she was a middle-class woman who had to work and because she was always in danger of losing her middle-class status and her "natural" morality. (14)

Esther repeatedly points out that she is not "clever," but her guardian Mr. Jarndyce tells her, "You are clever enough to be the good little woman of our lives here, my dear . . . the little old woman of the Child's (I don't mean Skimpole's) Rhyme: 'Little old woman, and whither so high?—To sweep the cobwebs out of the sky.' You will sweep them so neatly out of *our* sky, in the course of your housekeeping" (*Bleak House* 121). Esther acknowledges, "This was the beginning of my being called Old Woman, and Little Old Woman, and Cobweb, and Mrs. Shipton, and Mother Hubbard, and Dame Durden and so many names of that sort, that my own name soon became quite lost among them" (*Bleak House* 121). These names remain with Esther throughout the rest of the text and she willingly acknowledges she likes them and retains them, but they become ironic for Esther is even called Dame Durden by her husband (*Bleak House* 989). The nursery-rhyme connection is evident, and by possessing names linked to Mother Goose, Esther's characterization as the mother hen is metaphorically fixed.

Esther's nature, which includes the ability to be firm and confident, does not change, but her circumstances, like those of her Guardian do, even though he too retains his titles as she relates at the closing of the text, "I have never lost my old names, nor has he [Mr. Jarndyce] lost his; nor do I ever, when he is with us, sit in any other place than in my old chair at his side. Dame Trot, Dame Durden, Little Woman!—all just the same as ever; and I answer, Yes, dear Guardian! just the same" (*Bleak House* 988). Esther's awareness of her social value is evident in her speech as she has been saved, rather than left at an orphanage for the direct purpose of becoming a servant. The discarded daughter of someone with social value, Esther tries to make sense of her situation, but does not ask many questions when given the opportunity. Unlike Esther, however, Jo the crossing sweep, whose own situation mirrors Esther's, never finds out who his father is or receives any education.

Crossing sweeps during the Victorian period were not uncommon, and Jo is an illustration of such poor children and what they faced. Jo has no idea of his birth origin:

Name Jo. Nothing else that he knows on. Don't know that everybody has two names. Never heerd of sich a think. Don't know that Jo is short for a longer name. Thinks it long enough for *him*. *He* don't find no fault with it. Spell it? No. *He* can't spell it. No father, no mother, no friends. Never been to school. (*Bleak House* 177)

The speaker in this instance is not Jo but someone speaking for him. The additional stress Dickens places upon the *He* and *him* indicates that while Jo finds nothing wrong with his name or his situation, other people may. The speaker, Little Swills, comes from a working class background and outlines Jo's life for readers. Richard Altick notes in *Victorian People and Ideas*, "Even if a child possessed a minimal ability to read, the unpleasant circumstances under which he acquired it, as well as the general ignorance which the brevity of his schooling made inevitable, usually meant that he would seldom exercise his gift" (251). Jo's chances of bettering his life are very faint. In Chapter 54, readers later find out Mr. Snagsby is Jo's father, long after Jo's death. Jo speaks as a child of the working classes and often for their plight. As Chapman finds, "Much sadder are the preternaturally old children, worldly wise beyond their years. They often speak for the pressure of reality upon the poor, among whom childhood was brief and soon lost in the need to add to the family income" (167). While the imperfect child is usually an orphan, some sort of family exists for them in the shadows, as Mr. Snagsby's connection to Jo illustrates. Still, Jo must add to his own income through any work he can find.

Jo's death draws upon the readers' sentimentality as Little Nell's does, but with Little Nell readers are assured of her peace, whereas Jo is trying to reach an understanding of heaven as he is passing away. His life until this point in the text is full of suffering. The life of a crossing sweep allowed Jo a home on the streets he kept clean and he was at the mercy of the Victorian public and society. He knows words exist, but little of their meaning. When questioned as to where he lives, Little Swills explains:

> What's home? Knows a broom's a broom, and knows it's wicked to tell a lie. Don't recollect who told him about the broom, or about the lie, but knows both. Can's exactly say what'll be done to him arter he's dead if he tells a lie to the gentlemen here, but believes it'll be something wery bad to punish him, and serve him right—and so he'll tell the truth. (*Bleak House* 177)

Jo continuously keeps the streets of his home clean, but like the life he leads, it spirals into unstructured murkiness. Everything about Jo, his life, name, and situation, are defined and controlled by Victorian society. He seems to "know" some things, though he cannot recall where he learned them. He knows he has a name, but does not know how it was obtained. Jo knows little of anything except how to work and that there is something beyond his everyday existence. He serves a function and service for society, not for his own interests. Jo's understanding of his situation, his "truth," stems from what Lakoff and Turner term direct experience. In *Metaphors We Live By*, Lakoff and Turner suggest of such association," . . . none of them can be fully comprehended on their own terms. Instead, we must understand them in terms of other entities and experiences, typically other *kinds* of entities and experiences" (177). Jo's name rhetorically suggests his societal position and function as a "regular Joe" or person. He is seen as one of the great unwashed, not as an individual struggling in nineteenth-century society. Thus Jo realizes his value and place through contact with others in Victorian society. No one tries to help him challenge such a position, but rather those who do step in to help, such as Nemo, who gives Jo money but can barely help himself, only continue to keep him in his dreadful societal role. Dickens's own haunting reality of being little and unable to help his family as they spent time in the Marshalsea Prison surfaces in *Little Dorrit*.

Known throughout *Little Dorrit* by many different titles, Amy Dorrit develops as the protagonist. Called "The Child of the Marshalsea," "Little Mother," and most commonly "Little Dorrit," Amy's naming indicates the ever-changing roles she assumes and illustrates her versatility against characters, such as her father, who are unable to acknowledge the reality of the world they inhabit. William Dorrit, Amy's father, is known as "The Father of the Marshalsea," for he spends almost twenty-five years locked away in this debtor's prison. He is an oddity in this environment, for he is a former member of the upper class and has fallen into poverty. The inhabitants of the Marshalsea leave small tokens of food and money for him, but he ignores the sources of such items. Amy, however, has been born in the prison and knows no other life. She is also an idiosyncrasy in the Marshalsea, for her father largely ignores her education, yet she is able to obtain an education for herself and her siblings.

Dickens's use of the language of these characters never differs, for they are both distinct from the prison population surrounding them in that their formal language indicates their social background. This telling feature extends to Amy Dorrit as she initially has little control over her own naming, and when she eventually does she insists that Arthur Clennam call her "Little Dorrit." Dickens uses the term "little" to refer to Amy throughout the novel in many different ways, but ultimatelythis rhetorical use indicates irony and satire. The shifting between naming and the static nature of language as class indicator gives readers further access to the distortion Dickens utilizes throughout the text.

The designation of class becomes a powerful tool in *Little Dorrit* as Dickens is able to designate those of the upper class and those of the working class who are all imprisoned in the Marshalsea[8] prison. Language is the means by which Dickens is able to control this environment in a culture like Victorian England where the printed word and illustration were the most influential forms of media. William Dorrit's education comes from being "Brought up as a gentleman, he was, if ever a man was. Ed'cated at no end of expense. . . . As to languages—speaks anything. We've had a Frenchman here in his time, and it's my opinion he knowed more French than the Frenchman did. We've had an Italian here in his time, and he shut him up in about half a minute" (*Little Dorrit* 74). His education is classical whereas his children, especially Amy, must learn to fend for themselves among the poor. The above recollection clearly indicates the status of its speaker as being from the working class. Sylvia Bank Manning notes, "Mr. Dorrit's manner of speech, and the sentence-paragraph is worded in such a way as to make it equally—and truly—applicable to the whole man . . ." (164). William Dorrit's speech is more indicative of his upper class background, but Amy's remains that of the upper class although she has been born and raised in the confines of the prison yard.

As the "Child of the Marshalsea," Dickens clearly indicates Amy is thought of as a product of her environment, but this does not show in either her speech or internal drive to attain work and an education to provide for her family. The youngest child of three, Amy takes over the responsibilities of both father and mother upon her mother's death when she is just eight years of age. Dickens writes:

> At thirteen, she could write and keep accounts—that is, could put down in words and figures how much the bare necessaries that they wanted would cost, and how much less they had to buy them with. She had been, by snatches of a few weeks at a time, to an evening school outside, and got her brother and sister sent to day-schools by desultory starts. . . . There was no instruction for any of them at home; but she knew well—no one better—that a man so broken as to be the Father of the Marshalsea, could be no father to his own children. (81)

Amy learns about her father's incompetence from observing the world of the Marshalsea. Her care of her siblings and father begins when she is only eight years old, but "From that time the protection her wondering eyes had expressed towards him, became embodied in action, and the Child of the Marshalsea took upon herself a new relation towards the Father" (80). According to Sylvia Bank Manning in *Dickens as Satirist* (1971), Little Dorrit is " . . . pure goodness" (168), but this basic representation, which only furthers the image of Amy as the Angel in the House, is too simplistic. While Amy, like the Angel of the House figure, takes charge of her family and provides for them, she later shows her resistance through asserting her own identity and love for Arthur. Initially her identity is given to her and she embraces it, but she quietly creates her own individuality alongside the identity socially conscripted for her.

As Little Dorrit is the youngest of the Dorrit children, this term of endearment also signifies her place in the family, but Dickens uses this sarcastically and satirically in that it is Amy who provides for and tends to her entire family in a society where women of the upper class were to function as the Angel in the House. "The limitations on women's roles in society meant that there was not a class of achievers aspiring to a name they felt themselves to have earned" (111), writes Patricia Ingham in *The Language of Gender and Class: Transformation in the Victorian_Novel* (1996) in regards to the term "lady." This discussion extends to Little Dorrit, for she later asserts that her name will be Little Dorrit, but this is after she has socially risen and fallen when her father's inheritance dries up. As Ingham notes, women could not *outwardly* aspire to a particular role or title, but could do so through coercive means. Little Dorrit, on the other hand, does not allow society to define her but asserts she is to be called "Little Dorrit." As Arthur begins to call her by her given name, " 'I did,' said Arthur; 'but Amy told me—' " and here she interrupts him and states, " 'Little Dorrit. Never any other name.' (It was she who whispered it)" (*Little Dorrit* 781). In this instance, Dickens assures the reader that Amy has taken possession of her own identity as he specifically inserts "It was *she* [my emphasis] who whispered it" into the dialogue; but on the other hand, she also accepts the name society has long ago ascribed to her. In *Dickens and the Structure of the Novel* (1959), E. A. Horsman asserts, "It is this handling of words for purposes of ironical contrast that forms the very basis of the expression structure in a Dickens novel. . . . And so the whole expression structure of his novels is dominated by ironical contrast: between the abstract language which prefers the large claim and the concrete language which pricks the pretension . . ." (4). The very pathos in Amy's speech leads her to distinctly accept the name society has assigned and readers are able to see her distress, but it is Amy's ethos that prevents her from completely asserting her own identity.

The signifier "Little" represents how Amy is viewed both by her family and physically by society. Amy is labeled "little" upon her birth as the doctor notes, "A very nice little girl indeed . . . little but well-formed" (*Little Dorrit* 73), and it is this picture, which parallels the birth of Oliver Twist, that carries Amy into the world and indicates how others view her. Physically, Amy accomplishes more than her family and takes on the role of provider and nurturer willingly without outward complaint. If she were to assert herself in her father's fixed view of the world, one where he is settled and indicates no ambition to assist his family or leave his environment, William Dorrit would be shattered, for he does not even know or ever question where his food and clothing are obtained—just that they are present. In being addressed as "Little Dorrit," Amy loses any identity she may possess and becomes a member of the family rather than an individual in it. She is further assured the smallest recognition of both her place and role in the family unit. Dickens assures us that those who observe Amy are both taken and shocked by her appearance initially, as when Arthur first sees her he finds:

> . . . her diminutive figure, small features, and slight spare dress, gave her the appearance of being much younger than she was. A woman, probably not less than two and twenty, she might have passed in the street for little more than half that age. Not that her face was very youthful, for in truth there was more consideration and care in it than naturally belonged to her utmost years; but she was so little and light, so noiseless and shy, and appeared so conscious of being out of place among the three hard elders, that she has all the manner and much of the appearance of a subdued child. (63)

It is in this manner that Arthur, who inevitably becomes her husband, sees her through the text and he is not alone, for even those who do not know Amy believe her to be a child or frail. In *Invisible Writing and the Victorian Novel: Readings in Language and Ideology* (2000), Patricia Ingham reflects on Arthur's view of Amy and finds "He always thinks of her as 'Little Dorrit' not Amy, his 'delicate child,' his 'adopted child' " (158). Ingham further asserts, "His struggle is to free himself from an ingrained practice of denial and from any sense that sexual love for her would be pedophiliac" (158). Here Mr. Dorrit is mistaken. While Arthur is haunted by the difference in their ages, he is more concerned with the failures of his past relationships; most notably with Pet Meagles, than Amy's age.

Dickens is using a conceptual metaphor of the body in his representation of Amy Dorrit. While her actions are not "little" by any means, her body is stunted even when compared to other Victorian women. The image of the physical body allows for a variety of mappings to occur in *Little Dorrit*. The "belittling" Amy undergoes is indicative of this very practice. In *Metaphors We Live By*, Geoff Lakoff and Mark Johnson note, "The essence of metaphor is understanding and experiencing one kind of thing in terms of another" (5). Through this use of metaphor readers are better able to access Amy's position. Through an up/down metaphor readers are also better able to understand the "little" presence Amy is in the variety of settings she inhabits. Her role is larger than she is credited for. Interestingly, the metaphor of the Great Chain of Being can be applied to *Little Dorrit* as a whole because the hierarchical scale of life that Lakoff and Turner discuss, in *More Than Cool Reason: A Field Guide to Poetic Metaphor* (1989), is readily found in Dickens's frame of the idyllic family and caste systems.

Interestingly, Amy is referred to by her given name when her father's fortunes change, but she repossesses the name of "Little Dorrit" when she finds herself back in the Marshalsea prison. These shifts in her name further enhance the numerous aspects of Amy Dorrit's personality and character. Though Ingram finds, in *The Language of Gender and Class: Transformation in the Victorian Novel,* that Amy has a dual identity of mother/child, Amy is more complex than this as she asserts her own identity through action and naming and further hides secrets from most of the people in her life. Ingram also believes Amy to be "asexual-looking" (159), but again it is frequently reasserted though the text that she is a woman. However, one thing is clear to Ingram: "Thus Little Dorrit/ Amy herself is ultimately a contradictory and disruptive figure who sustains nothing more than a sadly dysfunctional family" (161), which, in part, is very true. Amy Dorrit resists the life her father wishes her to lead after his fortunes change, for she is happier participating in their old way of life. Before their fortunes change, Amy insists, " . . . in a burst of sorrow and compassion, 'No, no, I have never seen him in all my life!' " (*Little Dorrit* 230), but she has this view after the inheritance her father receives allows the family to leave the Marshalsea. Once again William Dorrit neglects his children and places them in the care of a maiden lady, Mrs. General, who is to teach his daughters the ways of society. After the death of her father, Amy returns to the Marshalsea, where Arthur is now residing for his own debts. Here Amy is finally able to overtly assert her identity. Dickens's use of satire is once again evident as "The satire of *Little Dorrit* envisions a world in which people have been so reduced to ciphers that names such as Bar of Bishop are perfectly adequate" (Manning 163) and so it is with "little" Amy Dorrit.

Amy Dorrit is aware of her physical size, but rarely laments that those around her demean her though a nickname like "Little Dorrit." As she tries to establish herself in a trade, she seeks out a milliner to teach her to sew, but the milliner finds Amy too fragile. Amy asserts, "I don't think I am weak, ma'am," though the milliner states, "And you are so very, very little, you see," to which Amy replies, "Yes, I am afraid I am very little indeed" (*Little Dorrit* 82). The milliner eventually takes Amy in and teaches her how to sew, but the satire and irony evident in this passage are representative throughout the text. While Amy admittedly is "little," her work and contribution to her family are larger than any made by other members of her family. She believes herself to be "little" to those around her, but does not deem herself as "little" in the same way her family and those in society find her. Chapman believes "The stronger woman is not always marked by overtly 'masculine' appearance and speech" (158), and Amy, though spiritually and psychologically strong, is not overtly assertive or physically robust. In marking Amy as "little," her potential and strength are both repressed, largely due to her social class and gender. This, I find, is what Dickens writes against in creating a character such as Little Dorrit, for she is socially and physically degraded with this nickname. Yet he makes her the savior of the family in a way that transcends the Angel in the House figure, for not only is she fulfilling her social role in the home but also works outside of it to provide for her family. Rhetorical practices were shifting during the nineteenth century and Dickens makes full use of these changes. Robert Connors explains, in *Composition-Rhetoric: Backgrounds, Theory, and Pedagogy* (1997), that the shift in nineteenth-century rhetorical practices:

> . . . shows many of the classic signs of the romantic shift, changes in the ways writers viewed themselves and in the way rhetoric viewed writing. . . . The world of external nature comes more into rhetorical consideration . . . as description became one end of rhetoric. The emphasis comes to rest on discourse as more organic than mechanical, needing to be nurtured, growing out of the writer's purpose. And, most important, the personal feelings, experiences, thoughts, and appreciations of the writer acquire a centrality and power in rhetorical education. . . . (302)

Amy's ability to eventually participate in her own naming is indicative of the organic nature Connors discusses. This also gives Amy some limited agency in the text.

While Amy's nickname is an ironic tool for Dickens that he also uses in other novels, such as with Little Nell in *The Old Curiosity Shop*, her various names throughout the text do indicate her multiple roles. Amy is known as "Little Dorrit" to some, "The Child of the Marshalsea," and the "Little Mother" to Maggy, a large, cognitively disabled woman. Amy acts as a mother to those close to her. Dickens's use of naming in the case of Amy Dorrit is conscious and he makes sure the audience is aware of her diverse roles. Harvey Sucksmith notes, in *The Narrative Art of Charles Dickens: The Rhetoric Sympathy and Irony of his Novels* (1970), " . . . more often than not Dickens is using language as an adequate, and sometimes as a subtle, narrative medium which helps to build and unfold his story, to give an organic impression of a world, its events and its characters, and to convey the significance of his vision. Moreover, as the manuscripts show, Dickens uses language in this way as the instrument of a *conscious* narrative art" (69). The intent of Dickens's use of Amy's nicknames, in this regard, establishes her as a character to the audience. In being "little" Amy has agency, for she acts, though covertly, to better her life in a society where women were not allowed a clear voice. Her power comes from the nature and effects of her actions. When she is recognized as "Amy," initially by her father, it is largely in cases where he is trying to assert his authority. This is not uncommon when we try to establish a serious tone with another individual. Amy later indicates her desire to be called "Little Dorrit," after she has established her feelings towards Arthur. Here she begins to construct her own identity.

Scholars and critics have often noted that Dickens's characters are merely caricatures and one- or two-dimensional at best. Amy Dorrit, for example, through the power of language, represents how inaccurate such interpretations of Dickens's characters can be. Her small stature and position as the last of the Dorrit clan, from which she receives the nickname "Little Dorrit," does not hinder her development or her contributions to her family and the world around her. Lionel Trilling observes in his essay "Little Dorrit": "Even the physical littleness of this grown woman, an attribute which is insisted on and which seems likely to repel us, does not do so, for we perceive it to be the sign that she is not only the Child of the Marshalsea, as she is called, but also the Child of the Parable, the negation of the social will" (100). Amy is the one member of the Dorrit family to survive poverty and establish her own identity. She defies social forces and is able to obtain a semblance of happiness as the text concludes, but still cares for her siblings and their children as well as her own family.

In *Charles Dickens: Linguistic Innovator* (1985), Knud Sørensen details the language Dickens uses throughout much of his work and dedicates one of his entries to "The Status of Human Beings Reduced" (94). That is what occurs in Amy's case. Early in *Little Dorrit* Arthur inquires after her and his mother's housekeeper claims "Oh! She? Little Dorrit? *She's* nothing; she's a whim of—hers [Arthur's mother]" (51). The status of Amy, as with Florence Dombey, is that of a pet and little more and she is deemed lower than a human being, for in this instance she is "nothing." Amy proves throughout the novel to be an asset to the world around her, but rarely receives the recognition she is due. This reconfiguration of the Angel in the House, though by no means feministic, illustrates the complexity Dickens's angels and imperfect children possess.

Death and Discourse

Dickens was not the only author to appeal to readers' sentiments through the use of the imperfect child's physical size and social conditions, for George MacDonald continues this tradition with Diamond in *At the Back of the North Wind*. Diamond is an imperfect character with clear connections to the sentimental and romantic views of children. Peter Coveney points out in *Poor Monkey: The Child in Literature*: " . . . the romantic symbol of growth, the innocence, the pathos, the nostalgia, the regret, the withdrawal, the "death"— the child—image contains not only the response of the artist to his condition, but the response of a whole society, to itself" (285). What makes Diamond a compelling sentimental child character is his rhetorical view of the world. His speech and language are almost too innocent to make him a believable character. Diamond's language borders on babyish and he offers surreal views of the Victorian period. Diamond's remarks on the rising and setting of the sun in *At the Back of the North Wind*, for example, illustrate both child observation and babyish delight as he claims, "What a strange light it is! . . . I have heard that the sun doesn't go to bed all the summer in these parts. Miss Coleman told me that. I suppose he feels very sleepy, and that is why the light he sends out looks so like a dream" (75). Many of Diamond's comments can be attributed to delusions and dream states, but the language he uses suggests he is doing more than simply observing, that he is also experiencing the circumstances around him, much as Nanny the crossing sweep does.

While many of Diamond's views are simplistic, his conditions and observations about Victorian England and his own situation in particular make him a dichotomy in that often his remarks illustrate his working knowledge of his sickness and impending death. It is these things in particular that he learns from North Wind as he slips in and out of consciousness throughout the text. In "Child's Work Is Child's Play: The Value of George MacDonald's Diamond," Lisa Hermine Makman suggests, " . . . *At the Back of the North Wind* (1871) not only presents the new toy-child but, strikingly, replays in its narrative the progressive development of the fantasy that children are toys" (119). Diamond's illness and eventual death contribute to the way adults treat him and as the view of children and childhood began to shift, so too does Diamond's value. It is not change in a straightforward fashion. Diamond's move from the barn to the house is indicative of his change in family and social value, but he remains an economic value for his family even as he is becoming an emotional resource. He understands this continuously developing position from the onset of the text. Upon Diamond's first meeting with North Wind she teaches him the difference between good and evil. Diamond says he will go with her because she is beautiful and she stresses, "You must not be ready to go with everything beautiful at once, Diamond"; and he posits, "But what's beautiful can't be bad" (*At the Back of the North Wind* 18). North Wind, who may be seen as a gentle Grim Reaper, exclaims, "No; I'm not bad. But sometimes beautiful things grow bad by doing bad, and it takes some time for their badness to spoil their beauty. So little boys may be mistaken if they go after things because they are beautiful" (*At the Back of the North Wind* 18). In the North Wind, MacDonald provides an ethereal teacher for Diamond. Diamond is drawing his observations of the world around him together with the lessons she constructs.

Diamond's nature is innocent, but he does know the difficulties of his life. Yet his name, which is often, like his character, seen as simplistic, illustrates his multidimensional qualities. A diamond, when initially found, is not a pure translucent smooth stone. It is a gem that must be honed, cut, and refashioned, much as Diamond is in *At the Back of the North Wind*. Its clarity, cut, color, and carat are estimated before purchase and often even those stones are imperfect. Maria Nikolajeva, in *The Rhetoric of Character in Children's Literature* (2002), suggests because some authors followed the standards of the conventional text, such as George MacDonald's individual characters, characters like those in the *Alice* books and *Heidi* are " . . . rarely complex psychological existents; rather they are actors in a plot" (68). Diamond's simplicity becomes MacDonald's cash nexus for readers and his wallet. In drawing upon the growing revaluation of children and childhood through characters like Diamond, MacDonald, like Dickens before him, was able to earn a living through constructing and marketing the imperfect child, which he continued to do with Princess Irene and Curdie.

In both *The Princess and The Goblin* and *The Princess and Curdie*, MacDonald again draws upon a fantasy world intermixed with realistic elements to express the world in which the imperfect child develops. Princess Irene, named after one of MacDonald's own children, acts little like a princess should. Her nanny questions Princess Irene's actions from the first time readers are introduced to her in *The Princess and the Goblin*. After Princess Irene tells her story of seeing her great-grandmother many times removed, the nurse finds it to be a tale rather than reality, claiming, "I know princesses are in the habit of telling make-believes, but you are the first I ever heard of who expected to have them believed" and goes on to note, as Princess Irene cries at this missive, " . . . it is not at all becoming in a princess to tell stories *and* expect to be believed just because she is a princess" (*The Princess and the Goblin* 20–21). Princess Irene does not fit the typical, metaphorical construct of what a princess "is" or ought to be, but MacDonald uses her to challenge many of the stereotypical characteristics of the traditional princess figure. Given trials as Curdie is, Princess Irene develops in the newly emergent ideas of what the child and childhood are, especially the female child. Her language is that of an educated child, but Curdie's speech reflects both an education and his working class status. Much like Curdie, Charles Kingsley's character Tom, in *The Water-Babies: A Fairy Tale for a Land-Baby,* also uses working class speech and is educated by a mythical fairy being, perhaps indicating that only in passing though a blended space of the fairy realm and reality might imperfect children attain the use of the Standard English of the middle class.

Tom's commercial value, like that of Jo in *Bleak House* and Oliver in *Oliver Twist,* is both intrinsically social and cultural. Tom's name, Kingsley notes, " . . . is a short name, and you have heard it before, so you will not have much trouble remembering it" (*The Water-Babies* 1). Tom's name is also that of his master, Tom Grimes. Kingsley addresses readers from the beginning of the text, much like MacDonald does, so immediately readers pay attention to the narrator's voice. Tom lives, readers are told, in an area where he and his master can earn a good living and he wants for little largely because he does not know any better (*The Water-Babies* 1).

The initial illustration of Tom by Linley Sambourne is that of an unhappy, dirty boy perched atop a chimneystack looking longingly at the sky. Tom is quite all alone, as is Jo, who lives in Tom's-All-Alone's in *Bleak House.* Nikolajeva finds, in *The Rhetoric of Character in Children's Literature,* Tom comes into contact with two "Emblematic characters . . ." (35) in the forms of Mrs. Doasyouwouldbedoneby and Mrs. Bedonebyasyoudo, which she finds to be characters used " . . . frequent[ly] in early didactic children's literature" (35). The image of the unhappy Tom and his future exposure to his fey teachers eventually show that through a proper education and again a shift through a blended space, there is hope Tom might become a productive member of Victorian society. John C. Hawley, S.J., notes, in "*The Water-Babies* as Catechetical Paradigm" (1989), Mrs. Bedonebyasyoudo "Significantly, becomes Kingsley's principal metaphor for social, religious, and in implied dialogue with scientists, physical evolution . . ." (21). Tom's ability to attain an education would not be socially likely and he was more than likely in reality to die before he became an adolescent. As Jordan explains, "Abrasions, falls, and burns were their [chimney sweeps] lot, and occasionally death" (36). When Tom becomes lost in the chimney flues of the house he is helping clean, Kingsley is presenting a painful reality.

Tom's reality is, however, as Kingsley illustrates, of his own making, for if given the opportunity, which many like him were not in Victorian society, Tom could make something of himself. His initial meeting with the Irish washerwoman, whom he later meets in his travels underwater, is Tom's first exposure to the notion that an alternate way of life is desirable. The Irish washerwoman warns Tom and his master Grimes: "Those that wish to be clean, clean they will be; and those that wish to be foul, foul they will be. Remember" (Kingsley 13). Tom later heeds this warning and obtains knowledge that the choice to be different is his own. Tom's speech patterns are not those of a typical working class boy, such as Jo. He speaks rather proper English that, like other imperfect children, parallels his ability to attain salvation. This is not the case for Jo, who speaks with the language patterns of his class. Even in asking simple questions like "What are bees?" and getting a response of "What make honey" (*The Water-Babies* 17), there is a distinction between Tom's speech patterns and other working class individuals in the text. A dragonfly Tom has befriended explains his metamorphosis, which parallels Tom's as being his choice, one earlier heeded by the Irishwoman for Tom when he explains that the underwater environment is " . . . a low place. I lived there for some time; and was very shabby and dirty. But I didn't choose that that should last. So I turned respectable, and came up to the top, and put on this gray suit" (Kingsley 100). This is the experience Tom has throughout the text. Tom undergoes a metaphorical death/rebirth through what Lakoff and Turner term the metaphor of Life is Fluid in the Body; Death is Loss of Fluid and "Metaphorically, life diminishes" (*Metaphors We Live By* 19). Tom experiences rebirth after he emerges from his underwater adventures and is thus reborn and his life renewed though his exposure to fluid. Tom's insight into the world of heaven and religion gives him Victorian salvation, as it later does for Hesba Stretton's Jessica in *Jessica's First Prayer*.

Jessica, unlike Tom or other street urchins that are imperfect children, has little social value. She undergoes more hardships due to her lack of societal value. With nothing to really offer society in the way of knowledge of a trade, Jessica exists on the very fringes of Victorian society; like a mouse, she picks up the crumbs and sulks in the shadows of Victorian culture. She even asks, as she becomes accustomed to a church building, "Isn't there a dark little corner somewhere that I could hide in?" (*Jessica's First Prayer* 27), but at this point in the text Jessica is forced to leave her dark corners and undergo her own introduction to Victorian society and culture. Jessica's understanding of her name relates directly to her experiences, for as Daniel questions what her name is, a curiosity he fights because in knowing her identity he has singled her out as an individual, Jessica explains her feelings towards her name: "It's Jessica . . . but mother and everybody calls me Jess. You'd be tired of being called Jess, if you was me. It's Jess here, and Jess there; and everybody wanting me to go errands. And they think nothing of giving me smacks and kicks and pinches. Look here! (*Jessica's First Prayer* 11). Her speech is that of a Victorian street child's and meeting Daniel, who later comes to care for her, allows Jessica a hopeful future. The meaning of the name Jessica is "He sees," both in her character and name. After being introduced to Christianity, Jessica's transformation begins. Nikolajeva explains, "Names are closely connected with identity, and since the identity quest is such a prominent part of children's fiction, the characters' names are not infrequently part of this quest" (269). Naming and speech are paramount in the development and construction of the imperfect child, for how society views them and the transformations they undergo are at the core of determining their imperfect status.

Becoming lost in a narrative is paramount for the imperfect child because they are often taught through a space that is both didactic and entertaining, a message Christina Rossetti tries to impart in her work. As Jessica comes to find and experience Christianity through wonder and piqued interest, so do Flora, Edith, and Maggie, in Rossetti's *Speaking Likenesses,* develop through the use of dialogue between Aunt and her nieces. Rossetti writes *Speaking Likenesses* as if readers are peering into a conversation they might have had themselves with someone. The nieces are being given lessons though story and the morals and instruction are not hidden in the dialogue. Flora, Edith, and Maggie represent ungrateful children who do not readily listen to their elders in some form during their trio of stories. While Flora and Edith are upper and middle class, Maggie comes from the upper working class and she is the one character who is relatively developed by the end of the story. In their respective stories each of these girls meets her "likeness" and learns from the dialogic exposure offered by Aunt. This rhetorical device offers Rossetti a form that makes her the author and not the didactic "preacher," which falls to the Aunt. In "Speaking Pictures: The Fantastic World of Christina Rossetti and Arthur Hughes" (1998), Andrea J. Kaston suggests, "In all three of these stories, the young heroine offers readers a version of girlhood that is markedly different from the Victorian idealized notion of a safe and pleasant space filled with love and governed by predictable rules" (309). Through the conventions that defy and define gendered spaces imperfect children are also able to develop. Later, E. Nesbit, who overtly speaks to readers as Kingsley does, entwines the metaphorical and elemental devices used in constructing the imperfect child in *The House of Arden* and *Harding's Luck* to illustrate the imperfect child in her own works. She would also keep the fantastical and realistic elements used by writers before her, such as Rossetti, to impart the developmental possibilities of the imperfect child.

Reinforcing the Economy of Heritage

In Nesbit's *The House of Arden* and *Harding's Luck*, Elfrida, Edred, and Dickie Harding's lineage is the key to their societal positions and value. The children, like many of the imperfect children examined previously, come from decaying English gentry. They come from what " . . . had been a great house once, with farms and fields, money and jewels—with tenants and squires and men-at-arms" (*The House of Arden* 1). The "house" not only refers to the actual homestead, but also the family as a body. Elfrida's name, as previously mentioned, suggests the blended space of fantasy and reality where the children must transition and meet their cousin, Dickie Harding. Their language is that of educated individuals, but Dickie, who is the rightful heir to the Arden estate, comes from a working class background and speaks as such. Dickie's working class speech is thicker than Jo's in *Bleak House*, but he, like Diamond, uses language much more like a child than Jo does. When asking for some seeds, for example, Dickie says, "Gimmie . . . gimmie a pennorth o' that there" (*Harding's Luck* 4). The conclusion of *Harding's Luck* finds Dickie no longer lame and, like Tom, choosing his own destiny, but in doing so he imposes another upon his cousins. Dickie's nurse tells him, " . . . now thou art a man; forget the dreams of thy childhood, and play the man to the glory of God and of the House of Arden. And let thy dreams be of the life to come, compared to which all lives on earth are only dreams" (225–26). Nesbit follows the tradition of encouraging her characters and thus her audience that to find their way to an imperfect status one must accept their hardships and embrace faith and spirituality. In *A Woman of Passion: The Life of E. Nesbit 1858–1924* (1987),[9] Julia Briggs points out that in *The House of Arden* and *Harding's Luck* the most important thing the children " . . . find is their lost father" (182) and thus the family name and fortune.

Imperfect children understand themselves in terms of how Victorian society and culture define them in either their given name or names they are called. Being "little," both physically and in the eyes of nineteenth-century England, is a key element in developing the imperfect child. The imperfect child must transition through a blended space as that explained by Lakoff and Turner in order to attain their imperfect status. They journey both physically and mentally and attain this label through both fantastic and realistic worlds. Dickens's Oliver Twist, Little Nell, Tiny Tim, Esther Summerson, Jo, and Little Dorrit are all representative of this trend in Dickens. In "Critical Opinion: Reading Children's Books" (1996) Julia Briggs notes, "No one recalled more vividly than Dickens how children felt, their continuous fascination and bafflement with the incongruous and illogical world created by the adults around them" (22). Later authors, such as MacDonald, Kingsley, Stretton, Rossetti, and Nesbit, writing for children and adults alike, use the metaphors and rhetorical elements Dickens draws upon in constructing the imperfect for the protagonists in their own texts. These characters, like Diamond, Nanny, Princess Irene, Curdie, Tom, Jessica, Flora, Edith, Maggie, Elfrida, Edred, and Dickie, understand themselves in terms of society and come to illustrate their own identities, as do Dickens's characters. Such transitions conclude happily with either a death or a relatively happy ending.

Chapter Four
A Beautiful Decay
Disease, Death, and Eternal Longing of the Imperfect Child

"A baby's cradle with no baby in it,
A baby's grave where autumn leaves drop sere;
The sweet soul gathered home to Paradise,
The body waiting here."
                    —**Christina G. Rossetti**, *Sing-Song: A Nursery Rhyme Book* (15)

The disease and possible death of any child creates a haunting and tragic image in the minds of parents, friends, and society. Such an idea is as applicable for the Victorians as it is today. For Victorians, the romanticization of disease, death, and decay, especially associated with children, was not only an emotionally evolving concept, but for some Victorians it becomes a favorable economic concept. Many occupations, such as morticians and doctors, in Victorian culture were able to capitalize on disease, death, and decay. Pictorial books of death[1] were created to remember loved ones and mourning jewelry fashioned from the hair of the deceased was worn in remembrance of someone dear who had died. Victorian culture also saw the rise of the romantic and sentimental notion of bodily difficulties. The romance associated with death for the Victorians lay in the promise of an afterlife; a place devoid of the evils of society. Children's writers capitalized on images and ideas of disease, death, and decay. Charles Dickens, George MacDonald, Charles Kingsley, Hesba Stretton, Christina Rossetti, and E. Nesbit all draw upon the romanticizing of the diseased, dying, and dead child in constructing the imperfect child character to illustrate the transition space one must move through in order to attain a semblance of harmony. Some sort of disease or death, and especially the decay of life, must strike imperfect children in order for them to realize a happy existence, whether it is through life or death.

Disease and death were not uncommon or taboo subjects in Victorian culture, including children's literature. These affected every level of Victorian society. Industrialization, concentrated living conditions, poor hygiene, and unsanitary conditions both in the home and at work were only small factors that led to mass illness and death. Richard Altick points out in *Victorian People and Ideas*:

> . . . whereas the old kind of deprivation and suffering was diffused, the new kind was concentrated and its effect upon the beholder intensified. Individual cases, thousands upon thousands of them, coalesced into a mass of misery. No ordinary exercise of private philanthropy would suffice to relieve it. Its magnitude was such that only a concerted effort on an unheard-of scale would have any hope of success. Thus history offered not guidance; the conditions to be remedied were the result of novel causes, yet the remedies had to be such as could be applied though existing institutions . . . it was a question that affected all of Britain, not the laboring poor alone. (41–42)

Diseases such as typhus and smallpox were both highly deadly and very contagious. This was especially true for those living in cramped living conditions, like Tom All-Alone's in Dickens's *Bleak House*. Children lived in misery and squalor at various levels of society. These children were impacted as terribly as adults in a society that did not completely understand the value of hygiene and quarantine.

Despite disease and death, Victorian's hope held. Writers used their texts and illustrations to enrich readers' understanding of the growing societal burden of the poor as well as to make a living. The child character became a symbol for these authors and Dickens capitalized on the developing vision of the Victorian child and childhood. The romanticized notions of the Victorian child set children apart from adults and childhood and children became something to be protected and preserved. Such children were presented as innocent, loving, religious, and, above all, untouched by human misery and knowledge. They were examples of mankind before Eve plucked her sinful apple, and thus a status to which culture and society could never return or attain. But try the Victorians did. The imperfect child, however, is never fully free from the evils of Victorian culture and society. Oliver Twist, for example, knows the misery of the workhouse, and Tom in Charles Kingsley's *The Water-Babies* knows what abuse is at the hand of his master chimney sweep. It is not enough that readers should learn about the accounts of such children. Exposure to the image of the imperfect child drew on the emotions of

Victorian society as the images presented in reading material were occurring throughout the Victorian world in both city street and country lane.

Depictions of Romantic children could be found throughout Victorian society and childhood was well ingrained in the culture. There was a vast wardrobe of Victorian children and authors had many options as how they may dress their characters, but the Romantic child was at the heart of every creation, for it represented unattainable perfection. Illustrations of such children were mass-produced and distributed throughout Victorian society. As Anne Higonnet points out in *Pictures of Innocence: The History and Crisis of Ideal Childhood* (1998), "According to Romantic pictures of children, innocence must be an edenic state from which adults fall, never to return. Nor can Romantic children know adults, they are by definition unconscious of adult desires, including adults' desires for childhood. . . . We [adults] long for a childhood we cannot reach" (28). The unconsciousness of the Romantic child separates them from the Victorian imperfect child. Just as "The image of the Romantic child replaces what we have lost, or what we fear to lose. Every sweetly sunny, innocently cute Romantic child image stows away a dark side: a threat of loss, of change, and, ultimately, of death" (Higonnet 28–29). The image of such a child, however, cannot die, for it is static unless marred by an adult's hand and this too illustrates the impact of society and culture upon the image of the Romantic child and childhood. The Romantic child came to be something to be socially preserved and was rarely touched by disease and death: imperfect children were not. This imperfection contributed to the social development of new social values being placed upon children and childhood.

The danger in relating stories like those of Oliver Twist and Tom is that in portraying them as fictional characters, their plights became fictional as well. Stories such as Oliver Twist's were largely portrayed as happening in the past even though the conditions and children were readily available in the present. Often the fictional accounts of children placed such experiences in the past, such as with Oliver's story occurring before its publication date. Reader's guilt, therefore, could be reduced since these were situations that they were not forced to confront outside the pages of novels. But writers, including Dickens, were ready to point out that the characters in his works, such as the imperfect child, were drawn from very real individuals and circumstances, as he notes in the preface to *Oliver Twist*. In giving readers the choice to recognize or ignore the conditions presented textually, authors could appeal to a reader's sense or sensibility. Disease and death were inherent social issues found throughout society and as writers drew attention to these problems, political and cultural changes began to come to fruition. Writers like Dickens saw it as their job to present a cause, and by doing so they brought social ills to light in their work; it was left to readers to determine what they would do with such information.

For many authors the construction of imperfect children did not stop at inflicting their character with disease and death. The child was meant to be beautiful and their journey illustrated a decay of Victorian ideals. Children that were diseased or died were bound in a moment and learned something of their value to society. Held in repose at times and frolic in others in illustration and text, a diseased or dead child was often a "happy" child. Higonnet states, "The beautiful child corpse is one morbidly logical conclusion of the Romantic child image" (29) and " . . . I would say that the image of the Romantic child is haunted by death. [For example,] Long before she actually died, Penelope Boothby's parents looked at her living beauty with death in their eyes" (30). This was, I argue, true for the majority of Victorian society. Not only were images and text of disease and death frequently to be found in Victorian homes, but also the dead themselves. In *Victorian Childhood: Themes and Variations*, Thomas E. Jordan explains, "In some respects, death was a theme of childhood and children's experiences in Victorian Britain. Routinely, they encountered the complex of events which surrounded death . . ." (85). Commonplace in the household and culture, " . . . death forced itself into children's lives as epidemics spread and communicable diseases . . . spread rapidly. Death had familiarity for children, and popular culture of the period provided an appropriate degree of response" (Jordan 86). A Romantic child was a dead child whereas the Victorian imperfect child had a chance at life because it had knowledge of experience.

Scholars argue whether Victorian adults placed their longing for a lost childhood upon their own children, but readily apparent is society's desire for the existence offered by childhood. Victorian adults would then be free from the harshness of Victorian reality and all it held. Conditions in Victorian England were terrible in both the country and city. People were impoverished and hungry. There was little escape from the harshness of industrial progress. If children were physically stunted and little, there was no account for what contributed to maladies that haunted those that were less than hardy. Altick suggests:

> Epidemics of typhoid and cholera—outbreaks of the latter killed 16,437 people in England and Wales in 1832, and some 16,000 in London alone in 1849—joined with diseases induced by malnutrition, exhaustion, and "vice" . . . to further increase the death rate, which in these conditions was several times the national average. One out of every two babies born in the towns died before the age of five. (44–45)

Despite all of the disease and death, Victorian society and culture flourished. The Victorians romanticized and longed for days of chivalry and innocence, much as our own society and culture romanticizes the nineteenth century in everything from literature and magazines, such as *Victorian Homes,* to film, such as with Jane Austen film adaptations of *Pride and Prejudice* (2005) and *Sense and Sensibility* (1995). Contemporary viewers think of upper class excess paralleled with the battle of the sexes. In adaptations of Victorian texts, like *Vanity Fair* (2004) or Roman Polanski's *Oliver Twist* (2005), even Victorian England becomes beautified and healthy in appearance. Our selective taste for the Victorian period and the types of children that developed out of it, especially the imperfect child, is still alive and well.

Idealism vs. Realism

The imperfect-child construction was and continues to be a problematic ideal for society and culture. The imperfect child is a societal and cultural possibility, but overtly Victorians longed for the romantically perfect child because it offered something they could not possess: a return to innocence. Such a child reflects the reality of Victorian society and culture so readers could relate their own experiences to those of such characters. The binary of romantic child and street waif was challenged in the development of the imperfect child as this character was a blend of characteristics from the former duality of good/bad. During the nineteenth century, children were deemed to be either intrinsically good or inherently evil by most in society and this was outlined in the two dominant schools of thought. The concept of the Romantic child was not altogether new to the Victorians, and they readily embraced the idea of the pure, innocent child who had inherent goodness. Penny Kane notes in *Victorian Families in Fact and Fiction* (1995):

> ... the concept of children as fresh from Heaven reinforced the alternative concept of children as unregenerate in redrawing the place of children in contemporary minds. ... Depending on one's religious views and personal temperament, this unique being might be envisaged as an innocent not yet contaminated by the world, or brimming with original sin. ... (50)

The imperfect child lies in this binary. Oliver Twist, for example, is not ignorant of the injustices of the world; he knows little of religion and has been brought up in poverty and in harsh circumstances. Oliver merely exists. When Oliver finally leaves and cultivates an existence on his own, he begins to understand his experiences in relation to his society and culture. The imperfect child is deemed imperfect through a societal lens. It does not meet the requirements for being labeled an angelic soul, but it is not unredeemable as are the feral children Oliver meets in Fagin's den. Even in individuals such as Charley Bates and Nancy, there is hope for redemption, but the children have to choose such a path.

Marketing Realism

There is still a vision of the child as inherently good in Western societies and cultures. Brooding parents and family members seemingly have a fresh chance with each new offspring. Children are uncontaminated by societal and cultural issues and we try to protect them at any cost. Programs such as DARE and Amber Alerts[3] are set in place with one idea in mind: protection. By telling children about such things, however, they are also exposed to the fact that people do drugs and children can be and are kidnapped and hurt. In offering protection, we must also offer information or the protection will not work effectively. Imperfect children all too often learn about the deficiencies on their own. While such hardships would be better off left between the fictional covers of texts, they do unfortunately occur and impact very real individuals. Harry Potter is not the first child to be forced to live under a staircase and Hesba Stretton's Jessica was not the first to be neglected and abused by her mother. These occurrences are very realistic and tragic. Still, children are shielded and often not credited for knowing and experiencing the difficult world around them. Disease and death are two tragic issues the Victorians did not try to hide from children. These two topics were considered as a necessary part of life, yet now we often screen such occurrences from children.

The imperfect child has characteristics of both the angelic/innocent and unredeemable/damaged children common in Victorian ideology. Imperfect children are romanticized and ultimately socialized through their illness and rebirth. In illustrating a child as ill, authors more readily draw upon the sympathies of their audience, as Dickens does with Little Nell in *The Old Curiosity Shop*. The impending death of Little Nell drew readers to its pages. The oft-cited story of how Americans lined the docks of Boston and New York, as Fred Kaplan outlines in *Dickens: A Biography*, waiting to find out the fate of Little Nell " . . . that might break their hearts . . ." (124) might be paralleled today to the anxious readers awaiting the next installment of a Harry Potter book and the desire to know whether the protagonist will live or die. Such fictional children are loved and beloved for more than just readers' desire to relive a childhood, something many critics have pointed out. When a child character is ill, readers have a certain amount of power over that child, just as with any sick individual. The power to pity and assist such a person allows readers to feel better about themselves. The imperfect child becomes romanticized as readers hope they regain health and vigor and may thus continue upon their journey towards recovery.

Sentimentality and Decay

The illustration of the diseased and dead imperfect child is not only romantic but also very sentimental. While the Romantic child is deemed pure and innocent, the imperfect child is romanticized so that while their heart may be thought to be pure, such a child is impacted by experience. These children become someone to be saved and their childhood something to be guarded. They are desirable because they can be viewed and have little ability to speak out against such treatment. Such depictions did not reflect the reality of Victorian life, as Elizabeth Thiel explores in *The Fantasy of Family: Nine-teenth-Century Children's Literature and the Myth of the Domestic Ideal* (2008) and suggests, "The destitute poor of the cities, reportedly breeding unchecked in their disease-ridden rookeries, posed a danger to social stability generally, but it was their 'vermin' offspring, 'swaddled' in evil and genetically destined for crime and depravity, that were viewed as potential contaminants of the future" (44). As the imperfect child becomes an object to be viewed as help-less, they often are idealized, and readers read their own stories and experi-ences into the lives of such children. The value of the imperfect child increases because of such idealization. Readers want them to live, as in the case of Little Nell, and overcome their difficulties, yet these are not necessarily children readers want to associate with on a daily basis. In bettering himself/herself, the imperfect child will live, whether it is in heaven or in the confines of some-one's home, but we typically don't want them to live in *our* homes.

The hands-off approach indicates our continued desire for the angelic, untouched perfect child. Socially this is overt as can be seen in the number of "unadoptable" children in orphanages. James R. Kincaid points out in *Erotic Innocence: The Culture of Child Molesting*, "Not all children are truly adorable children, dream children. None are. And we might be asking whether our cud-dling of fantasy cute kids, kids with sticky kisses and fistfuls of dandelions, is what other kids need, the kids who flock around us in the flesh" (109). Oliver Twist, for example, needs the kind of love and attention given to children, but he is still touched by societal and cultural experiences with which the angelic dream child is not. The imperfect child is a child of modernity, but its roots lay in the Victorian period and it develops through characterization in what are deemed texts for an adult audience. Kincaid discusses the modern child as "... both radiant and oddly repellant, the object of fawning and not-so-secret resentment" (*Erotic Innocence* 53). This modern child, or as Kincaid dubs it a "new child," has much in common with the imperfect child. The value in such a child lies in what it is and is not, what readers want to view, but not possess. As the imperfect child becomes ill, the more it is romanticized and untouch-able. When the imperfect child reaches death or is close to it, it is longed for even more. Anne Higonnet suggests in *Pictures of Innocence: The History and Crisis of Ideal Childhood*:

> If the child's body appeals sensually to adults because it is unconscious, then the deeply sleeping, possibly dead body will be very appealing. The dead child's body is one that never did and never will know desire, that al-lows adults to project the full measure of their longings. In a more specific sense, these images of dead children deal with a terrible parental fear, the actual loss of one's own flesh and blood. (30)

Higonnet's contention is questionable, but the stillness of the dead child does allow for such projection. Fears may develop with the death of a child or a family line, as in the case with Paul Dombey, may die. With a death occurring early in life, we may also recognize that childhood is rarely innocent and that adults project the desire of innocence on children. While readers might project their own desire to regain their lost childhood or remember what it is like to be innocent, there is still an intrinsic desire for such a child physically and emotionally.

Historically this desire has been for the perfect, unsullied Romantic child, but a secret longing that has long been denied is for the imperfect child because readers can relate to their cultivation of experience. The diseased and dead child has knowledge of societal and cultural ideologies and this makes them both a threat and an asset. They do not fit the image of the "dream child." As images of JonBenét Ramsey, a contemporary example of what the perfect image is supposed to resemble, filter across different media images, we both revile in horror and yet secretly envy her image. Seemingly, there is repulsion for those othered socially and culturally, as there was in the Victorian period. People may no longer be put in side shows or locked in someone's attic, but we do lock them away in asylums and from the majority of society through media displays. While some strides have been made for reflections of such individuals in the public eye, such as with Geri Jewell's representation of a disabled individual on HBO's series *Deadwood* (2004–2006) or Chris Burke's character on *Life Goes On* (1989–1993), who has Down syndrome, all too often these individuals represent the milder cases of those with such disorders.

Western culture still wishes for the perfect, healthy child, but realistically there is a desire for the imperfect child who better represents real children. Kincaid points out, "It's another matter with children who aren't cute to begin with: poor children and most children of color, fat and skinny and diseased children, and children who are simply plain. When the construction of adolescence is forced on them, they become officially eroticized on their own account and thus lose all erotic interest for the rest of us" (*Erotic Innocence* 107). Such children are either overlooked if plain or viewed as part of the side show if diseased and/or disabled. Supposedly there is no wish to look or create an "other," but Western culture is still peeking at the individual behind the curtain. From a pedagogical perspective, presenting texts with an othered protagonist, such as the imperfect child, often creates more reading interest among students. If the protagonist were the innocent Romantic child, the desire to read the text is not as high overall. Teachers may use a variety of texts that include both imperfect and romantic children to help compliment all learning styles and open a wide discussion base.

Enhancing Pedagogy: Death and the "Classic" Text

Using *Oliver Twist* in the classroom helps students both confront and understand disease and death. What makes such texts "classical" is their continued applicability to the world in which contemporary readers exist. Though children might not mine for coal or sweep chimneys in first world countries (at least not legally), there are still children who work for pennies a day and contract terrible diseases. The problems of child labor, sickness, and death have not disappeared; they tend to be overlooked in Western culture or have just outsourced to other countries. Western society may believe such hideous problems no longer affect "us," and an account like Oliver's become almost fictionalized. The starving and diseased "they" seem to exist only on the margins of society or are a world away. "Classic" literature should be used to enlighten and perhaps enact action. As the imperfect child learns through experience, so too can contemporary students use this literature to think about the larger context of the world in which they live. Such texts can not only inform and entertain readers, but also help make individuals better citizens.

All literature cannot be understood in terms of one's own experiences. In "Does Theory Play Well in the Classroom?" (1996) Barbara Christian uses the phrase "literary geography" to show students that a text is produced out of a specific social and cultural context (248). Christian explains that "literary geography" helps students understand " . . . the text that they're reading from the nineteenth century is looked at in a completely different way because of what we're dealing with right now" (248). What Christian does not note is the problematic nature of this approach in not showcasing how the text was produced during the nineteenth century and how it developed out of a Victorian climate. If students discuss the various types of illness children at different levels of society caught and then how those diseases still exist or have been treated in relation to they way they are dealt with in the text, they may better understand the importance and applicability of "classic" texts. There needs to be a strong emphasis on making sure historical elements in a text are not taken out of context. Students should be encouraged to apply contemporary ideologies to a text as they will come to read it through the lens of their own experience, but must also be taught the text in its historical context. Reading a text like Oliver Twist can help students understand experiences such as Oliver's, such as when he is "raised by hand." These issues have been around for centuries and perhaps discussion may help to shed light on how they have been dealt with and are applicable globally today.

Rightly, Christian tries to illustrate that the world of the academy and the world of text are one and that the academy exists in what is typically called the "real world,"[4] or that outside of the academy. Educators might encourage students to both view the academy and that which they learn in the classroom as the "real world" for heightened understanding of both the literature they read and world they participate in every day. Students often ask how what they are learning applies to not only the "real" world but to their future employment. Disease and death, for example, are topics students can relate to on many levels. Ways in which disease and death have impacted the sociological and cultural ideologies of children and childhood are enhanced through reading texts such as Oliver Twist. Though not every student may have personally encountered death, they will have had some experience with disease. The way we currently treat diseases, especially those encountered in texts such as *Oliver Twist*, is different from our Victorian counterparts. Advances in medicines and treatment have allowed for better treatment options and opportunities for patients, but the treatment is still a very personal matter. Many of the diseases the Victorians faced on almost a daily basis, such as tuberculosis and smallpox, have virtually been wiped out in Western society, but since 9/11 we have reexamined these diseases and realized the impact they might have if they were to be administered to the population at large. Many of these diseases still pose threats to children, but the theme of the imperfect child might illustrate the character overcoming disease and/or death whereas the Romantic child may die peacefully never knowing they were ill and this can be found in both contemporary and "classical" texts.

Through teaching texts labeled "classics," students are offered not only exposure to literature and history but also knowledge of how the concept of humanity has developed. "Classic" texts help instructors to illustrate the parallels of society and culture and we may come to see that we are not wholly divorced from Victorian ideologies as a Western culture. Many of our medical practices are the same as the Victorians, but contemporary American culture's attitude towards death is very different. The ways we honor our dead and face death are also similar, but these are now a much more private affair. For example, it is no longer a common practice to lay out a body for home viewing or to wear widow's weeds. If a deceased loved one's family clips a lock of hair from the corpse, it is usually done in private and stowed in a drawer rather than turned into a piece of jewelry to wear in public. In teaching "classics" we teach about culture and society and how our current ideologies have been shaped though such lenses. Challenging personal ideologies through the use of "classic" texts can be problematic. Students may react with statements such as "This does not apply to us as we have advanced culturally since the Victorian period" or "Why should we care?" Teachers should try to dispel these notions, for if we do not care about what has occurred before, how are we to care about our current social and cultural conditions, which extend to other geographic locals?

Using feminist pedagogy, instructors need to be careful about how they present text. The teachers' views on issues such as heath care, for example, might not mirror those of students. Through analytical discussion and application of the analysis, teachers can help bridge gaps for students and illustrate how Oliver's story can apply to current sociocultural conditions. In so doing, teachers must emphasize that we cannot read as a nineteenth-century reader would, and that we can not simply bring our own set of twentieth- and twenty-first-century ideologies to the work. Students do not have to always "relate" to a work or character, but in teaching texts such as *Oliver Twist* they may learn more about sociocultural ideologies and practices.

Berenice Malka Fisher suggests, in *No Angel in the Classroom: Teaching through Feminist Discourse*, "For feminist teaching, the confluence of individual and collective passion seems especially important to the exercise of authority. I see this occurring in two particular forms in my own teaching: in the power of passion for *initiating* activity and in the tendency of passion to lead to *idealizing* others and ourselves" (97). Both of these forms do present dangers, especially as the world becomes internationalized, for many prejudices and discriminations still exist.

The overly applied phrase for a "classic," a work that "stands the test of time," is problematic, for that does not really apply to a context. The term "classic" is problematic enough, and key phrases are easy for students to use, but they provide little context for a text. In seeing sociocultural parallels through texts like *Oliver Twist*, students are more apt to understand, even if they are not engaged by the work, our own ideologies about issues such as disease and death and how we have developed constructions of the child and childhood.

Application of classroom material to the "real" world becomes essential for understanding the development of current ideologies of the child and childhood and even more so when such individuals face disease and death. The imperfect child falls ill and may face death, or outright die in the narrative. While Dickens and authors who followed him use disease and death in the narrative of construction of the imperfect child to indicate a turning point in not only the text but also the imperfect child, these authors often drew upon their own reality to illustrate these issues. The social and cultural value of such children has cyclically developed along with economic shifts in society and culture. Viviana A. Zelizer, in *Pricing the Priceless Child: The Changing Social Value of Children,* explains:

> The nineteenth-century revolution in child mourning as well as the twentieth-century campaign for child life are less significant as measures of changes in private sentiment, that is, an improvement in mother-love, than as dramatic indicators of a broader cultural transformation in children's value. As children, regardless of their social class, were defined as emotionally priceless assets, their death became not only a painful domestic misfortune but a sign of collective failure. Individual and group responses were therefore shaped by a cultural context that upheld child life as uniquely sacred and child death as singularly tragic. (32)

Authors such as Dickens contributed to changes in the development of the child and childhood, for these were a focal point of not only the narrative but also a sociocultural concern.

Death and Realism

Since disease and death were not uncommon in the everyday lives of the Victorians, it is not surprising they are common subjects in written work during the nineteenth century. Dickens's own life was filled with various diseases and deaths among his friends and family, and he encountered these on a daily basis as he walked the streets of London as a child, young court reporter, and later as a writer. Such associations undoubtedly impacted the sensitive Dickens and these images appear in many of his imperfect child characters. Throughout his life Dickens was preoccupied with disease and death, as is apparent in the majority of his works. He also loved children and they became protagonists for many of his texts, as was the case for many authors.

As L. Frank Baum, a father of four boys, was noted to have given his wife her Dorothy through his *Oz* (1900) series after the death of their niece Dorothy, Dickens also preserved the memories of many of those he had loved who had passed away in his own tomes which then became another tomb for their dearly departed. One oft-cited example of this occurred with the death of his sister-in-law, Mary Hogarth, whom it is widely suggested was the inspiration for Nelly Trent in *The Old Curiosity Shop*. Kaplan believes Dickens's " . . . own experience had made the child figure central to his imagination, the sensitive youth whose sense of his worth is assaulted by a hostile world from infancy onward" (95). In characters like Oliver Twist and Paul Dombey, we see neglect of the child and their childhood, though their value lies in their commodity.

Devaluation through Orphanhood

Disease and death impacted Dickens through the loss of his beloved sister-in-law, Mary Hogarth (1820–1837), his infant daughter Dora (1850–1851), as well as many friends and family members, and this is apparent in his work. However, with characters like Oliver Twist the narrative is not just personal, but public. Kaplan explains, "The most powerful expression in his fiction of such loss and deprivation is to be born an orphan or near orphan, as are Oliver, Pip, Little Nell, David Copperfield, and Esther Summerson, or to have lost one parent, like Nicholas Nickleby, Florence Dombey, and Amy Dorrit" (95). I would further suggest that the loss of one parent is significant for the latter group of these characters as the remaining parent is often ineffectual and shortsighted, caring little for their offspring. These children become imperfect at the beginning of their lives through the love of their guardians, a desire that lies in their commodity and socialization. Such a child's destiny, unless they apply the knowledge they attain and renegotiate their own value, is doomed from birth, such as with Oliver Twist's friend Dick.

Oliver Twist is born both from and into experience. He gains knowledge of Victorian life from the perspective of a working class orphaned child, and his initial understandings in life come from disease and death. Oliver is born sickly and his mother dies at his birth. As Oliver is issue from a marriage-less relationship, he is socially labeled a "bastard" and thus the sickness and death associated with his birth were often superstitiously blamed upon the conditions under which he was conceived. The surgeon's response to Oliver's mother having no wedding band on her left hand shows that such conditions are all but uncommon (*Oliver Twist* 47). Shifts in such ideologies, however, were occurring as when Oliver's half-brother Monks calls Oliver a "bastard" and Mr. Brownlow reflects a different idea when he explains such language only diminishes the ethos of the speaker and suggests Monks should "Let that pass" (*Oliver Twist* 457). Oliver has a marginal chance of survival from birth, but the outlook for a happy, healthy productive life is unlikely. At birth Oliver has trouble with his respiratory system and the doctor determines that he will live after his first labored breaths. Dickens credits this to "Nature" and goes on to note, " . . . after a few struggles, Oliver breathed, sneezed and proceeded to advertise to the inmates of the workhouse the fact of a new burden having been imposed upon the parish . . ." (*Oliver Twist* 46). Disease haunts Oliver for the rest of the narrative, as does its brother, death, and they are not only imposed upon Oliver but also his intimates.

Dick, a contrast to Oliver, is Oliver's friend in suffering at the hands of Mrs. Mann, and is represented as the innocent child, a perfect child who knows of God and Heaven and is happy to die even after knowing the misery of being farmed. On his trek to London, after running away from his apprenticeship with the undertaker Mr. Sowerberry, Oliver crosses in front of his old home and Dick is outside. In a sentimental picture, Dickens depicts Oliver hugging his friend good-bye while Dick explains that he knows he will be better off after his death and states, "I know the doctor must be right, Oliver, because I dream so much of Heaven, and Angels, and kind faces that I never see when I am awake" (*Oliver Twist* 96–97). Dick imagines a beautiful place where there will be no more beatings, sickness, or hunger. His journey to what Jacqueline Banerjee illustrates, in *Through the Northern Gate: Childhood and Growing Up in British Fiction, 1719–1901* (1996) as a happy death (37), has begun. Dick accepts his fate whereas Oliver struggles against those elements in culture and society that seek to restrain him.

Dick has no social value and his death will be little more than an inconvenience for those who have cared for him, but Oliver has an established value and his desertion of his apprenticeship, as he well knows, could result in his being badly beaten or killed. While Oliver is able to resist his apprenticeship as a chimney sweep, he is eventually sold to Mr. Sowerberry, an undertaker. Though he resists death as a chimney sweep, he is forced to deal in death as a trade. Dickens describes this change in Oliver's fortunes as placing him in " . . . a new scene of suffering" (*Oliver Twist* 72). Oliver learns about death before coming into contact with Mr. Sowerberry, but through his apprenticeship he learns first hand about death as a career and how people relate to it. Accompanying Mr. Sowerberry during a consultation to a working class household, Oliver is exposed to the funeral arrangements of a young mother. Her family is present and a male family member says that the dead mother " . . . was starved to death. I never knew how bad she was, till the fever came upon her;

and then her bones were starting through the skin. There was neither fire nor candle; she died in the dark—in the dark! She couldn't even see her children's faces, though we heard her gasping out their names" (*Oliver Twist* 82). The young woman's funeral is held in a small church cemetery and her placement in the pauper's corner reflects her societal economic value.

Oliver learns not of the good of Christianity at this point, but rather how easily those in power can corrupt its ideologies. Catherine Gallagher and Stephen Greenblatt point out, in *Practicing New Historicism* (2000), "Involuntarily taking something 'on faith' because it cannot be otherwise established is the outcome of exhaustion, finitude, or laziness, whereas believing in something is the result of vigilance" (165), and Oliver learns to believe in his own agency as he leaves his miserable living conditions. The service for the young mother is very short so he learns little of Christian doctrine, something that Dickens illustrates Oliver would learn on his own. The four-minute service and her burial atop other coffins in the same grave, paralleled with the " . . . ragged boys whom the spectacle attracted into the churchyard [who] played a noisy game at hide-and-seek among the tombstones, or varied their amusements by jumping backwards and forwards over the coffin" (*Oliver Twist* 84), indicate the triviality of the death of a Victorian working class individual. A pauper child, such as Dick, would have been lucky to receive the burial the young mother received as his societal value would have been even less than that of the young mother.

As social and cultural notions of the child and childhood changed, so did the economic value of their death. A new market in the death trade opened up for children's caskets, life insurance policies, burial clothing, and grave markers. Special sections in graveyards were set aside for burying children. Zelizer acknowledges that insurance policies " 'bought' a dignified death for children" (132), and during the Victorian period such policies were purchased as " . . . a token of respect for the dead child . . ."; but during the twentieth century this shifted, so they now became an illustration " . . . of love for the living child . . ." (136).[5] While there were no insurance policies or benefits for children such as Dick or Oliver, they were insurance that people like Mr. Bumble and the Board would have continuous employees. Dickens's use of the imperfect child and its relation to disease and death shows not only what such individuals experience socially and culturally, but also how they came to gain their knowledge of Victorian society and culture. Throughout *Oliver Twist* the protagonist is continuously exposed to and experiences disease and death.

Though readers know Oliver is born gasping for air, they are told little about the illness Oliver experiences in the care of Mrs. Mann. Yet Dickens notes more than once he was starved, beaten, and abused daily during this portion of his life. Interestingly, Oliver, as one can imagine children of his ilk would, runs away from the undertaker's home and employ and thus from the grip of living surrounded by such a bleak existence. Upset by continuous acknowledgment that his mother was better off dead, Oliver beats on Noah Claypole, a fellow worker, and after he is punished runs away to London. During his incarceration before he runs away from the Sowerberry family, Oliver:

> ... gave way to the feelings which the day's treatment may be supposed likely to have awakened in a mere child. He had listened to their taunts with a look of contempt; he had borne the lash without a cry: for he felt that pride swelling in his heart which would have kept down a shriek to the last, though they had roasted him alive. But now, when there were none to see or hear him, he fell upon his knees on the floor; and, holding his face in his hands, wept such tears as ... few so young may ever have cause to pour out before him. For a very long time, Oliver remained motionless in this attitude. (*Oliver Twist* 95)

At this point, Dickens indicates Oliver has suffered more than any one human can and also illustrates Oliver's tenacity to live. When Oliver, much like Little Nell later in *The Old Curiosity Shop*, sets out, not really knowing where he is going, it is "With the first ray of light that struggled thought the crevices in the shutters ..." (*Oliver Twist* 95–96); he passes Dick, who the doctors have said is dying, and thus Oliver leaves both the trade in death and the possibility he will die at the hands of Mrs. Mann.

Though he does not undergo years of schooling in the undertaker's business, Oliver is exposed to disease and death as he reaches London and is afflicted with fainting spells throughout the narrative. Such exposure illustrates Oliver's new education will come from firsthand experience, much like a real street waif would obtain. The first time he is weakened is by a beating and this indicates a shift in Oliver's luck. In trying to pickpocket Mr. Brownlow, Oliver is caught and set upon by a mob. At the inquest of the events, Oliver faints dead away and, upon being found innocent in this incoherent state, is thrown on the street pavement, where "Little Oliver Twist lay on his back ... with his shirt unbuttoned, and his temples bathed with water; his face a deadly white; and a cold tremble convulsing his whole frame" (*Oliver Twist* 124). Here Oliver's innocence becomes an asset, for Mr. Brownlow takes pity on him and takes Oliver home with him to care for the boy. Mr. Brownlow sees potential in Oliver and his potential as social currency. Oliver's innocence and looks are what peaks the old bachelor's interest. In *Erotic Innocence: The Culture of Child Molesting*, Kincaid suggests, "For Dickens, it was not the child's innocence that was in danger but its life; he did not think people loved children in a sick or perverted way but that they did not love them at all, simply did not care" (290), but in Mr. Brownlow, there is a sense of caring though we may question why. Mr. Brownlow muses, "There is something in that boy's face ... something that touches and interests me. *Can* he be innocent? He looked like—By the by ... God bless my soul! Where have I seen something like that look before?" (*Oliver Twist* 119). Oliver's innocent countenance is what first compels Mr. Brownlow to take him in. Dickens uses Oliver's illness for shifts in the narrative as well as to indicate the sickly nature of his first imperfect child protagonist.

Oliver faces not only illness, but also encounters death on personal and public terms. After his apprenticeship to Mr. Sowerberry and discussion with Dick, Oliver is repeatedly ill and faces death by the hangman's noose for the pickpocketing he is accused of doing. His encounters with disease and death become darker as he is taken in and out of Fagin's custody, as when he reads on, " . . . the lives and trials of great criminals . . . of dreadful crimes that made the blood run cold; of secret murders that had been committed by the lonely wayside; of bodies hidden from the eye of man in deep pits and wells: which would not keep them down, deep as they were, but had yielded them up at last, after many years . . ." (*Oliver Twist* 196). Such tracts, often found in texts like the *Newgate Calendar* (1750) and *The Terrific Register* (1825), were read throughout Victorian society. The latter of these, Peter Ackroyd acknowledges in his biography *Dickens* (1990), was young Charles's favorite reading material and later in life Dickens was to write that he treasured the text for " . . . making myself unspeakably miserable, and frightening my very wits our of my head, for the small charge of a penny weekly; which there was always a pool of blood, and at least one body . . ." (109).[6] Dickens found much of the literature available for children too didactic;[7] the pools of blood and bodies found in sensational literature we now consider unfit for children were to stay with him throughout his life. He drew such scenes in his own texts, and the imperfect child is impacted by this everyday Victorian reality both bodily and spiritually. This becomes a way of not only ensuring the audience's sympathy and desire for the imperfect child, but also a way to demonstrate how such children were romanticized and socialized by Victorian society and culture.

Though Oliver escapes disease and death repeatedly in *Oliver Twist*, their constant presence affects him, much like it does Nell Trent in *The Old Curiosity Shop*. Oliver's unknown half-brother, Monks, wishes him ill, whereas Nell faces Quilp, a perverse bookie to whom her grandfather owes unknown amounts of money. Quilp wishes to take it out in trade with Nell physically. Nell's grandfather has taken over as her guardian and his gambling habit has led him to sacrifice his granddaughter on the alter of Victorian society and culture. He leaves her unprotected and alone, but she is strong enough, like many of Dickens's heroines, to make her own way. As Oliver is given up to make his own way, Nell traverses the recesses and byways of nineteenth-century society and culture alone, though often at the behest of her grandfather. While Oliver must make his way if he is to survive, Nell is pushed out into the world and readily exposed to it by those who are supposed to care for her. Gallagher and Greenblatt note that such child sacrifice " . . . suggest[s] that pauper children [are] view[ed] as, specifically, a *social* problem inside the skeptical, individualist mentality . . . for it is there that the very concept of 'society,' with its lateral class divisions, takes shape" (178). Unlike Oliver, Nell's journey leads to her death, which is painted with the happiness surrounding Dick's description of what he sees when he dreams of angels.

The death of Little Nell has been frequently discussed by critics and scholars, especially its sentimental overtones. It is not my purpose here to focus on the idea of sentimentality connected with the death scene of Little Nell, but rather to explore its relation to her status as an imperfect child and how such a scene romanticizes and socializes her character. In *Ministering Angels: A Study of Nineteenth-Century Evangelical Writing for Children* (1979), Margaret Nancy Cutt explains, "Dickens also used the industrial city as a background to pathos. Oliver Twist in Fagin's school; Nell's flight from the city; the night spent on the ash-heap of the furnaces stay in the reader's mind; the helplessness of children in these grim situations strengthens the emotional impact" (112). As Cutt suggests, Dickens drew on the sentimental nature of such scenes so they would haunt readers and thus they would continue to purchase the next installment in a storyline. Little Nell's death occurs at the end of the text and her life is filled with disease and death, like Oliver's, both on personal and public levels. Hilary M. Schor claims of Little Nell in *Dickens and the Daughter of the House* (1999), "She must be preserved at the moment before sexuality, before reproduction, so that she can stay a 'trace,' a 'souvenir,' a 'memento.' Nell, in that way, is not only a monument, she is her own epitaph; more, she stands in the place of the whole novel, and for that reason, the novel can become 'the death of Little Nell' " (42). Nell's journey to her death, rather than her death itself, is the "monument" of how such children are constructed and the reality in which they exist.

There is an erotic undertone to Little Nell's death. As Higonnet has pointed out, in the deaths of children this was largely attributed to the characterization of their innocence. Higonnet believes this is linked to the child's body " . . . both because the child's body was supposed to be naturally innocent of adult sexuality, and because the child's mind was supposed to be blank" (8). Little Nell's body is physically innocent of adult sexuality, but her mind is not "blank" of adult experience. She has knowledge. Typically noted by critics and scholars and echoed in the words of Schor is that " . . . Nell dies not only of exhaustion and malnutrition, but of becoming a woman—or of excess femininity. On the verge of reproductive possibility, Nell must die precisely so she can stay a miniature, she can both stay small and leave behind no double of herself, she can stay a "one-er" (4). This is the physical connection between Little Nell and her development toward her death. That her death results because she is on the brink of adulthood[8] paints her as the perfect child sacrifice, but her lack of mental innocence has been neglected.

The actual death of Little Nell has long been credited to John Forster, Dickens's close friend and first biographer. Forster personally takes credit for putting the thought of killing Little Nell into Dickens's mind as he claims in his biography *The Life of Charles Dickens* (Vol. 1):

I was responsible for its tragic ending. He had not thought of killing her, when, about half way through, I asked him to consider whether it did not necessarily belong even to his own conception, after taking a mere child through such a tragedy and sorrow, to lift her also out of the commonplace of ordinary happy endings, so that the gentle pure little figure and form should never change to the fancy. (188)

Little Nell's death makes her a spectacle, much like one in the freak wax-works show she works for a time. Death, Dickens relates, takes all of Little Nell's cares away. The experiences of tragedy are erased and her passing allows her to be happy. Readers are told upon Little Nell's death in the final chapters of *The Old Curiosity Shop*, "Where were the traces of her early cares, her sufferings, and fatigues? All gone. Sorrow was dead indeed in her, but peace and perfect happiness were born; imagined in her tranquil beauty and profound repose" (Dickens 540). There is no punishment or cruelty in Little Nell's passing, nor does she die being a cruel child. Little Nell's death is a positive experience without the guilt associated with a life of vice. She does not fear death but, like children in many earlier texts which feature a child dying, welcomes such an ending with dignity and calm joy. Little Nell, however, is not fully innocent or experienced; she is an imperfect child with a perfect death.

AT REST

Figure 4.1 "At Rest." Illustration from Charles Dickens's *The Old Curiosity Shop* (1841), illustration by Geroge Cattermole, Rpt. in *The Old Curiosity Shop*, (London: Oxford University Press, 1901) 693.

The description of Little Nell's death is drawn out over many pages of text. Dickens spends time crafting her death, as he does her illness and journey, almost to explain and thus justify to his readers his reasons for killing a treasured character. Many mourners come to Little Nell's funeral and she lays in state for a few days, as indicated in Figure 4.1, as if to give readers time to grieve alongside her fictional friends and family. Dickens explains to readers after Little Nell's death in *The Old Curiosity Shop*, "When Death strikes down the innocent and young, for every fragile form from which he lets the panting spirit free, a hundred virtues rise, in shapes of mercy, charity, and love to walk the world, and bless it" (544). Never once should readers doubt Little Nell's innocence, for this characteristic is repeated throughout the text. Her death brings sorrow as well as joy to her friends. Little Nell's innocence, like that of all imperfect children, lies in her heart, but she does not have an unclouded brow. Kincaid finds "Innocence was such a pure conception in the nineteenth century that we may be struck with the difference between the adored literary child—little Alice or Oliver Twist or Ragged Dick—and the chimney sweeps dying of cancer of the scrotum . . . cast-off kids being left to wander the streets and peddle their bodies" (54). Alice and Oliver Twist, however, are not purely innocent. The construction of the Romantic child, pure of heart and head, became sullied with the experience and knowledge these characters gained through interactions in Victorian society and culture. The imperfect child offers a balance between depravity and innocence, something more realistic than the Romantic child could offer.

Little Nell is not a representation of the Romantic child and her interactions with disease and death are indicative of the conflicting nature of her existence. Her experiences parallel those of Oliver Twist. She is both parent and caretaker to herself and her grandfather. Suffering from malnutrition, mental and physical fatigue, and stress, Little Nell observes disease and death along her journey. Her final illness and death come, as with the dying child Harry West, upon meeting the kind schoolmaster for the second time. Her initial meeting begins with Harry's death and Dickens explains Nell's grief, despite her young age, "And though she thought as a child herself, and did not perhaps sufficiently consider to what a bright and happy existence those who die young are borne, and how in death they lose the pain of seeing others die around them . . . still she thought wisely enough, to draw a plain and easy moral from what she had seen that night . . ." (*The Old Curiosity Shop* 199–200). This passage describes death in a romantic vein, almost harkening back to the view of child death in the eighteenth century. Through experiencing the death of Harry West, Little Nell understands what death can mean and bring, not just the beautified idea of death that allows him to leave his earthly troubles behind. Harry is an illustration of the Romantic child whereas Little Nell is imperfect, for she has experienced more hardships than Harry could comprehend. Yet she lives with a hope in her heart as befitting an innocent.

NELL'S GARDEN

Figure 4.2 "Nell's Garden." Illustration from Charles Dickens's *The Old Curiosity Shop* (1841), illustration by H.K. Browne. Rpt. in *The Old Curiosity Shop*, (London: Oxford University Press, 1901) 529.

As they begin their life with the schoolmaster, Little Nell settles into a daily routine and is content with their final destination where she and her grandfather are surrounded, as Oliver is in the employ of Mr. Sowerberry, by death and decay. As Oliver learns early on of disease and death, Little Nell has as well, and while both children fight becoming victims, both become inflicted with disease and accepting of death if it happens to them.

In a series of five illustrations towards the conclusion of *The Old Curiosity Shop*, some of which are by different artists, Little Nell is depicted working, taking solace, dying, and being taken by angels in the decrepit churchyard they call their final home. As she begins to work alongside her grandfather in one illustration, she labors to build a garden with him, indicating that life will hopefully renew itself for the pair. They are depicted in Figure 4.2 as being set apart from the bachelor, holding onto one another and digging in the cold graveyard ground as they will soon join one another in the very soil they mean to work. Readers are invited to gaze upon the loving nature of the tired pair who seems to be digging their own graves, for there is no one, save the bachelor, to help them. Little Nell, who, James Kincaid notes in *Annoying the Victorians* (1995), " . . . is a child, which is good, is extraordinarily pure and innocent, and that's good, too, since it means she is empty and can be occupied" (45). This ideal paints her as the Romantic child, something

THE SPIRIT'S FLIGHT

Figure 4.3 "The Spirit's Flight." Illustration from Charles Dickens's *The Old Curiosity Shop* (1841), from illustration by Geroge Cattermole, Rpt. in *The Old Curiosity Shop*, (London: Oxford University Press, 1901) 715.

she cannot be. Digging in the dirt, as indicated in Figure 4.2, she and her grandfather are both destined for a grave, away from the experiences they have recently undergone. Kincaid recognizes, in *Annoying the Victorians*, " . . . Nell pushes past desire to a kind of complete fulfillment in death, a fulfillment that works against perpetuating desire. In addition, she is a kind of voyeur herself; throughout the novel she keeps looking—and looking right back at us. . . . She is, that is to say, in control; she guides her grandfather and stares assertively even at Quilp" (45). Little Nell is a "good" individual, but her inner resolve and experiences gives her status as one of Dickens's imperfect children.

The death of Little Nell provides solace, though ironically, for readers, and Dickens's constant reference paints her ascension to heaven as a beautiful picture and justifies her passing. Dickens is not only describing the ideal Victorian child death, but is also defending his decision to kill off his beloved character. In *The Old Curiosity Shop*, Dickens depicts those who attend the wake and funeral as being young, old, and in all stages of health, " . . . to gather round her tomb. . . . the deaf, the blind, the lame, the palsied, the living dead in many shapes and forms to see the closing of that early grave. What was the death it would shut in, to that which still could crawl and creep above it!" (543). The mourners[9] are a motley group who attend and share in reminiscing about Little Nell's life and the interactions and times they viewed her. This last gathering offers one final voyeuristic viewing of Little Nell's body, something readers, whoever they are and no matter their health, are invited to participate in. Readers become a part of the crowd that can "creep and crawl" above her grave. Though angels take her away, as Figure 4.3 indicates, Little Nell is left objectified and imperfect and dies peacefully while readers weep and creep and crawl away from the text. As Kincaid points out in *Annoying the Victorians*, Little Nell's demise allows us control as readers, for she will forever be on exhibit, as were the waxworks she shows for Mrs. Jarley (37). Yet, Kincaid acknowledges, "We really want always to be moving in that direction, always about to take possession but never doing it. In other words, what we want is desire, not an ending to desire . . . we want Nell always dying, always about to become an object. We do not want her dead. Death ends desire. We are voyeurs, not necrophiliacs" (*Annoying the Victorians* 37). With Quilp and her grandfather dead and her own passing, Little Nell and the idea of her is preserved in the minds of readers.

Though Little Nell's progress of decay spans a considerable portion of time, Dickens did not take much time in exploring Tiny Tim's questionable existence in *A Christmas Carol*. Disease and death are as readily present in *A Christmas Carol*, and Tiny Tim's life, as they are for Little Nell and the imperfect children to follow her in Dickens's works. In the very first lines of *A Christmas Carol* death is presented as "Marley was dead: to begin with" (33). For Scrooge, Marley's living partner, death is present in the way he lives and it pervades his bones. He even finds it is a remedy for what ails Victorian society and culture because death can help do away with the poor, who belong in prisons and workhouses (*A Christmas Carol* 38–39). Tiny Tim, the son of Scrooge's sole worker Bob Cratchit, is an illustration of a happy but poor child at Christmas. As he is initially described as a child with a crutch (79), Dickens draws upon readers' pathos to help establish where their focus for this character should fall. Tiny Tim's economic value lies in the sentimentality Dickens infuses into his character. As luck is stacked against him due to his family's poverty, Tiny Tim is destined to die unless someone cares, as Kincaid has noted his creator wanted. Zelizer finds, "While in the nineteenth century, the market value of children was culturally acceptable, later the new normative ideal of the child as an exclusively emotional and affective asset [that] precluded instrumental or fiscal considerations" (11). Tiny Tim has no economic value for his family or society as he cannot participate in the types of work available for such an individual. The outlook, as the text suggests, is grim for Tiny Tim unless someone, such as Scrooge, shows concern for his plight.

Tiny Tim is afflicted with a disorder readers are never told exactly what it is and one that is never treated. Tiny Tim's handicap may be due to polio. His crippling, much like Dickie Harding's in E. Nesbit's *House of Arden* and *Harding's Luck*, becomes an unexpected sight for Victorian society and culture. Tiny Tim's experiences with disease and death are similar to those of Oliver and Little Nell, who were also surrounded by these issues on the London streets and at early ages. Though some would pity him, others would, as Scrooge notes, believe he and those like him should not exist unless they can add to rather than draw upon the surplus economy (*A Christmas Carol* 38–39). Tiny Tim lives, unlike Marley, through the grace of Scrooge and his desire to share his financial resources with the Cratchit family. But the cost is questionable. Scrooge spends the majority of the text, along with the reader, gazing on all that has occurred in the past, what is occurring presently, and what may happen in the future. Many readers want Tiny Tim to live so a continued gaze on his handicap can occur, which is another reason Dickens does not indicate if he is ever cured. Little Nell's death was at the behest of Forster. Additionally, Dickens's beloved sister-in-law Mary Hogarth had just died, so it is often attributed to these factors that Little Nell's death was both cathartic for Dickens and helped preserve the memory of the child for readers. Tiny Tim, on the other hand, was developed during the Christmas season and Dickens's third son was just born, so while Dickens might have been feeling generous, life and death become powerful plot devices for concluding the narratives of these stories. Tiny Tim's life offers readers hope, as does Little Nell's death. While disease and decline frame the narrative of *A Christmas Carol*, Tiny Tim is able to escape the clutches of Dickens's death pen, whereas Little Nell and other imperfect fictional children were not so fortunate.

Disease and death for Little Nell allow readers to move on, for there is a conclusion, wrapped snuggly in a coffin. But Dickens seeks to gratify our desire and offers yet another child. This time it's a boy, in the form of sickly Paul Dombey in *Dombey and Son*. Like Oliver asking for more, Dickens, as the indulging parent, gives it to readers, who are left begging for yet another child sacrifice. After *The Old Curiosity Shop*, Dickens offers up another dose of decay for readers, who seemingly plead, "Make us cry again!" and they are served a wonderful helping of the imperfect child in Paul Dombey and his sister Florence. Paul is born a sickly child and the passage of time does not alleviate what ails him, for even with much care, no remedy could improve his state:

> Naturally delicate, perhaps, he pined and wasted after the dismissal of his nurse, and . . . seemed but to wait his opportunity of gliding through

their hands, and seeking his lost mother. . . . Every tooth was a break-neck fence, and every pimple in the measles a stone wall to him. He was down in every fit of the whooping-cough, and rolled upon and crushed by a whole field of small diseases. . . . (*Dombey and Son* 107)

These childhood diseases, which are commonplace and part of natural growth, were frightful maladies during the Victorian period. Already a weak child, Paul's health is not improved through his struggles with childhood illnesses, but he still holds value for his father as he is the only Dombey heir. Yet, it was not the value to the father Dickens intended as the primary focus, but the loss of the child to the sister, Florence, that Dickens wanted to highlight to readers. Forster notes, in *The Life of Charles Dickens* (Vol. 2), that Dickens wrote him on July 25, 1846, stating, " . . . the natural affection of the boy will turn towards the despised sister. . . . When the boy is about ten years old (in the fourth number), he will be taken ill, and he will die; and when he is ill, and when he is dying, I mean to make him turn always for refuge to the sister still, and keep the stern affection of the father at a distance" (311). The imperfect brother in Paul Dombey turns to the imperfect sister in Florence, who has long been dismissed by her father as something easily discarded and of little value.

Florence is a dutiful Victorian daughter and self-sacrificial, to a point. As Dickens continued to create his characters he began to focus on Paul's death and referred to it in letters to Forster; he would not " . . . kill him until the fifth number" (324) on October 3 and again speaks to it in November (Forster does not give a day) that "Paul, I shall slaughter at the end of number five" (328). The mirth Dickens uses in the language of Paul's passing serves as an example of the tone the child's passing would take. Forster finds Paul's death changed the way writers and readers constructed child death scenes as it " . . . quite took the death itself out of the region of pathetic commonplaces, and gave to it the proper relation to the sorrow of the little sister that survives it. It is a fairy vision to a piece of actual suffering; a sorrow with heaven's hues upon it, to a sorrow with all the bitterness of earth" (329). Paul's passing turns his father even further away from his sister, but Florence does try to love their father while he resists all of her attempts, and even before this tragedy Paul questions his own staying power. In speaking to Mrs. Pipchin, a caretaker, Paul notes, "That's what I mean to do, when—He stopped and pondered for a moment. . . . If I grow up . . ." (*Dombey and Son* 214). His old-fashioned nature coupled with fey characteristics, mark Paul as only temporarily visiting this world. Not long after his discussion with Mrs. Pipchin his sister takes over and nurses him until his death.

Florence is a dutiful daughter as well as her own person, for she eventually looks out for herself and leaves her father to his grief. During Paul's passing, Mr. Dombey is present to the boy in only a feeling on his cheek, but his sister holds and cares for him until he is gone. Paul's spirituality is overtly evident as

Dickens states, "He [Paul] put his hands together, as he had been used to do, at his prayers. He did not remove his arms to do it; but they saw him fold them so, behind her [Florence's] neck" (*Dombey and Son* 253). Florence is the one, as Dickens states, whom Paul will turn to until the last when:

> The golden ripple on the wall came back again, and nothing else stirred in the room. The old, old, fashion! The fashion that came in with our first garments, and will last unchanged until our race has run its course, and the wide firmament is rolled up like a scroll. The old, old fashion— Death! Oh thank GOD, all who see it, for that older fashion yet, of Immortality! And look upon us, angels of young children, with regards not quite estranged, when the swift river bears us to the ocean! (*Dombey and Son* 253)

Dickens planned Paul's death, unlike that of Little Nell's, with whom he struggled. Little Nell's passing spans many pages of text, whereas Paul's life ends more abruptly, even with his perpetual sickness as a child. Florence becomes helpmate to her brother and, in eventually leaving her father's home, though she later returns of her own volition, her father's memory is preserved. Florence establishes her own identity by leaving behind the name of Dombey, which also ends with Paul's death. Paul and Florence do not need to search for their name, which is all-important to their father.

Jo and Esther Summerson in *Bleak House*, like Oliver Twist, are never told of their parents and must find out their true, estimated societal value on their own, even as they face illness and death. As a street orphan, Jo's economic value parallels his service as a crossing sweep. His death is more of a burden to society than his life, as Dickens depicts it. Jo realizes he is ill and dying and repeatedly notes he is heading for the "berryin-ground." His final request is to be buried alongside Nemo as he relates to Dr. Alan Woodcourt, " . . . him as wos wery good to me, wery good, he wos. It's time fur me to go down to that there berryin-ground, sir, and ask to be put along with him. I wants to go there and be berried" (*Bleak House* 733). Burial in a pauper's field was commonplace for the poor, but this was still a luxury, as Dickens illustrated in the death of the young mother in *Oliver Twist*. The death of a working class child of the streets was often deemed to be little more than pollution added to the cobblestones of the London metropolis. Jo's body is also dishonored, as indicated by his having to beg to be put in the "berryin-ground" alongside Nemo. Tom's-All-Alone, where Jo tries to hide and live, is rank with illness and death; sections of London such as that existed where many bodies went unclaimed and were left for dumping in the Thames River. Kincaid explains that Jo " . . . is murdered by a society that doesn't care if he sells his body, doesn't care at all about anything to do with the boy. He is always told to 'move along,' resting nowhere, given no home and no peace" (*Erotic Innocence* 291). As an imperfect child, Jo exists on the margins of a society that does not want him and uses him only for the minimal amount of work he can produce as a crossing sweep.

Like Oliver, Little Nell, Tiny Tim, Paul Dombey, and Esther, Jo is exposed to death and decay throughout his life. Jo, as does Little Nell, finds spirituality in his final moments, but it is religious dogma he knows nothing of as he holds onto Woodcourt's hand and repeats the Lord's Prayer as he passes away (*Bleak House* 734). Dickens chides society as he writes of Jo and those like him, "The light is come upon the dark benighted way. Dead! Dead, your Majesty. Dead, my lords and gentlemen. Dead, Right Reverends and Wrong Reverends of every order. Dead, men and women, born with Heavenly compassion in your hearts. And dying thus around us every day" (*Bleak House* 734). For a child like Jo, there would be little opportunity to change his societal position and the constant moving on and shoving about by everyone he comes into contact with would not have been uncommon, for he exists as an invisible child on the Victorian streets. Shuffled from space to space and never stopping in one place for long, Jo serves as visible social evidence that everything was not as perfect as the Victorians wished to depict. Esther, unlike Jo, is able to escape such a fate through the duty her aunt feels to her religious beliefs, though neither child receives the love a parent or guardian should bestow on a child.

As an orphan, Esther is also viewed through the service she can eventually provide for society and culture. She has no value as a person and is clearly told this throughout her childhood. What is unique about Esther's illness and near-death experience is that readers are given it from her perspective. Though the illness is never overtly named, it is probably smallpox, which was prevalent during the nineteenth century and would explain the marks left on Esther's face after the disease has passed. Her fever induces life-changing thoughts for Esther and she claims, "In falling ill, I seemed to have crossed a dark lake, and to have left all my experiences, mingled together by the great distance, on the healthy shore. . . . I had never known before how short life really was, and into how small a space the mind could put it" (*Bleak House* 555). Through her illness, Esther finds value in herself as household duties are put aside and she states that though this distressed her, they " . . . were soon as far off as the oldest of the old duties at Greenleaf . . ." (*Bleak House* 555). Esther's illness does not take place when she is a child, but it helps restructure her sense of individual value. This transition also occurs for Amy Dorrit in *Little Dorrit* after a similar illness.

Illness for Amy Dorrit, as for Esther Summerson, changes her ideological focus on life as she becomes more overtly assertive through its impact. Her initial fainting away allows for a narrative transition, as Dickens employs with Oliver Twist. This also occurs after Amy has asserted herself to her sister and resists dressing to illustrate their newfound family fortune, instead choosing to stay in the dress she has worn while living in the Marshalsea Prison. Such a change for Amy, the daughter of the Marshalsea, would indicate a change in persona and identity. Arthur Clennam, whom Amy later marries, carries her out of the prison as the family makes its way towards their new life. Amy states to her sister, Fanny, "She has been forgotten. . . . I ran up to her room . . . and found the door open, and that she had fainted on the floor, dear child. She appeared to have gone to change her dress, and to have sunk down overpowered. It may have been the cheering, or it may have happened sooner. Take care of this poor, cold hand . . ." (*Little Dorrit* 414). The assembled crowd, like that at Little Nell's funeral, is not seen by Amy as her illness allows her to retain her individuality because she is passed out and is in a static state, though she is viewed by the crowd around her. Amy's sense of identity, like that of the imperfect child, is not a simple binary. As Kincaid suggests, in *Annoying the Victorians*, "Many characters in Dickens cannot be understood in the linear, developmental terms appropriate to individuals. They are the 'we' of one another. . . . The move towards alternate, boundaryless, conceptions of being is played out throughout the Dickens canon" (84). This is the experience disease and death allow for characters like Amy because the borders she must face are not straightforward. Authors such as George MacDonald later carried out this tradition when they examined disease and death in conjunction with their own constructions of the imperfect child, as is readily noticeable in Diamond in *At the Back of the North Wind*.

At the Back of the North Wind is a tale of illness and death with Diamond at its center. From the beginning of the story, Diamond is depicted as an ill child. MacDonald documents stage by stage Diamond's journey with a literal death, in the form of the North Wind. Diamond is often thought of as a depiction of a perfect, Romantic child, but Diamond's is a working class child who takes part in the family business when needed. He understands and accepts his families' social position, though he does try to better their situation with whatever help he can provide. Diamond, like Jo, has a spiritual ending. As MacDonald writes, he is told, "But at least there is one thing you may be sure of, that there is a still better love than that of the wonderful being you call North Wind" (*At the Back of the North Wind* 345). Illness for Diamond becomes a space of transition where he learns more about the Victorian world in which he lives, but will leave. His repeated questioning of North Wind about nineteenth-century society and culture provides readers with answers, albeit through the eyes of MacDonald. As he passes away, the narrator of *At the Back of the North Wind* explains, "I walked up the winding stair, and entered his room. A lovely figure, as white and almost as clear as alabaster, was lying on the bed. I saw at once how it was. They thought he was dead. I knew he had gone to the back of the north wind" (346).

North Wind, largely regarded as MacDonald's representation of Death, allows Diamond, as Lisa Hermine Makman notes in "Child's Work is Child's Play: The Value of George MacDonald's Diamond," "His proximity to death, like that of other fictive Victorian children, grants him a special power, the power to transform his world and to create in it a secure home" (120). Diamond helps his family and friend Nanny, a crossing sweep like Jo in Dickens's *Bleak*

House, and transforms their social conditions. As he leaves them behind, he transitions into a new space where, as an imperfect child, he challenges social and cultural boundaries and overcomes them. MacDonald continues this tradition in his other fantasy texts *The Princess and the Goblin* and *The Princess and Curdie,* though Princess Irene and Curdie do not have to face North Wind overtly. The fairy tale of Princess Irene and Curdie crosses boundaries, as Kincaid has indicated, and thus puts forth the message anything is possible. In order for this to occur, illness and death, for the imperfect child, must be faced on different fronts, whether personally or publicly, as readers see with Tom in *The Water-Babies.*

Tom, an orphan child much like Oliver Twist and Jo, faces illness and death through his career in Kingsley's *The Water-Babies.* Tom's death, like that of Diamond, Jo, and Little Nell, is literal. Unlike his dead counterparts, however, Tom's physical death leads to his rebirth after his transition underwater. Tom must, like other imperfect children, cross boundaries between life and death in order to redefine his social and cultural position. His transitory space is uniquely underwater. In "A (Sea) Green Victorian: Charles Kingsley and The Water-Babies," Naomi Wood explains, "In Kingsley's view, Nature is resilient, powerful, and redemptive; ignorance of Nature's processes will eventually cost humans too much. Setting his fairy tale primarily underwater allows Kingsley both to satirize contemporary foibles and to posit a place governed by those natural laws that we ignore at our peril" (238). This occurs at Tom's peril, but it is society that sacrifices Tom for its own needs and, in such a way, feeds on its own children. Tom feels, "I must be clean, I must be clean" (55) throughout the narrative of *The Water-Babies,* and Kingsley posits that this can only occur if Tom learns at the hands of nature. Consequently, he must die and abandon his old lifestyle in order to have a virtuous life. Tom manages to escape the trade Oliver was offered. The transitional space between life and death, sometimes in the form of a fantasy world underwater or with goblins or on the real streets of London, offers this to the imperfect discarded child, as happens in Hesba Stretton's *Jessica's First Prayer* to the protagonist, Jessica, another street orphan.

Children like Jessica who inhabited the London streets were commonly overlooked and ignored in Victorian society and culture; yet this extensive group undertook many jobs, such as those of crossing sweeps, flower sellers, and chimney sweeps, that the regular tradesman rejected. Henry Mayhew's series on the London working classes highlighted how children and people were able to see in print not only what was occurring around them, but also hear first-person accounts from individuals. Disease and death were everyday incidents on the streets of London and Jessica has not been spared any of the harshness, such as abuse and disease. Though Jessica does become ill and is " . . . cuffed and beaten by her mother, and over-worked and ill-used by her numerous employers . . ." (*Jessica's First Prayer* 22), she also faces death, as was common for a child in her situation. Jessica faces a very sentimental passing as she contracts a fever and is on the brink of death. In her disorientation, "Jessica, who was light-headed and delirious, but in the wanderings of her thoughts and words often spoke of God, and prayed for her Mr. Dan'el" (*Jessica's First Prayer* 70). Facing illness and death, as imperfect children must, they ultimately save themselves and those closest to them as spiritually and religiously. Patricia Demers, in "Mrs. Sherwood and Hesba Stretton: The Letter and the Spirit of Evangelical Writing for Children" (1991), finds " . . . Stretton personalizes, concretizes, and lavishly dramatizes the moral choices that for her constitute engaged Christianity" (147). Jessica not only learns about Christianity, for that would not be enough, but through suffering she attains understanding.

Like Tom in Kingsley's *The Water- Babies*, Jessica transitions through a space while sick so that she can obtain firsthand knowledge of the healing power of religion, and she, like Tom, becomes a more accepted member of Victorian society and culture. Her transition of her social and cultural value increases and her romanticized, street waif status is replaced by a romantic view of the socialized child. Jessica is "tamed" and can thus become a productive member of Victorian society with little threat to Victorian sensibility by her shift in class standing. The spirituality that the imperfect child must know is not only found in learning of a higher power than man's such as Jessica does, but is also depicted in works such as Christina Rossetti's *Sing-Song: A Nursery Rhyme Book* (1872), where the subjects of her poems progress through birth, life, and death and learn about the tenets of proper social and cultural behavior.

Rossetti's series of 121 lyrics in *Sing-Song* are meant to be read with children and explore such topics as the complexities of life and death, the joys and sorrow of child/parent relationships, and the change of the seasons. The lyrics illustrate the progression of life and how it might end for either parent or child. Knoepflmacher reminds readers in *Ventures Into Childland*:

> Whereas the opening and concluding lyrics are cradle-poems that celebrate an unself-conscious symbiosis between mother and child, the sequence soon accommodates a growing awareness of temporal units, diurnal and seasonal, and dwells on contraries that a maturing "self-consciousness" must acknowledge and master. (330)

Sing-Song is meant to be read throughout childhood and the lyrics encompass the learning that comes with different stages of development. Topics such as death, however, do not alter, but are used throughout the text, for such events can happen throughout the course of one's life. In the lyric in *Sing-Song*, "I have but one rose in the world," for example, a mother is depicted with her child, "I have but one rose in the world, / And my one rose stands a-drooping: / Oh, when my single rose is dead / There'll be but thorns for stooping" (85). The child, being the one bright spot for the speaker, is ailing and it is evident the child will die, for it is stated in line three "when my single rose is dead" rather than *if* the rose were to die. A flower, the rose, will be dead and there will only be thorns left on the stem when the speaker visits the gravesite to "stoop" down. Children would learn about death through poems such as "I have but one rose in the world."

Poems like those in Rossetti's *Sing-Song* explore how life was as imperfect as many of the children who lived in Victorian England. Rossetti indicates through her lyrics that death does not just impact parents, but also children with deceased parents. In the two-lined lyric "Motherless Baby and Babyless Mother," Rossetti interchanges the concepts of the meaning of loss from the parent to the child. She states, "Motherless baby and babyless mother, / Bring them together to love one another" (*Sing-Song* 125). There is also a woman in the illustration reaching over a grave marked with a cross to receive an infant from the hands of a nurse. Readers assume that this woman has lost her child as the child has lost its mother and the nurse is bringing them together, which reflects "proper" Christian tradition. In this vein, death was not destructive, for tragedy also offered possibility. The way the imperfect child is impacted by illness and death in *Sing-Song* is as overt as how characters such as Oliver Twist and Jessica must face them. As texts developed and became aimed at specifically diverse audiences, such was the case with *Sing-Song* and E. Nesbit's *The House of Arden* and *Harding's Luck*, Victorian imperfect children had to encounter illness and death to become properly socialized.

Disease and death are not just themes, but significant realities for the imperfect child. These events become healing rather than destructive elements in their lives. Authors like Dickens, MacDonald, Kingsley, Stretton, Rossetti, and Nesbit construct the imperfect child so that it must undergo and come into contact with illness and death to be properly socialized. The illnesses and deaths that occur for Oliver Twist, Little Nell, Diamond, Tom, Jessica, and Dickie, as well as other imperfect children, expose them to spirituality and metaphorical rebirth. The authorial critique of Victorian society and culture by Dickens, MacDonald, Kingsley, Stretton, Rossetti, and Nesbit expresses the ultimate sacrifice imperfect children must make in order to be accepted by society and culture and participate in it. The position of the imperfect child in Victorian society and culture reflects the market reality of the child and childhood. Trading in the concepts of the child and childhood, often with the flesh and bone of the imperfect child, helped drive the Victorian economy and this resulted from the social desire for this child. This is a trend that continues in our contemporary construct of the child and childhood, especially in terms of our longing for the imperfect child.

Chapter Five
Mining the Missing Link
Contemporary Constructions of the Imperfect Child

"To try to see blots in the sun, and to pick holes in Dickens, seems ungrateful, and is indeed an ungrateful task; to no mortal man have more people owed mirth, pleasure, forgetfulness of care, knowledge of life in strange places. There never was such another as Charles Dickens, nor shall we see his like sooner than the like of Shakespeare."

—**Andrew Lang** (*Essays in Little* 130–31)

The characterization of the imperfect child has not been abandoned to the Victorians or Edwardians as media continues to publish this construction in print and on screen. Dickens's texts are still widely introduced and read by adults and children, and it is the children in his texts, especially Tiny Tim, that open a gateway into his work for younger audiences. The majority of post-Dickensian authors' works explored here are readily available in bookstores and online for both adults and children.[1] MacDonald, Kingsley, and Nesbit are now regarded primarily as children's literature authors while Rossetti retains her status as an author for both groups. Stretton, unfortunately, has largely been forgotten and when she is discussed it is mainly in the context of her religious texts, while her other writing is typically overlooked, even among scholars. The imperfect child lives on in the writing of many modern writers such as Joan Aiken, L. M. Boston, Philip Ardagh, Lemony Snicket, J. K. Rowling, Lois Lowry, Philip Pullman, and Eoin Colfer.

Minor modifications in the development of the imperfect child character may be evident in contemporary representations. For example, some contemporary authors draw upon Victorian environments in their narratives or they include more sentimentality in their plots than most contemporary writers. Joan Aiken, in her creation of Dido, a working class imperfect child whose adventures are chronicled in her eleven-book *Wolves Chronicles*, draws upon Victorian backdrops for the narrative of her cunning and overt imperfect child. Authors such as Philip Ardagh, in *The Eddie Dickens Trilogy*, use the Victorian era for their texts, but, in the vein of Lemony Snicket's thirteen-volume *A Series of Unfortunate Events*, use dark melodrama, satire, and irony to chronicle the awkward life of Eddie Dickens, another contemporary imperfect child. Although these are not the only contemporary representations of the imperfect child, they denote the use of this character over the last century in relatively overlooked authors, such as Joan Aiken, or recent popular writers like Lemony Snicket.

The imperfect child, alongside changes in how childhood and the child are viewed, has shifted somewhat in that he/she now more overtly demonstrates power and desire, such as in the case of L. M. Boston's children, especially Tolly, in *The Children of Green Knowe* series. As Kincaid explains in *Erotic Innocence*, this contemporary child is " . . . inherited from the Victorians [and] is both inside us and distant from us, a repository of nostalgia and a hope for the future, weak and powerful, alluring and revolting. One oddity of this 'child' is that it has seized hold of the power to define *us*" (68). While the contemporary child is evident in children's books, so too is the continued use of the imperfect child in characters such as Harry Potter from J. K. Rowling's *Harry Potter* series or the Baudelaire orphans from *A Series of Unfortunate Events*. Adults and children read these texts, much like the Victorians, and this is largely due to the staying power of the imperfect child. Due to its complex nature, the imperfect child keeps readers interested in their development even when the narrative is of little appeal, which texts like *Oliver Twist* may be for contemporary readers. If a reader stays interested in such a character, they may be more likely to find a narrative they are not drawn to compelling. Using texts like *The Eddie Dickens Trilogy* in a classroom, for example, may compel audiences to keep reading, for Eddie's ridiculous struggles make the rich narrative livelier. The imperfect child has given way to the contemporary child. However, many readers still find the imperfect child captivating as their balance of innocence and experience makes them a representation of what individuals face on a daily basis, even if they possess a wand and graduate from an esteemed school of magic.

The distinction between the contemporary imperfect child and the nineteenth- and early-twentieth-century imperfect child is not evident through markers such as gender, but is sometimes more evident in social class. The characterization of the contemporary child developed out of the imperfect child construction, so elements in developing this child, such as independence and the necessary movement from reality into a fairy realm and back again, are used by authors. The contemporary imperfect child, however, manipulates the environment, whereas the nineteenth- and early-twentieth-century imperfect child is more, though not completely, altruistic in his or her actions. If they do manipulate someone or a situation, it is typically unintentional. The elements evident in the characterization of the imperfect child can be found in Kincaid's description of the building of the American Dream Child from the Romantic child:

> . . . in the nineteenth century as a way of keeping alive the image of the child of power, somehow in contact with sources of primal energy (not excluding sexual energy) adults would like both to deny and to claim as our own. This child, then, strikes us as both valuable and dangerous, familiar and very strange. We are never sure whether to worship this child or spank it. The key point is that this Romantic child has become central to the way we structure our world of desire. He reappears throughout the nineteenth century and the twentieth as Bomba and Tarzan and a host of other savage children. He is also domesticated, in a variety of middle-class imps, leading to a parade of mischief makers. . . . Our own distinctive national spin on romanticism's wild child of power is also cute, in need of taming, and discardable after use—but adds the charged issue of class. America's adorable bad kids are often poor and ask for more. . . . (*Erotic Innocence* 63)

Such children are the descendants of Oliver Twist and his imperfect brethren, and, like Harry Potter, they face extraordinary situations from birth. The imperfect Victorian child, like the contemporary imperfect child, can come from any social class, but Victorian imperfect children typically had to face their extraordinary situation on their own while contemporary imperfect children, like Harry Potter, have more friends and support as they face their travails. The Victorian imperfect child also tends to come into contact with issues that are more individual concerns that relate to the larger social condition. Inversely, contemporary imperfect children are typically confronted with social situations that then impact them personally, such as the event that begins Harry Potter's battle.

Contemporary Imperfect Children

Potentially the most popular imperfect child in contemporary literature is Harry Potter. His story begins much like Oliver Twist's in that his parents die and he is left an orphan. Unlike Oliver, who is born into cruelty, Harry is unknowingly given into it when the loveable giant Hagrid hands him off to his terrible relatives, the Durselys. The narratives for Oliver and Harry are also similar in that, after presenting the story of their births, both Dickens and Rowling do not bother relating the next phase in the children's lives, but shift their narrative to when they are both nine years old. It is as if Dickens and Rowling suggest these missing years of development are as uninteresting as yesterday's pudding. Yet, while Oliver is on his own, Harry's saviors seek him out. Harry lives in a dark cupboard at the beginning of *Harry Potter and The Sorcerer's Stone* and is characterized by " . . . a thin face, knobbly knees, black hair, and bright green eyes. He wore round glasses held together with a lot of Scotch tape because of all the times Dudley [his cousin] had punched him on the nose. The only thing Harry liked about his own appearance was a very thin scar on his forehead that was shaped like a lightening bolt" (Rowling 20). He is abused and looks as if he has lived alongside Oliver in Mrs. Mann's home and was raised by hand. Harry's world is fantasy blended with reality, for he shifts from the Durselys' home to Hogwarts. Not knowing why his parents were killed, Harry, like Oliver, is left to fend for himself until he is rescued and taken to a magical realm of witches and wizards that exists alongside the Muggle, nonmagical realm he has lived in for his first nine years. While Harry finds friends, education, and support at Hogwarts, Oliver lives with Fagin and his band of child thieves in a hidden world that is found, much like Harry's magical realm, behind the existence of the respectable middle class.

Oliver sets out on his own for London and the Victorian imperfect children show independence in the face of personal injustice as do contemporary constructions of this character. Characters like Harry Potter, however, have character elements very similar to those of the Romantic child. Jack Zipes points out in *Sticks and Stones*:

> . . . goodness is, of course, embedded in Harry and his friends. And unlike most children entering puberty, they have pure souls; in fact, they do not drink, smoke, or take drugs. They do not curse or fail to show their elders respect. They study hard and attend all classes. They rarely break the rules of Hogwarts, and when they do, they have a good reason or guilty consciences. (182)

Despite this innate goodness, however, Harry and his friends Ron and Hermione are imperfect children. Hermione is belittled at school because she is half Muggle and Ron comes from a working class family. Harry is an outsider and remains so throughout his tenure at Hogwarts. Throughout a series of seven books, this misfit trio fights against the evil pervading the school and world of magic until they defeat it once and for all.

Harry, Ron, and Hermione's story concludes with a typical fairy tale ending in that all are married and have successful careers. Such endings parallel the marriage plot of many nineteenth-century novels. Unlike traditional fairy tales, however, Rowling puts a modern spin on her happy ending, for Harry and his crew are all blessed with children. Goodness prevails in a world where a neutral space has seemingly disappeared when confronted with pure evil. Harry and his friends are modern constructions of imperfect children, but their goodness and overdone happy ending elicits the sentimentality readers have supposedly outgrown and ridicule today. In a modern-day formula for a short story in *Glamour* magazine, Harry, Ron, and Hermione, as Zipes suggests, "Left alone, they would probably grow up and become dutiful and pleasant wizards and witches like the gentle and conscientious ones who teach in their school. Goodness is doing unto others what you would like done to you, and Harry and his friends are gentle Christian souls" (182). They are not left alone, however, and though the narration of the story is formulaic, the characters are not simple constructions as they face both public and personal crises.

While there are parallels that can be drawn between many contemporary imperfect characters and those in Victorian children's texts, my point here is not to establish a list of similarities and differences, but to illustrate the way in which this character is still used and how readers respond to this overlooked construction of childhood and the child. The imperfect child challenges, either knowingly or unknowingly, cultural and societal boundaries and Harry, Ron, and Hermione lead imperfect lives. As the Victorian and Edwardian imperfect child must challenge societal and cultural boundaries, so too must Harry, Ron, and Hermione challenge such ideals. Their lives and characters are imperfect, and therefore realistic, and this illustrates the nature of their imperfection. They do not, as does their arch-nemesis Draco Malfoy, come from wealth or have familial pedigree. Instead, they must prove themselves in other ways to their community. From the beginning of the *Harry Potter* series, it is doubtful that these children can make it in the wizarding world. Rowling makes the old prejudices evident in Draco Malfoy's words when he first meets Harry, unaware to whom he is speaking: "I really don't think they should let the other sort in, do you? They're just not the same, they've never been brought up to know our ways. Some of them have never even heard of Hogwarts until they get the letter, imagine. I think they should keep it in the old wizarding families" (*Harry Potter* 78). Harry, Ron, and Hermione do not fit Malfoy's traditions, as they are either orphans, poor, or do not have wizarding in their family lineage. In the hallowed halls of Hogwarts, these children must make their own stand against evil and class prejudice. In using the imperfect-child construction, Rowling does not need to overtly discuss the presence of Christianity or lead her characters to faith, which is already innately built into this new form of the imperfect child.

Is This Thing On?

Many versions of "Dickensian" texts for children exist and while abridged versions of such work are not uncommon, the question begs to be asked: How many children readily pick up such books on their own? Instructors must encourage children to read Dickens's work even when they draw away from long description and prefer action and adventure. While some readers might skim the description in a text, the importance of the "skipped-over" description is not always readily apparent to readers. The desire to omit these portions of text may be due to the too ready supply of films and television programs that then give audiences the visual representation of a scene rather than challenging them to envision it themselves. As long as readers are spoon-fed others' visual representations of narrative, there will be resistant readers. The imagination, and thus the fancy Dickens believes we should preserve and encourage, is no longer present, but rather is presented. Illustrations were also provided in Dickens's works, but these did not have accompanying three-dimensional figures. Readers had to use their imagination to put the written narrative into visual form. Visual representations of popular characters like Harry Potter are given to readers via the screen and thus the imagination does not have to work to draw the characters in action. This has obvious drawbacks, but illustrations also supply images for readers. Though in no way is it suggested literary transactions be abandoned or we reject three- dimensional figures nor those found in illustration, readers' imagination should ultimately construct the character or scene based upon their experiences with the text and different mediums that bring the story to life.

Elements that are considered "Dickensian,"[3] however, are still readily popular and can be found in various examples of contemporary children's literature. Such elements are dark and gothic, for they illustrate a contemporary use of satire, irony, and morbidity. They hearken back to the fairy tales of the Brothers Grimm, Hans Christian Andersen, and Charles Perrault. Harry Potter, for example, starts his life as an orphan, as does Oliver Twist, and this motif is still widely used in children's texts. These elements were used long before Dickens began to write, but there is something unique in the way Dickens uses these tropes and themes and it is that which survives today. The Baudelaire orphans in Lemony Snicket's *A Series of Unfortunate Events* books face more "Dickensian" challenges than Oliver Twist. Ardagh's *The Eddie Dickens Trilogy* is set in the Victorian period, details the miserable life of Eddie Dickens, and is both humorous and dark. Texts such as these where the imperfect child is present allow readers to experience the Victorian atmosphere through the use of morbid humor and dark wit. While many of the situations such characters face are nonsensical and improbable, they help bring readers to texts such as *Oliver Twist*, and Oliver, whose experiences contemporary readers may find just as outlandish.

Location, Location, Location

Many authors who use the contemporary imperfect-child character in their narrative also draw upon Victorian settings for backdrops and tone, as in *A Series of Unfortunate Events*. This nineteenth-century setting and the feeling of it are not necessary for the development of a text that has a contemporary imperfect child present. Some imperfect children, like Harry Potter, find this in the fantasy world of the narrative, as is the case with Hogwarts. The contemporary imperfect child is in all genres of literature. Barbara Park's *Junie B. Jones* series provides an example in Junie of a young, contemporary imperfect child, as does Christopher Paul Curtis's Byron from his historical-fiction text *The Watsons Go to Birmingham—1963* (1997). Contemporary representations of the imperfect child illustrate that these children face real concerns and overcome them through perseverance and hope. The world faces as much, although different, hardship and possibility as it did during the Victorian period and through learning these difficulties potentiality can be achieved.

Feminist pedagogical practices offer some of the necessary tools that will allow instructors to not only teach but also help build strong communities in the classroom that may eventually extend to those outside of the classroom environment. In *No Angel in the Classroom: Teaching Through Feminist Discourse*, Berenice Fisher discusses the practice of consciousness-raising in the classroom and finds, "It promotes awareness of gender injustice and cultivates women's capacity to make their own decisions about how to respond to that injustice, even when these decisions differ" (39–40). By using texts which feature the imperfect child, a child of reality, readers may be more compelled to continue delving into even the dreaded description portions of the narrative, for they may be more likely to relate to the text and/or character once they can parallel the experiences of the imperfect child with their own or make social and cultural connections. Fisher notes that consciousness-raising leads students to examine what she terms " . . . relations between personal and political life. The feminist insistence that women's liberation requires a radical questioning of the division of labor implies an analysis that must go beyond individual needs and desires that emerge in daily life" (42). Fisher's work is important because it helps establish that authority must always be questioned and teachers need to create a safe yet strong community in their classroom. Such ideology is applicable to any text, as is evident with Dickens's work.

Dickens's social criticism can be a crucial point of discussion, and therefore understanding it allows students to draw parallels between the text and contemporary social issues as well as outline the class and gender issues of the Victorian period. In looking at the conditions of orphanages in the nineteenth and early twentieth centuries, as Oliver would have been brought up in, and examining contemporary orphanages in Western culture, students have seen the differences and similarities in these environments. In reading fantasy texts, such as *Harry Potter and the Sorcerer's Stone* or *The Children of Green Knowe*, Tamora Pierce suggests in her essay "Fantasy: Why Kids Read It; Why Kids Need It" (1996), "Fantasy, more than any other genre, is a literature of empowerment. . . . In fantasy, however short, fat, unbeautiful, weak, dreamy, or unlearned individuals may be, they find a realm in which those things are negated by strength" (181). The imperfect child is able to obtain a sense of agency and empowerment through spending even a modicum amount of time in a transitory space like the realm of faery. In contemporary fantasy literature, as well as in Victorian texts like MacDonald's *At the Back of the North Wind* and Nesbit's *The House of Arden*, the fantasy space like Hogwarts that exists is often set apart from the real world. In this alternate reality, the imperfect child is free to explore and obtain knowledge about personal existence. They gain experience and bring this back with them into their other reality. For Dickens, such an alternate reality for the imperfect child did not exist in a separate realm of wizards and dwarfs; instead, those fairy creatures were a part of the real Victorian landscape; characters such as Little Nell in *The Old Curiosity Shop* had to trod to obtain bittersweet happiness. In *The Children of Green Knowe* from *The Green Knowe Chronicles* series, this is what Tolly experiences as he learns of the ghost children that haunt his great-grandmother's house at Green Knowe.

L. M. Boston has long been neglected in scholarship and many of her books are simply out of print, but her *The Green Knowe Chronicles* are still widely available. In Dickensian tradition, Boston's creation of a fading family aristocracy paralleled with a dilapidated familial house, Green Knowe, brings together the real world in which Tolly and the ghost realm where his deceased relatives still enjoy taunting and playing with the houseguests exist. Tolly, whose given name is Toseland after his grandfather, has only a stepmother and father and is sent to live with his great-grandmother. When Tolly initially encounters his great-grandmother Mrs. Oldknow, "She had short silver curls and her face had so many wrinkles it looked as if someone had been trying to draw her for a very long time and every line put in had made the face more like her. She was wearing a soft dress of folded velvet that was as black as a hold in darkness" (*The Children of Green Knowe* 11). Mrs. Oldknow is, like Princess Irene's great-grandmother is to the castle in *The Princess and The Goblin* and *The Princess and Curdie*, a part of the castle Green Knowe. When Tolly questions Mrs. Oldknow as to why she resides in a castle as he " . . . thought that was only in fairy tales," she replies that it is a real castle and things do, like in fairy stories, happen in its walls (*The Children of Green Knowe* 14). Green Knowe has a timeless feel to it, and when Tolly begins to explore the winding corridors and land surrounding the castle, he interacts with a variety of ghosts who become protectors and friends during his stay. This interaction brings together the reality and fantasy realms Tolly as an imperfect child must negotiate.

The ghosts Tolly has the most contact with are children who are family members. Tolly's exposure to death occurs daily, but for him these creatures represent company and play, not long-dead relatives. They are children who will never grow up, forever frozen in a painting and ghostly form and they will always be desired. In the painting of the Oldknow family, Tolly sees:

> . . . three children and two ladies. There were two handsome boys, wearing lace collars and dark green silk suits. They had long hair but looked

anything but girlish. The elder of the two [Toby], who might be fourteen years old, was wearing a sword, . . . The younger brother [Alexander] had a book under his arm and a flute in his hand. The little girl [Linnet] has a smile of irrepressible high spirits that seemed to defy the painter to do a serious portrait of her. She was holding a chaffinch, and beside her on the ground was an open wicker cage. (*The Children of Green Knowe* 23)

The ghost children provide Tolly with playmates, relations and most importantly encourage his independence. Pierce suggests, "Fantasy . . . is a literature of *possibilities*. It opens the door to a realm of 'What If,' challenging readers to see beyond the concrete universe and to envision other ways of living and alternative mindsets. . . . Intelligent readers will come to relate the questions raised in these books to their own lives" (180). Tolly's interaction with his ghostly relatives provides him and readers with pleasure. These are children who will never go away and much can be accomplished when one's playmates are made of ectoplasm. Tolly is happy in his new home and over the course of the series becomes more independent and resourceful. He is predominantly unselfish, which is a trait the imperfect child inherits from the Romantic child. Experience for Tolly is comforting, for he has someone, Mrs. Oldknow, to look after him, even in his abandoned state. This is not the case for all contemporary imperfect children, however, as Joan Aiken illustrates in her character Dido from the *Wolves* series.

Dido Twite is a strong female protagonist whose adventures are chronicled over the course of eleven books in Aiken's *Wolves Chronicles*. While Dido does not appear until the second book in the series, *Black Hearts in Battersea*, she becomes the primary focus of the majority of texts to follow. In some of the texts in the series her sister Is, who is psychic, becomes the protagonist, but Dido develops into the main character throughout the many different books in the sequence. Dido first appears to Simon, an heir to the Battersea throne, when he tries to rent a room from her working class family in Southwark, and she is described as " . . . a shrewish-looking little creature of perhaps eight or nine, with sharp eyes of a pale washed-out blue and no eyebrows or eyelashes to speak of. Her straw colored hair was stringy and sticky with jam and she wore a dirty satin dress two sizes too small for her" (*Black Hearts in Battersea* 14). While Dido and Jessica from *Jessica's First Prayer* have much in common in that both come from abusive homes and have waifish appearances, Dido is headstrong and willful. Throughout her adventures she rarely appears in traditional female clothing, instead preferring to dress up in boys' attire. Even as Simon falls in love with her, Dido, in a feminist twist, does not wish to be brought into his upper-class world of society and culture, for she recognizes she would be ostracized. In the tenth book, *Midwinter Nightingale*, Simon explains to Dido, "The only person I've met so far . . . who would be right for me is you, Dido"; and she makes clear, "Not if you're a-going to be a king, Simon. I'd *never* do as a queen, never! Not me. It's too high a step from Rose Alley to Saint Jim's Palace.

You'll have to look for someone classier. Or turn down the job" (240). As an imperfect child, Dido recognizes her status as seen by Aiken's alternative early-nineteenth-century culture and does not challenge that positioning, but this is her choice to make and not socially prescribed.

As Aiken began publishing her *Wolves Chronicles* in 1962, Dido became a role model for young women since her adventures challenged social and cultural norms. Dido's actions, such as when she foils a plot to blow up Castle Battersea in *Black Hearts in Battersea*, illustrate her independence and unconventional nature. Simon decides he will not take any wife if he cannot be with Dido. Consistently, Dido challenges social norming through what she wears, her adventures, and unconventional actions. Dido is a heroine in an era when they were not supposed to exist as tomboys. Aiken does not take liberties with her plot, such as with her use of The Bow Street Runners, established in 1749 by author Henry Fielding, in her depictions of the early nineteenth century in *Black Hearts in Battersea*. Though everyone who comes into contact with Dido grows to admire her, she recognizes that as a part of the culture in which she belongs she has a certain social status. Her position as working class allows her personal sovereignty. In her introduction to *Children's Literature: New Approaches* (2004), Karin Lesnik-Oberstein questions what new approaches in children's literature criticism are out to accomplish and suggests, " . . . the maintenance of the real child is part of a maintenance of a real world, which can be sensed and known" (18). As Dido leads her own life, a life of adventure and freedom, she is satisfied with her existence. Through lessons such as this, the real child is encouraged to seek out personal freedoms, but they are "maintained" as is the world in which they live. Dido rightly recognizes her reality and it is *she* who turns down an invitation to become part of upper-class society and culture. She is not keeping her place, but rather resists being absorbed into a sphere where she would be unwelcome.

After Aiken's death in 2004, her books, and especially those in her *Wolves* series, became noted "classics" in children's literature. Both adults and children read them, although the series is not as popular as the *Harry Potter* series. For adults, reading texts primarily aimed at a children's audience may be partially because of childhood nostalgia or readers may wish to know what one's child is being exposed to. The desire for adults to peep into children's spheres is common and sometimes illustrated in children's works, as in Robert Munsch's *Love You Forever* (1986). This can be easily done as is seen with the special adult editions of the Harry Potter series. If adult readers appear to be reading adult material, or if the material is presented in an adult fashion, there is little threat to how the adult is viewed socially and culturally. However, if an adult were to be seen reading one of the *A Series of Unfortunate Events* books children read, then the impression may be given that that person is not adult. Adults who read and collect comic books are thought of similarly. As Alison Lurie points out in *Don't Tell the Grown-Ups: Subversive Children's Literature* (1990), "The line between adult and juvenile fiction was less strict then than it is now, and adult writers like Charles Dickens, William Thackeray, Oscar Wilde, and Christina Rossetti . . ." (75). As childhood and the child have become more distinct from an adult sphere, their literature has also become "othered." Comics and graphic novels, however, are read by and marketed to adults and children. Society and culture do not just hand down texts such as traditional fairy stories, but rather assign children their own reading material. This children's sphere is a place adults continuously try to invade and by applying "classic" to such literature, grown-ups feel safe reading children's books like Aiken's *Chronicles* series or the popular Lemony Snicket's *A Series of Unfortunate Events* texts.

Orphans of Outrageous Fortune(s)

While *A Series of Unfortunate Events*, where each text has thirteen chapters and concludes with book thirteen, is aimed at readers ages 9–12, it has become immensely popular among children and adults. The books are published so that they resemble Victorian texts with uncut pages, 5 × 7 inch hardcovers, bookplates, and black-and-white illustrations by Brett Helquist. He embeds hints about each successive chapter and book in his drawings that are reminiscent of Victorian woodblocks. Snicket, who has written other books for adults, including *The Basic Eight* (1999). *Watch Your Mouth* (2002), and *Why We Broke Up* (2011),[4] has called *A Series of Unfortunate Events* "neo-Victorian" and "mock-gothic" ("Lemony Fresh"), but the series developed out of what Daniel Fierman reports in his May 23, 2002, *Entertainment Weekly* article "Lemony Fresh," Snicket " . . . decided to rework a failed neo-Victorian novel for adults into a kids book. . . ." Yet Snicket's series has kept readers across age groups very interested in his work. His characters in the series, though not originally supposed to have reflected any particular ethnicity, undergo a series of trials and tribulations while being pursued but the ever-present Count Olaf. In league with Count Olaf are a band of merry thugs who assist him in his evil endeavors. The Victorian setting of the texts also reflects their gloomy, morose tone. Snicket suggested to Vicki Haddock in "Shivers Under the Covers" (2002), Victorian London was not the original place he had in mind for the setting and he, in fact, " . . . had no place in particular in mind when his imagination conjured up the damp, gloomy and often creepy settings in which the orphans often find themselves." Snicket's use of tongue-in-cheek writing, satire, irony, dark humor, and references to literature, pop culture, and social issues illustrate his perspectives and social critiques in plaited strands of mock absurdity and serious frivolity as his writing is often critical of itself.

Snicket notes feeling antipathy towards fairy tales and children's literature in general as he " . . . concluded early on [during childhood] that much children's literature left something to be desired" and commonly calls such work "crap," according to Haddock ("Shivers Under the Covers"). It is fair to say that Snicket's work is not similar to fairy tales. As Laurie Langbauer points out, in "Ethics and Practice of Lemony Snicket: Adolescence and Generation X" (2007), "In numerous reviews and countless interviews, Handler argues for the breakdown of boundaries in literature as a response to our times" (503). Handler, like many contemporary readers, desires fresh new approaches to storytelling. Drawing upon the imperfect child character in his construction of the Baudelaire orphans, Snicket illustrates the complexity of modern life for contemporary orphans whose situation has much in common with Oliver Twist's and other nineteenth- and early-twentieth-century imperfect children. While Handler's popularity is still on the rise and he has a long way to go to reach Dickens's fame and staying power, his work is similar. Kathy Boccella writes, in "Kids Sweet on Lemony Snicket" (2002), "Like a modern-day 'Oliver Twist' each installment recounts the travails of the Baudelaire children." Boccella goes on to state: "The books' style has been described as Dickensian, but Handler says he was more influenced by Edward Gorey and Roald Dahl. . . ." Handler tells Boccella, "I liked books where something dramatic happens and there wasn't this sort of moralistic tone." Though Handler does not wish to take on a "moralistic tone" in his writing, there are nonetheless instances where readers are encouraged to think through, along with the Baudelaire children, about the consequences of actions. Such is the case, for example, when the children must decide if they should save their Aunt Josephine or flee the scene of her death in the third book, *A Series of Unfortunate Events: The Wide Window.*

The three Baudelaire orphans are portrayed as loving, caring children who have just had a serious case of bad luck. They are reminiscent of Dickens's orphans Oliver Twist and Little Nell. The Baudelaire surname is taken after the nineteenth-century French poet Charles Baudelaire. The oldest sibling, Violet, is fourteen and very similar to Little Nell, for it is often through her quick-thinking skills that the children are saved. She ties her hair in a bow when she is inventing and is spatially gifted. Klaus, the only boy in the group, is the middle child and is about twelve. His temperament, stature, and the situations into which he falls make him comparable to Oliver Twist, although he is more bookish than Oliver. As Oliver must toil in a workhouse, so too do Klaus and his sisters in *A Series of Unfortunate Events: The Miserable Mill.* Klaus is an avid reader and able to learn and retain huge amounts of information rather quickly. Whereas Violet is a thinker and works well with her hands, Klaus learns rapidly and then acts. Their younger sibling, Sunny, is perhaps the oddest member of the trio. She is a baby; readers are not told her exact age but she does seem to be growing slightly as the series progresses. Sunny's special skill is biting anything and everything with her four very sharp teeth. Many times she helps her siblings escape through the use of her teeth, which also came in handy when she was employed as a secretary in book five, *A Series of Unfortunate Events: The Austere Academy.* Sunny largely speaks gibberish, which Handler readily translates for readers, though her siblings can understand her without paraphrase.

The actions of the Baudelaire orphans are very overt throughout the texts, but what are not are their features. Handler does say that the children are "charming, and resourceful, and had pleasant facial features . . ." (1) in the first book, but he stays away from ever clearly describing their specific features. The children are Caucasian and have distinct features in the illustrations by Brett Helquist, but Handler has wanted to paint them to be representative of any children, anywhere. The features of imperfect children are not often overly distinct and they can appear as any children from anywhere. Though some characters, such as Harry Potter, may have a distinguishing mark, their physical appearance is overly unremarkable. This helps indicate both their worldly nature and ability to fit into any environment. In "Shivers under the Covers" Haddock notes, "There is precious little physical description of the Baudelaire children—no race, no hair color." However, their arch-nemesis, Count Olaf, has quite a few distinctive traits which include a tattoo of an eye on his ankle and a unibrow. He is able to fashion himself any disguise and tries to lure the children into trusting him in almost every book. He is after their enormous fortune, but is unable to touch even a small amount of their wealth. Unfortunately, the orphans also cannot access their money as they are wanted on murder charges.

Violet, Klaus, and Sunny are homeless, penniless, and often friendless as they are on the run from the law. They, like Oliver and Little Nell, have had to learn to live on their own since every grown-up they can trust perishes before they have a chance to gain assistance. In constructing such lonely paths for the imperfect child, authors challenge not only societal and cultural norms, but compel their characters to take action and responsibility for their own lives and situations, which is something children are not always encouraged to accomplish. The imperfect child becomes adept, as do most protagonists when going through such ordeals, at solving problems and making decisions. In *Humor in Contemporary Junior Literature* (2011), Julie Cross, who defines texts like those of Snicket and Ardagh as comic gothic, explains, " . . . I believe that comic Gothic texts do set out to entertain and amuse but, at the same time, they offer the possibility of encountering profound questions about beliefs and identity, encouraging 'intellectual skepticism,' through the detachment afforded by the comic mode" (172). This challenges the ideology that we must protect children and therefore exposing them to experiences, such as showing them a homeless shelter or encouraging them to volunteer at an orphanage, becomes unfavorable for many individuals. Langbauer suggests, "By setting its orphans adrift in a world bereft of stable guidelines, Snicket's series also recasts ethics—from fixed code to something more fluid, knowable ultimately only in action" (503). Both challenges and ethics breaching tactics become evident as the orphans move from home to home.

Their environments parallel the wandering nature of their lives and there is little permanence. After their disastrous encounter with Count Olaf in the first book, the first relation that they can trust is Uncle Monty in *A Series of Unfortunate Events: The Reptile Room*. Uncle Monty dies from what seems to be a snakebite, but the children are the only ones able to figure out that his assistant, Stephano, is really Count Olaf, who killed him by injecting him with poison. The Baudelaire orphans regularly face this type of tragedy throughout the series. Count Olaf is repulsively similar to Daniel Quilp in Dickens's *The Old Curiosity Shop.* Olaf also wishes to marry a young girl; although his motives to wed Violet may be slightly different, they still relate to the economy each potential bride can bring to the marriage. In *A Series of Unfortunate Events: Book the First: The Bad Beginning,* the Beaudelaire children find themselves locked in Count Olaf's tower, where he has imprisoned them until the performance of "The Marvelous Marriage," a play in which he will actually marry Violet. Through ingenuity, Violet, who is right-handed, signs the marriage document with her left hand, which is enough to render the marriage void. Count Olaf escapes with his henchmen and the orphans are safe until the next volume.

The popularity of *A Series of Unfortunate Events* is due to its ironic tone and the imperfect children who serve as its protagonists. Readers clamor for the next book in the series, in part because of the destructive nature of the circumstances surrounding the Baudelaire siblings. The destructive nature of their circumstances, very imperfect circumstances, illustrates the like disaster their lives become. Children who are born into wealth, such as the Baudelaire orphans, are not thought to be able to tackle the circumstances life throws at the siblings. Yet, they overcome the stereotype and are not depicted as having perfect lives, despite their finances. Like a train wreck readers love to watch, the Baudelaire orphans overcome great odds, greedy relatives, and plenty of terrible food in order to be left stranded in a boat on an ocean with an adopted baby. Snicket leaves readers in the final volume, *The End,* having to accept "It is not the whole story, of course, but it is enough. Under the circumstances, it is the best for which you can hope" (324). Snicket never uses the words "the end" to finalize his story, but rather suggests, "There are some words, of course, that are better left unsaid—but not, I believe, the word uttered by my niece, a word here which means the story is over. Beatrice" (*The End* 13). Readers do not know exactly what the outcome is for the Baudelaire family, but they are certainly not unaware of the cruelty of their environments. They, like Oliver Twist, Diamond, Tom, Jessica, Harry, and Dido, plod on with hope that their circumstances will be "the best for which you can hope." In *Erotic Innocence,* Kincaid finds, "We have it in us to reimagine a set of stories not so tied to safety, not so cringing and cautious. There are stories of potential and risk, of excitement and possibility, stories that take pleasure in the present and look forward to the future. We need stories that aren't afraid to leave home" (294). These are stories found in *A Series of Unfortunate Events* and Ardagh's *The Eddie Dickens Trilogy.*

Snicket and Ardagh draw upon satire and dark humor in *A Series of Unfortunate Events* and *The Eddie Dickens Trilogy.* In these contemporary narratives a sense of parody is built into the traditional struggles of the imperfect child, such as establishing an identity and application of experience and knowledge to their societal and cultural positions. This negates a portion of the seriousness surrounding their situations and makes the text more believable to readers. Readers believe in the text because of the unbelievable nature of the circumstances. Divorced from such situations, readers have little or no responsibility for the social and cultural conditions faced by the protagonists in *A Series of Unfortunate Events* or *The Eddie Dickens Trilogy*. Readers can simply enjoy the stories as exaggerated narratives. The contemporary imperfect child is sometimes mocked in these situations, but their circumstances are depicted as fantastical. This occurs throughout *A Series of Unfortunate Events* as the heroic attempts of the orphans to clear their names and escape Count Olaf are undercut and mocked no matter what they try to do. The more overt displays of power and independence shown by the Baudelaire orphans and Eddie Dickens are due, in part, to the additional challenges they face as contemporary imperfect children.

The Eddie Dickens Trilogy begins with *Awful End*, in which Eddie is sent to live at Saint Horrid's Home for Grateful Orphans after his parents take ill, and his irresponsible relatives he is sent to live with forget who he is. The series becomes an attempt to rewrite Dickens texts and Dickens's own life with humor. As an imperfect child, Eddie is able to escape the orphanage and frees all of the other children incarcerated in its walls. He strikes back at Mrs. Cruel Streak, a woman in charge of the orphanage, after she hits him over the head with a spoon (*Awful End* 106–7). In a situation similar to Oliver Twist's when he asks for more, Eddie " . . . wasn't like the other boys and girls in the St. Horrid's Home for Grateful Orphans. He wasn't weak from years of bad food, hard work and no hope" and he "Without a moment's hesitation . . . snatched up THE GOOD BOOK in both hands, raised it high above him and then brought it crashing down on Mrs. Cruel Streak's head" (*Awful End* 108). A hero for saving the orphans of St. Horrid's, Eddie moves in with his family at Awful End. Though he sought to free himself from his forced habitation at St. Horrid's, he saves the orphans, who take up with a band of traveling actors (*Awful End* 128). Ardagh, as do authors like MacDonald, Kingsley, and Snicket, overtly addresses his audience throughout his series and this draws upon active reading skills. Eddie's experiences are humorous, but Ardagh, through directly speaking to his audience and explaining some of the situations Eddie faces, allows readers to better bridge the fiction of the text with the real world in which they exist. *In Books, Children and Men* (1975), Paul Hazard notes:

> Children reject the books that do not treat them as equals and which call them "dear little readers"; the books which do not respond to their won nature, which do not attract their eye through pictures, or their spirits by liveliness; books which teach them only what they can learn at school, books which put them to sleep but not to dream. (50–51)

In speaking directly to an audience through the text, authors alert readers that a story is for them. The imperfect child becomes more realistic and tangible and such parallels help ground it as a child of reality.

The real child is inherently imperfect, despite what societal and cultural notions of the child and childhood suggest. As Kincaid has indicated, innocence cannot be preserved and to do so is unnatural. What can be retained, as indicated through the construction of the imperfect child, is hope. If one does not possess experience and knowledge, such as Little Nell or Harry Potter, then one cannot have hope. The contemporary imperfect child is defined in terms different from his/her Victorian precursors, for the concept of childhood and the child has socially shifted. A wider separation exists today between the notions of childhood/adulthood and child/adult. In many cases, we try to create small adult sexless clones, but their innocence, we believe, is still intact. Adult and child readers still enjoy reading about the imperfect child. The desire for the imperfect child has increased the production of texts about them through Dickens's serialization, L. M. Boston's *The Green Knowe Chronicles*, continued series like that of Lemony Snicket's *A Series of Unfortunate Events*, or Joan Aiken's *Wolves*. Readers crave continuity in stories representing the imperfect child and that is why such children continue to live.

Conclusion
The Perfection of Imperfection—The Consummation of the Misunderstood

"Innocence is a lot like the air in your tires: there's not a lot you can do with it but lose it. Besides, it doesn't amount to much in the first place. Innocence makes you vulnerable, badly in need of protection, which is one reason adults like it to be in others . . . in the course of the nineteenth century it gravitated more and more toward a passive nullity, a pure point strangely connected to its opposite, depravity."

—James Kincaid from *Erotic Innocence* (53–54)

The most often discussed constructions and interpretations of both the child and childhood in literary criticism are in the binary of the Romantic and deprived child who is socially unredeemable. Other constructions and ideas regarding the concepts of the child and childhood are mentioned sporadically in criticism, but they have not been brought together and thoroughly examined. The imperfect child is one of these constructs. What is unique in the development of the imperfect child is the transmitting this character from literature that was primarily meant for a family audience to literature written specifically for children. Charles Dickens's constructions of the imperfect child in *Oliver Twist, The Old Curiosity Shop, A Christmas Carol, Dombey and Son, Bleak House,* and *Little Dorrit* greatly impacted future constructions of the child and childhood.

Dickens, who wrote for many audiences, uses the child protagonist throughout his work both to indicate the influences society and culture have on children and to show how this, in turn, affect society and culture. Other nineteenth-century authors such as George MacDonald, Charles Kingsley, Hesba Stretton, Christina Rossetti, and E. Nesbit, who also wrote for adults and children, construct the imperfect child who is also impacted by social and cultural issues. Despite the label of author of adult literature being applied to these writers, many of their texts, such as *At the Back of the North Wind*, *The Princess and the Goblin*, *The Princess and Curdie*, *The Water-Babies*, *Jessica's First Prayer*, *Speaking Likenesses*, *Sing-Song: A Nursery Rhyme Book*, *The House of Arden*, and *Harding's Luck*, have become known as children's literature in the same vein as many of Dickens's novels.

The imperfect child, as are many children, is born innocent though not always under the purest of conditions. Dickens points out with Oliver Twist's birth in *Oliver Twist*: "Oliver cried lustily. *If* [my emphasis] he could have known he was an orphan . . . perhaps he would have cried the louder" (47). Immediately following his birth, Oliver has no knowledge of his status, but soon learns what his social position is in Victorian England. The imperfect child faces and deals with social and cultural hegemonic ideologies regarding class, gender, and socioeconomic standing while either overtly or covertly staking personal claim for independence and individuality. Romantic children are loving, pure, and ignorant of the problematic nature of Victorian social and cultural ills and they thus become the blank ideal. As Kincaid explains in *Erotic Innocence,* the Romantic child " . . . was strangely hollow from the start: *un*corrupted, *un*sophisticated, *un*enlightened. The child was without a lot of things, things it was better off without, presumably, but still oddly dispossessed and eviscerated, without much substance" (53). Yet, as the imperfect child shows, such ideals cannot be maintained.

The struggles the imperfect child faces play upon readers' emotions, and while sentimentality is evident, perhaps at times overly used by authors, it is an important element in the narrative of these characters. Dickens frequently used sentimentality in his work to illustrate what children faced in the difficult social and cultural conditions of the Victorian era, but as critics have suggested, he drew upon his own negative feelings of his childhood as a cathartic tool. The use of sentimentality in literature was also used by future authors, though it did become less frequently and overtly drawn upon as time progressed. Coveney points out varying forms of sentimentality in *Poor Monkey: The Child in Literature* and states, "There is the sentimentality of sadness which indulges the pathetic; and there is the sentimentality of optimism which idealizes. There is, of course, the other sentimentality of the squalid with which we have become so familiar in modern literature, which, for no evident purpose, makes things . . . seem absolutely . . . squalid, and worse than they are" (116). This can be seen in today's literature, such as Lemony Snicket's *A Series of Unfortunate Events*. Little Nell's death in *The Old Curiosity Shop* or Jessica's struggle in *Jessica's First Prayer* to live in the squalid streets of London, for example, provides sentimental depictions of children overcoming overwhelming odds which imperfect children must do, but it is at the cost of their untouched souls.

The imperfect nature of these characters does not mean that they have been polluted, somehow tarnished, or do not have inherent worth, but rather that they exist as individuals impacted by their social and cultural conditions and are able to overcome great odds. Their image is belittled, authors indicate, in their naming and they must transition between the reality of Victorian society and the fantasy of an idealized fairy realm, where, as readers see, not everything is perfect. For all of the societal and cultural abuses the imperfect child faces, these characters are ever hopeful, like Tiny Tim in *A Christmas Carol*. They construct their own identities and destinies, either overtly or covertly, such as Florence Dombey does in *Dombey and Son*. The projection of the author's own social and cultural struggles in the construction and employment of the imperfect character shows the interconnected nature of humanity through society and culture in that they often express not only their own ideas, but call attention to the hypocrisy evident in their surroundings. Williams rightly states in *Culture & Society 1780–1950*:

> The one vital lesson which the nineteenth century had to learn—and learn urgently because of the very magnitude of its changes—was that the basic economic organization could not be separated and excluded from its moral and intellectual concerns. Society and individual experience were alike being transformed, and this driving agency . . . had, in depth, to be taken into consciousness. (280)

As the Victorian Era progressed, social and cultural consciousness regarding the plight of the poor was improved through the rise in literacy, journalism, literature, and many other mediums. Social and cultural conditions, which characters like Tom the chimney sweep in *The Water-Babies* and Diamond the youth, forced to drive his father's cab in *At the Back of the North Wind* faced, changed because of the considerable contributions literature made to raising awareness of these issues.

Victorian society and culture, in the way many societies and cultures are imperfect, were as imperfect as the imperfect child, but if such children were ignored, so too were the problems of the Victorian period. Societal and cultural change did not occur overnight, but as it did take place, ideas of the child and childhood also evolved, as evidenced in Thomas Jordan's *Victorian Childhood*. The child and childhood were something to be preserved as their social value shifted from the physical contributions they could make to emotional ones. Imperfect characters like MacDonald's Princess Irene and Curdie from *The Princess and the Goblin* and *The Princess and Curdie* or Elfrida, Edred, and Dickie Harding in E. Nesbit's *The House of Arden* and *Harding's Luck* are a part of or enter fantasy realms more overtly than earlier illustrations of the imperfect child. These fantasy spaces became more important to and divorced from Victorian reality. There are, however, events, such as with the return of Elfrida and Edred's father, occurring in such spaces that happen in the real world to which the imperfect child must eventually return and face. These imperfect children are socially and culturally challenged, but they find faith and do not lose hope that their situations will improve or those facing Victorian society.

The "ideal" Victorian child was a desire but not a possibility in Victorian culture, though the imperfect child was attainable. The ideas of children and childhood developed rapidly over the Victorian Era, along with increased literacy and availability of reading material for the emerging mass reading public. Children's literature was one of the developing areas for publishers and readers, but this did not stop the public from bringing home books not expressly intended for children and reading to their family. In the idealized middle class family circle, authors such as Charles Dickens were read and appreciated by members of all ages. The upper and working classes also found pleasure and delight in reading Dickens's work. While Dickens rarely wrote expressly for children, his books, which frequently focus on children and childhood, were admired and read by many authors. As such, his work continues to influence contemporary children's writers.

Recent writers, such as Joan Aiken, L. M. Boston, J. K. Rowling and Lemony Snicket, have used the construction of the imperfect child character to illustrate the difficulty children still face in society and culture. Harry Potter and the Baudelaire orphans are alone and they know their situations and experiences are uncommon and not what society and culture deem "normal." Langbauer notes that in an interview for the *New York Times* after September 11, Handler stated, "Stories like these aren't cheerful, but they offer a truth—that real trouble cannot be erased, only endured . . ." ("The Ethics" 506). For the imperfect child, the harshness life has to offer is a reality and while there might be an idyllic notion of a perfect, happy existence, it is not truthful. The contemporary imperfect child typically has a support system of peers or guiding adults to help them traverse their problematic paths, whereas the Victorian imperfect child usually has to make decisions for themselves and seek out assistance. Contemporary imperfect children do not replace Victorian imperfect children, but are rather a continuation of this character. What has developed for the contemporary imperfect child is the reflection of the changes in attitudes towards the child and childhood. Their situations might not be more positive, but society and culture are much more helpful in assisting them through their troubles as is evidenced in the many charities and programs such as WIC available to them and their families. In either case, the imperfect child is a representation of the real child, one readers want to tame, but secretly hope still runs wild and free. Some contemporary authors, such as Lemony Snicket and Philip Ardagh, mock the situations and experiences of the imperfect child and draw upon Victorian conventions of setting and the common use of powerful sentimentality. Contemporarily, society and culture deride and criticize overt sentimentality, so its use becomes humorous and satirical in texts like *A Series of Unfortunate Events* and *The Eddie Dickens Trilogy*. While readers may hope to see the imperfect child face challenges and win, they really desire to see these children continue to fight, and therefore these children can never win.

Feminist pedagogical practices offer some of these necessary tools that allow instructors not only to teach but also help build strong communities in the classroom that may eventually extend to those outside of the classroom environment. In *No Angel in the Classroom: Teaching Through Feminist Discourse*, Berenice Fisher discusses the practice of consciousness-raising in the classroom and explains how such pedagogical methodologies can help increase both instructor and student awareness of cultural and social issues (39–40). Analyzing the role and experiences of the Victorian and contemporary imperfect child in the classroom is crucial in helping students explore the different constructs of the child and childhood. Feminist theory is one of the most accessible approaches for students as it explores and challenges what defines the "other." Fisher's consciousness-raising approach becomes a cornerstone for much of what we accomplish when reading "classics" because it helps us negotiate the boundaries between text and life, fantasy and reality. Through encouraging students to apply what they were reading to the world outside our classroom door, they became more interested in the situations they were encountering in the text and the text itself. Fisher notes that the consciousness-raising leads students to examine what she terms "relations between personal and political life. The feminist insistence that women's liberation requires a radical questioning of the division of labor implies an analysis that must go beyond individual needs and desires that emerge in daily life" (42). Fisher's work helps establish the fact that authority must always be questioned and educators need to create a safe yet strong community in their classroom. By utilizing such principles, students may feel more secure in their abilities not only as writers and readers, but also as participants in a dynamic classroom atmosphere. It is the day-to-day concerns of life Dickens is concerned with and presents in his texts. The social criticism that resounds throughout much of his work can be a crucial point of discussion and therefore understanding it allows students to draw parallels between the text and contemporary social issues.

Exploring ways in which teachers can help students enjoy and appreciate "classics" and examining why a resistance may be formed to them in the first place may help break apprehension for reading these texts. Yet, drawing students to imperfect child characters allows them to see that while the world outside of a text is not perfect, happy endings are not always found in the covers of a book either. A text can, and often does, reflect reality and through this understanding students may became more engaged in such literature. In *Arts of Living: Reinventing the Humanities for the Twenty-First Century* (2003), Kurt Spellmeyer notes:

And both sides keep looking resolutely backward, conservatives pleading for the same great books, while radicals want the great books as well, though as targets for a harsh "interrogation" rather than as sacred icons. The culture wars not withstanding, the crisis in the humanities has not been caused by our teaching, or failing to teach, certain books. The humanities are in trouble because they have become increasingly isolated from the life of the larger society. (4)

Spellmeyer continues to say that this path has been chosen continuously by the humanities over the twentieth century (4), and while this notion may be a bit excessive there is truth in such a claim. The fear and trepidation students have when assigned a text they might not "get through" in two hours or that might cause them to develop helpful reading strategies is all too apparent. The appeal for and to the imperfect child by readers can help bring audiences back to the texts that have, according to Spellmeyer, become secluded. While readers do read in many cases to "escape" from reality, though presenting realistic problems, such as with Oliver Twist's experiences or Harry Potter's struggles, readers can relate to or become open to such situations and explore ways these issues can be better handled. While not all humanities disciplines have distanced themselves from larger society, many fields have resisted incorporating progressive resources, such as iPads, and traditional teaching methodologies.

Oliver Twist, *The Water-Babies*, *Jessica's First Prayer*, and many other texts which incorporate the imperfect child are still popular, but what makes them interesting and well-liked amongst contemporary readers is complex; and while these books remain on bookshelves for young and old alike, audience reception is an important part of why they have become "classics." Stories by Dickens, Kingsley, Stretton, and other authors using the imperfect child in their stories were a part of the Victorian middle- and upper-class reading habits and as such, the stories contained both adult concerns for children as well as entertainment for the impressionable young audience. The family audience openly read stories like these together. Many people remember reading such stories with their families, but these types of recollections may disappear as children are no longer read to but either simply given books or handed computerized reading assistance by devices like the Leap Frog readers. In her essay "Dickens for Children" (1982), Margaret Hodges remembers her childhood and Dickens being a staple in the family reading diet and recalls, "After morning church and midday dinner that would have pleased Charles Dickens himself, many winter afternoons were spent with a walk from which we retuned to an open fire—and Dickens" (626). This became a strong memory for Hodges and she explains that they began with *A Christmas Carol* and feels Dickens is at his best when he "Makes us see what he had seen as a child and remembered as a man" (626).

While this type of memory may disappear, it is this nostalgia for childhood and treasured characters like Tiny Tim, an imperfect child, that may keep audiences returning to such texts. There is also a grim reality that as books like *Oliver Twist*, *A Christmas Carol*, *The Water-Babies*, *Jessica's First Prayer*, and others like them are being taught throughout many schools, teachers may hear the old phrase "Why do we have to read this? It's old and I can't understand it." Educators may make such books more accessible to readers by including selected modern adaptations in either written or visual form to accompany such literature. A study conducted by Jim Cope in 1990, outlined in "Beyond Voices of Readers: Students on School's Effects on Reading" (1997), examined what a group of twelfth-graders were assigned to read, notably works by Dickens and Shakespeare, and how they responded to the literature. These authors were the most widely complained about amongst students, and it is largely due to what Cope terms "Moby-Phobia," avoiding reading what one is unfamiliar with or having difficulty relating to ("Beyond"). The teaching methods of instructors also played a large factor in Cope's study as many students cited problems with teaching models that were primarily concerned with such things as symbolism and plot structure rather than keeping students focused on the story content.

This makes for a very negative reading experience and, as many students pointed out in Cope's study, they did not want to attempt reading Dickens or Shakespeare again. Fisher's model of consciousness-raising would be helpful in teaching such literature, for it both empowers readers and provides a better understanding of the text as a whole. Instructors can also turn to Louise M. Rosenblatt's classic text *Literature as Exploration* (1996) in which she explores the periphery between reader and text and subject and object. She seeks to find the marginal area where these binaries meet and develop an understanding of the effect of one upon the other. This has been somewhat controversial with reader-response theorists, but Rosenblatt's insistence that readers are *active* allows us to view reading as something readers engage with and intentionally *do*. While readers may come to a text with preconceived ideas due to the label "classic," they may be less intimidated by this title if they appreciate their stake in the reading experience. An aversion to "classics" only further damages an already apprehensive reader's desire to seek out such literature. In placing *Oliver Twist* and *A Christmas Carol*, among other books originally intended for a family audience, on children's shelves there comes the responsibility to make such literature accessible for contemporary readers and abridged texts do not offer a complete answer, for they often omit much of the importance of the original tale. Feminist approaches to teaching may meet with resistance initially, but once understood and implemented they may make teaching "classics" more rewarding for teachers and students alike.

Dickens's works *Oliver Twist, The Old Curiosity Shop, Dombey and Son, Bleak House, Little Dorrit,* and *A Christmas Carol*, some of which were written for children, all contain the imperfect child. When they are placed alongside other works, such as *The Water-Babies* or *The Eddie Dickens Trilogy*, the construction, romanticizing, and socializing of the imperfect Victorian child is evident. These authors use elements of religion, naming, death, irony, fairy worlds, gender, and class to illustrate the intrinsic need for the ideal child and yet the impossibility of achieving such a construct. Though our contemporary ideas of the child and childhood differ from that of those in the Victorian period, we still long for this version of the Victorian child in contemporary literatures. While debates rage over how to define children's literature, imperfect children such as Oliver Twist, Jessica, and Jo, though somewhat changed, can still be found in the most popular of literatures read by children. The imperfect child is a depiction of a real and not an ideal child, a child whose perfection is found in their complex and engaging imperfection.

Notes

Notes to the Introduction

1. Throughout the text my reference is to the Romantic child of Wordsworth rather than Blake, who framed such a child through a more realistic lens.
2. See Falconer, Rachel. *The Crossover Novel: Contemporary Children's Fiction and Its Adult Readership.* London: Routledge, 2008, for a detailed discussion on the topic. Print.
3. See the work of noted critics: Kaplan, Fred. *Dickens: A Biography.* New York: William Morrow & Co., Inc., 1988.; Forster, John. *The Life of Charles Dickens. Vol. 1–3.* Boston, Estes and Lauriat P, 1872. Print.; Tomalin, Claire. Charles *Dickens: A Life.* London: Penguin Press, 2011.; Slater, Michael. *Charles Dickens.* New Haven, CT: Yale University Press, 2009, as well as many others. Print.
4. For an interesting overview of this subject see Winter, Alison. "Mesmerism and Popular Culture in Early Victorian England." *History of Science* 32 (1994): 317–43. Print.
5. My focus on these works, which were primarily targeted at child audiences, is to illustrate the way in which Dickens's fictional children influenced not only later writers but also child characters and literature for children. These works were popular texts throughout the Victorian period and many continue to be today. The imperfect child Dickens perfected can be seen in these later works.

Notes to Chapter 1

1. Dickens was not the first author to use the child as a protagonist in his work. Earlier depictions, such as Horace Walpole's Matilda in *The Castle of Otranto* (1764), Daniel Defoe's Moll Flanders from *Moll Flanders* (1721), can easily be found as well as a wide array of books targeted towards children. See the informative Demers, Patricia. *From Instruction to Delight: An Anthology of Children's Literature to 1850.* Oxford: Oxford University

Press, 2008, for an excellent overview of the history of children's literature. Print. Philip Ariès and his well-known work *Centuries of Childhood* also provide an informative examination on the ways in which children and childhood have been constructed socially and culturally throughout history. His work is, however, contested as with Linda Pollock's *Forgotten Children* (1983), who challenged many of his ideas. Works such as *The Castle of Otranto* and *Moll Flanders*, however, were not aimed at child audiences, so they provide a better parallel for Dickens's work.

2. See the work of John Locke, such as *Some Thoughts Concerning Education* (1693) or his *An Essay Concerning Human Understanding* (1689), for a background to this ideology. Jean-Jacques Rousseau's "child of nature," the idea of the child being born pure and ultimately corrupted by society and culture, was to follow in the eighteenth century. Romantic poets such as William Wordsworth were to further believe and promote the idea of the child as pure and untarnished.

3. The debate as to how children's literature is defined is ongoing. Jacqueline Rose's seminal work *The Case of Peter Pan: The Impossibility of Children's Fiction* (1992) is widely examined and contested and many other works, such as *Kiddie Lit: The Cultural Construction of Children's Literature in America* (2004) by Beverly Lyon Clark or Marah Gubar's recent work *Artful Dodgers: Reconceiving the Golden Age of Children's Literature* (2010), add important voices to this debate.

4. The increase in media available, whether it is through film or toys, for works like the *Harry Potter* series has also contributed to awareness of such literature as well as its societal and cultural value.

5. *Household Words* ran from 1850 to 1859 and after it was canceled, Dickens was to establish *All the Year Round,* which was published from 1859 to 1895. His eldest son, Charles Dickens Jr., was to serve as editor and owner after his father's death in 1870.

6. Many series like this exist but Dickens did not always approve of their publication. His copyright battles, both at home and abroad, were a constant issue throughout most of his career.

7. The term "classics" is problematic by its nature. It assumes much about a text and places a value on the work that cannot be wholly qualified or quantified. I use the term here because it is widely utilized and thus familiar.

8. This further illustrates the value of such individuals. As part of the "Great Unwashed," they were placed into a group and labeled rather than seen as individuals with disparate needs.

9. Education is one of the critical themes in Dickens's work and he was a proponent for reforms to education in the Victorian era. The reverberations of Thomas Gradgrind's "Fact, Fact, Fact!" (Ch. II) from *Hard Times* (1854) provides commentary on the way in which many schools avoided developing students' critical thought and ignored imaginative pedagogy; or encouraging the development and use of fancy altogether.

10. These types of relationships reflect the idea of many Victorians, the known "child-savers" among them, who felt that if assistance and education were provided for the working classes they could better their chances for a more productive life.

Notes to Chapter 2

1. The impact Disney has had upon global understanding of the fairy tale has been widely discussed and is still debated. While some suggest Disney has helped fairy tales retain their significance, others feel the company has done little more than capitalize on their legacy by stripping them of societal and cultural significance. For further discussion see *Breaking the Magic Spell: Radical Theories of Folk & Fairy Tales* (2002) by Jack Zipes; Eleanor Byrne's *Deconstructing Disney* (2000), *From Mouse to Mermaid: The Politics of Film, Gender, and Culture* (2008), edited by Elizabeth Bell, Lynda Haas, and Laura Sells; Douglas Brode's *Multiculturalism and the Mouse: Race and Sex in Disney Entertainment*; and *The Mouse That Roared: Disney and the End of Innocence* (2010) by Henry A. Giroux.

2. Applying the term "original" to traditional fairy tales is problematic, for it connotes ownership, on some level, of a body of stories that should be free from such constraints.

3. More recent work by companies like DreamWorks Animation has helped depict these stories in new ways. Pixar, purchased by Disney in 2006, has created thirteen feature-length films to date and *Brave* (2012) will be its first overt attempt at the fairy tale genre.

4. This was also in response to the growing interest in spiritualism, mesmerism, and occultism in the Victorian period.

5. Fagin is depicted throughout much of *Oliver Twist* as an unearthly creature and is seen by many to be Dickens's indication that he is a/the Devil. This is commonly supported through Cruikshank's illustration "Oliver Introduced to the Respectable Old Gentleman," where Fagin is shown holding a sausage fork with two tongs over an open flame. Dickens further indicates Fagin, who is characteristically labeled as "the Jew" throughout the text, is not part of genteel society because of his underhanded dealings and ability to lead young children down a path of vice.

6. See Demers, Patricia. *From Instruction To Delight: An Anthology of Children's Literature to 1850*. Oxford: Oxford University Press, 2008. Print.

7. Henry Mayhew's (1812–1887) series *London Labour and the London Poor* (1851) is noted as being one of the first sociological examinations of the working classes in Victorian England. He wrote three volumes and cowrote a fourth on the plight of London's downtrodden. Mayhew offers detailed accounts of interviews and settings throughout his series that have proven invaluable to scholars. He also edited *Punch* (1841), which he had cofounded, with Mark Lemon (1809–1870), a friend of Dickens.

8. Penny dreadfuls were cheaply produced thrillers that were printed on cheap paper and available to anyone inexpensively. Some of the most famous stories are *Varney, the Vampire; or the Feast of Blood* (1845–1847) and *Black Bess; or the Knight of the Road* (1866–1868), a series loosely based on the crimes of Dick Turpin. These would often, as with the life of Dick Turpin, romanticize the exploits of villains and criminals.

9. Like penny dreadfuls, *The Newgate Calendar* was widely read. Initially, it chronicled the monthly executions at Newgate Prison and was supposed to deter crime. Writers began to draw upon the stories of the criminals at Newgate through the initial monthly bulletins and created romantic versions of their crimes. *The Newgate Calendar* was popular from the middle of the eighteenth century through the early nineteenth century. Dickens was, like many middle- and upper-class individuals, said to have read them out of the gaze of others. *The Newgate Calendar* and penny dreadfuls were considered base literature and not to be read by members of the middle and upper classes.

10. See Demers, Patricia. *From Instruction To Delight: An Anthology of Children's Literature to 1850.* Oxford: Oxford University Press, 2008. Print.

11. The short vignettes in *Speaking Likenesses* are told orally by an aunt to her charges that reflects the original method of delivery for fairy tales.

Notes to Chapter 3

1. For further discussions on this, see *Rethinking Race, Class, Language, and Gender: A Dialogue with Noam Chomsky and Other Leading Scholars* (2011) by Pierre W. Orelus; Lisa Heldke and Peg O'Connor's edited collection *Oppression, Privilege, and Resistance: Theoretical Perspectives on Racism, Sexism, and Heterosexism* (2003); and Chela Sandoval's *Methodology of the Oppressed* (2000).

2. This is reminiscent of the "othering" nineteenth-century "freak" shows and carnivals contributed to well into the twentieth century. Difference could mark one as a pariah with little value. In this vein, such an individual would be marked as someone who would not contribute to society but would rather only take from it throughout his or her lives.

3. It is important to note that while abuse was rampant throughout all levels of society, there were groups and individuals that did try to combat this during the Victorian period. One such group, the National Society for the Prevention of Cruelty to Children (1884), is still in place today, which speaks to its longevity and mission.

4. The phrase "Fallen Woman" could be applicable to female prostitutes, those who had been sexually abused, actresses, etc. One had "fallen" if one defied societal conventions of womanhood. In essence, such an individual was seen as having "fallen from God's grace" and had lost her innocence, though this need not be sexual in nature.

5. The Board is comprised of well-off locals who serve as the administration for the workhouse. Dickens describes these gentlemen as "well-fed," thus alluding to their greed, which provides a parallel to the starving orphans within their jurisdiction.

6. Designed to help the poor, the English Poor Laws went back to the late sixteenth century. During the nineteenth century, the Poor Law Amendment of 1834/New Poor Law, later reformed in 1845, it was determined that the old Poor Laws were not working and ways were found to try to help the situation. Under the New Poor Law, local parishes would form into Poor Law Unions that would then oversee workhouses in their area. In 1840, it was established that the only poor relief that could be provided was in the workhouse. For further discussion, see Kathleen Jones's *Making of Social Policy in Britain: From the Poor Law to New Labour* (2006) and *Workhouse Children: Infant and Child Paupers under the Worcestershire Poor Law 1780–1871* (1997) by Frank Crompton.

7. For further consideration, see *A History of the Modern Fact: Problems of Knowledge in the Sciences of Wealth and Society* (1998) by Mary Poovey and her work *Genres of the Credit Economy: Meditating Value in Eighteenth- and Nineteenth-Century Britain* (2008).

8. Dickens's family had spent time in the Marshalsea Prison (1824), which was located on the River Thames in the part of London known as Southwark, for outstanding debts. The prison officially closed in 1824.

9. For further discussion on E. Nesbit, see Betty Greenway's *Twice-Told Children's Tales: The Influence of Childhood Reading on Writers for Adults* (2005) and *Childhood in Edwardian Fiction: Worlds Enough and Time* (2009) edited by Adrienne E. Gavin and Andrew F. Humphries.

Notes to Chapter 4

1. With the innovation of family photography during the nineteenth century, mourning albums were widely made. Photos of the deceased would be posed to illustrate the grief of loved ones or to preserve the image of a family member. Some of these photos would depict those who had died as still alive or perhaps reclining as if they were simply sleeping. See *The Victorian Celebration of Death* (2005) by James Stephens Curl, *Death in the Victorian Family* (2000) by Patricia Jalland, and Mary Holtz's *Literary Remains: Representations of Death and Burial in Victorian England* (2010).

2. For further treatment of this subject, see *The Healthy Body and Victorian Culture* (1978) by Bruce Haley.

3. Amber Alerts were begun in 1996. The name derives from missing nine-year-old Amber Hagerman, who had been abducted and murdered near her grandparents' Arlington, Texas, home.

4. See Alastair Pennycook's *Language as Local Practice* (2010).

5. As funerals became more common, people began to spend more money on lavish embellishments to showcase their wealth and social position as well as their taste. Such expenditures could also indicate the social and cultural value of the deceased.

6. Dickens enjoyed such works, as well as fairy tales, and would draw upon such writing in much of his own work. *Oliver Twist* is considered by many to be a Newgate Novel, which were especially popular during the early nineteenth century, though the writing of such novels had begun in the late eighteenth century.

7. See Dickens's essay "Frauds on the Fairies."

8. Though the majority of Dickens's imperfect children could be contemporarily categorized as tweens, this not need be the case for the imperfect child overall.

9. For some funerals, individuals would be paid to serve as mourners and this became a recognized form of employment. Mr. Sowerberry thinks of using Oliver for just such a purpose because of his innocent countenance.

10. *Sing-Song*, aimed at a younger audience, predates *Speaking Likenesses* and illustrates the dark imagery and tone Rossetti was to use in her later work.

Notes to Chapter 5

1. With the increasing popularity of e-readers, there might be more interest in "classic" works. However, it must be recognized that potential readers must possess an e-reader in order to access e-books.

2. This is one of most significant developments for the imperfect child of the post-Victorian period. Victorian imperfect children tend to have solitary journeys and develop their own agency, whereas contemporary imperfect children rely more on the strength of friends/groups in order to solve dilemmas and develop a notion of self.

3. The growing Steampunk movement may also play an important part for developing future reading interest in nineteenth-century literature.

4. Snicket has also published picture books for younger children such as *13 Words* (2010) and *The Composer Is Dead* (2009), though due to their content it might be argued these books are more likely to be read by older child audiences.

Bibliography

Ackroyd, Peter. *Dickens*. New York: HarperCollins. 1990. Print.

Aiken, Joan. *Black Hearts in Battersea*. London: Red Fox, 2004. Print.

———. *Midwinter Nightingale*. New York: Dell Yearling, 2003. Print.

———. *The Wolves of Willoughby Chase*. New York: Dell Yearling, 2001. Print.

Altick, Richard. *Victorian People and Ideas*. New York: W.W. Norton & Company, 1973. Print.

Ardagh, Philip. *Awful End*. London: Faber and Faber Ltd., 2000. Print.

Banerjee, Jacqueline. *Through the Northern Gate: Childhood and Growing Up in British Fiction 1719–1901*. New York: Peter Lang, 1996. Print.

Baum, L. Frank. *The Wonderful Wizard of Oz*. Chicago: George M. Hill Co., 1900. Print.

Boccella, Kathy. "Kids Sweet on Lemony Snicket." *Arizona Daily Star,* 29 May 2002. Web. 14 November 2002. http://whoswhohp.tripod.com/lemony/articles/ads05292002.html.

Bosmajian, Haig A. *The Language of Oppression*. London: UP of America, 1983. Print.

Boston, L. M. *The Children of Green Knowe*. New York: Harcourt Young Classics, 2002. Print.

Briggs, Julia. *A Woman of Passion: The Life of E. Nesbit 1858–1924*. New York: New Amsterdam Books, 1987. Print.

———. "Critical Opinion: Reading Children's Books." *Only Connect: Readings on Children's Literature*. 3rd Ed. Eds. Shelia Egoff, Gordon Stubbs, Ralph Ashley, and Wendy Sutton. New York: Oxford UP, 1996. 18–31. Print.

Butler, Judith. *Gender Trouble: Feminism and the Subversion of Identity*. London: Routledge, 1999. Print.

Carpenter, Humphrey. *Secret Gardens: The Golden Age of Children's Literature from Alice's Adventures in Wonderland to Winnie-the-Pooh*. Boston: Houghton Mifflin Company, 1985. Print.

Carroll, Lewis. *Alice's Adventures in Wonderland* and *Through the Looking-Glass*. Ed. Hugh Haughton. London: Penguin, 1998. Print.

Chapman, Raymond. *Forms of Speech in Victorian Fiction*. London: Longman, 1994. Print.

Christian, Barbara. "Does Theory Play Well in the Classroom?" *Critical Theory and the Teaching of Literature: Politics, Curriculum, Pedagogy*. Eds. James F. Slevin and Art Young. Urbana, IL: NCTE, 1996. 241–57. Print.

Clayton, Jay. *Charles Dickens in Cyberspace: The Afterlife of the Nineteenth Century in Postmodern Culture*. Oxford: Oxford University Press, 2003. Print.

Cockshut, A. O. J. "Faith and Doubt in the Victorian Age." *The Penguin History of Literature: The Victorians*. Ed. Arthur Pollard. London: Penguin, 1993. 25–49. Print.

Connors, Robert J. *Composition-Rhetoric: Backgrounds, Theory, and Pedagogy*. Pittsburgh: Pittsburgh UP, 1997. Print.

Cope, Jim. "Beyond Voices of Readers: Students on School's Effects on Reading." *English Journal* 86.3 (1997): 18–23. Print.

Coveney, Peter. *Poor Monkey: The Child in Literature*. London: Rockliff Publishers 1957. Print.

Cross, Julie. *Humor in Contemporary Junior Literature*. London: Routledge, 2011. Print.

Cruikshank, George. *The Cruikshank Fairy-Book*. New York: Capricorn Books, 1969. Print.

Curtis, Christopher Paul. *The Watsons Go to Birmingham-1963*. New York: Yearling, 1997. Print.

Cutt, Margaret Nancy. *Ministering Angels: A Study of Nineteenth-Century Evangelical Writing for Children*. Broxbourne, UK: Five Owls P, 1979. Print.

Demers, Patricia. "Mrs. Sherwood and Hesba Stretton: The Letter and the Spirit of Evangelical Writing for Children." *Romanticism & Children's Literature in Nineteenth-Century England.* Ed. James Holt McGarvan, Jr., Athens, GA: University of Georgia Press, 1991. 129–49. Print.

———and Gordon Meyers, eds. *From Instruction to Delight: An Anthology of Children's Literature to 1850.* Toronto: Oxford UP, 1982. Print.

Dickens, Charles. *A Child's History of England.* London: Chapman and Hall, 1870. Print.

———."The Magic Fishbone." *Victorian Fairy Tales: The Revolt of the Fairies and Elves.* Ed. Jack Zipes. New York: Routledge, 1987. 89–100. Print.

———. *Bleak House.* Eds. Nicola Bradbury and Terry Eagleton. London: Penguin, 2003. Print.

———. *The Old Curiosity Shop.* Ed. Norman Page. London: Penguin, 2000. Print.

———. *Hard Times.* Ed. Kate Flint. London: Penguin, 1995. Print.

———. *The Speeches of Charles Dickens.* Ed. K. J. Fielding. London: Oxford UP, 1960. Print.

———. "Frauds on the Fairies." *Household Words* 184. 8 (1853): 97–100. Print.

———. *Little Dorrit.* Eds. Stephen Wall and Helen Small. London: Penguin Books, 1998. Print.

———. *The Life of Our Lord.* New York: Simon and Schuster, 1999. Print.

———. "A Christmas Carol." *A Christmas Carol and Other Christmas Writings.* Ed. Michael Slater. London: Penguin, 2003. 27–118. Print.

———. *The Haunted House.* London: Hesperus P, 2003.

———. *Great Expectations.* Eds. David Trotter and Charlotte Mitchell. London: Penguin, 2003. Print.

———. *Oliver Twist.* Eds. Peter Fairclough and Angus Wilson. London: Penguin, 1985. Print.

———. *Dombey and Son.* Ed. Andrew Sanders. London: Penguin, 2002. Print.

Fierman, Daniel. "Lemony Fresh: Daniel Handler's Zesty Kid-Lit Series Has Broken the Spell of the Boy Wizard." *Entertainment Weekly* #655 (2002). 14 November 2002. Web. 12 December 2002. http://whoswhohp.tripod.com/lemony/articles/ewmay2002.html.

Fisher, Berenice Malka. *No Angel in the Classroom: Teaching through Feminist Discourse.* Lanham, MD: Rowman and Littlefield Publishers, Inc., 2001. Print.

Flegel, Monica. *Conceptualizing Cruelty to Children in Nineteenth-Century England: Literature, Representation and the NSPCC.* Surrey, UK: Ashgate, 2009. Print.

Forster, John. *The Life of Charles Dickens.* Vol. 1–3. Boston, Estes and Lauriat P, 1872. Print.

Frost, Ginger S. *Victorian Childhoods.* Westport, CT: Praeger, 2009. Print.

Gallagher, Catherine, and Stephen Greenblatt. *Practicing New Historicism.* Chicago: U of Chicago P, 2000. Print.

Greg, W. R. "Why Are Women Redundant?" *National Review* 14 (April 1862): 434–60. Rpt. in *Uneven Developments: The Ideological Work of Gender in Mid-Victorian England.* Mary Poovey. Chicago: U of Chicago P, 1988. 14. Print.

Haddock, Vicki. "Shivers Under the Covers." *San Francisco Chronicle,* 26 May 2002. Web. 14 November 2002. http://whoswhohp.tripod.com/lemony/articles/sfc05262002.html.

Harvey, John. *Victorian Novelists and Their Illustrators.* New York: New York UP, 1971. Print.

Hawley, John C., S.J. . "The Water-Babies as Catechetical Paradigm." *Children's Literature Association Quarterly* 14.1 (1989): 19–21. Print.

Hazard, Paul. *Books, Children and Men.* Trans. Marguerite Mitchell. Boston: The Horn Book, Inc., 1975. Print.

Higonnet, Anne. *Pictures of Innocence: The History and Crisis of Ideal Childhood.* London: Thames and Hudson Ltd., 1998. Print.

Hodges, Margaret. "Dickens for Children." *The Horn Book Magazine* 58. (Dec. 1982): 626–35. Print.

Horsman, E. A. *Dickens and the Structure of the Novel.* Dunedin, New Zealand: U of Otago P, 1959. Print.

Ingham, Patricia. *Invisible Writing and the Victorian Novel.* Manchester: Manchester UP, 2000. Print.

———. *The Language of Gender and Class: Transformation in the Victorian Novel.* London: Routledge, 1996. Print.

James, W. L. G. "The Portrayal of Death and 'Substance of Life': Aspects of the Modern Reader's Response to 'Victorianism.' " *Reading the Victorian Novel: Detail into Form.* Ed. Ian Gregor. London: Vision Press Ltd., 1980. 226–42. Print.

Jordan, Thomas E. *Victorian Childhood: Themes and Variations.* Albany: State University of New York P, 1987. Print.

Kane, Penny. *Victorian Families in Fact and Fiction.* New York: St. Martin's P, 1995. Print.

Kaplan, Fred. *Dickens: A Biography.* New York: William Morrow & Co., Inc., 1988. Print.

Kaston, Andrea J. "Speaking Pictures: The Fantastic World of Christina Rossetti and Arthur Hughes." *The Journal of Narrative Technique* 28.3. (1998): 305–28. Print.

Keightley, Thomas. *The World Guide to Gnomes, Fairies, Elves, and Other Little People.* 1887. New York: Gramercy Books, 2000. Print.

Kincaid, James R. *Erotic Innocence: The Culture of Child Molesting.* Durham, NC: Duke UP, 1998. Print.

———. *Annoying the Victorians.* New York: Routledge, 1995. Print.

Kingsley, Charles. *The Water-Babies: A Fairy Tale for a Land-Baby.* New York: Macmillan and Company, 1896. Print.

Kirk, Robert. *The Secret Commonwealth: An Essay on the Nature and Actions of the Subterranean (and for the Most Part) Invisible People, Heretofore Going under the Name of Elves, Fauns, and Fairies.* 1815. Intro. Marina Warner. New York: The New York Review of Books, 2007. Print.

Knoepflmacher, U. C. *Ventures into Childland: Victorians, Fairy Tales and Femininity.* Chicago: U of Chicago P, 1998. Print.

Kotzin, Michael. *Dickens & the Fairy Tale.* Bowling Green, KY: Bowling Green Popular Press, 1972. Print.

Lakoff, George, and Mark Turner. *More Than Cool Reason: A Field Guide to Poetic Metaphor.* Chicago: U of Chicago P, 1989. Print.

———and Mark Johnson. *Metaphors We Live By.* Chicago: U of Chicago P, 2003. Print.

Lang, Andrew. *Essays in Little.* New York: Charles Scribner's Sons, 1901. Print.

Langbauer, Laurie. "The Ethics and Practice of Lemony Snicket: Adolescence and Generation X." *PMLA* 122.2 (2007): 502–21. Print.

Larson, Janet. *Dickens and the Broken Scripture.* Athens, GA: U of Georgia P, 1985. Print.

Lesnik-Oberstein, Karin. "Essentials: What Is Children's Literature? What Is Childhood?" *Understanding Children's Literature.* Ed. Peter Hunt. London: Routledge, 1999. 15–29. Print.

———. Introduction. *Children's Literature: New Approaches.* Ed. Karin Lesnik-Oberstein. New York: Palgrave Macmillan, 2004. 1–24. Print.

Lurie, Alison. *Don't Tell the Grown-Ups: Subversive Children's Literature.* Boston: Little, Brown and Co., 1990. Print.

MacDonald, George. *The Princess and Curdie.* London: Puffin, 1994. Print.

———. *The Princess and the Goblin.* London: Puffin, 1996. Print.

———. *At the Back of the North Wind.* New York: Tor, 1998. Print.

———. *At the Back of the North Wind.* London: Everyman's Library, 2001. Print.

———. "The Fantastic Imagination." (1893) *The Complete Fairy Tales.* Ed. U. C. Knoepflmacher. London: Penguin, 1999. Print.

Makman, Lisa Hermine. "Child's Work Is Child's Play: The Value of George MacDonald's Diamond." *Children's Literature Association Quarterly* 24.3 (1999): 119–29. Print.

Manning, Sylvia Bank. *Dickens as Satirist.* New Haven, CT: Yale UP, 1971. Print.

Mayher, John. *Uncommon Sense: Theoretical Practice in Language Education.* Portsmouth, UK: Boynton/Cook, 1990. Print.

Mayhew, Henry. *London Labour and the London Poor: A Cyclopaedia of the Condition and Earnings of Those That Will Work, Those That Cannot Work, and Those That Will Not Work.* Vol. IV. London: Frank Cass & Co. Ltd., 1967. Print.

Munsch, Robert. *Love You Forever.* Ontario, Canada: Firefly Books, 1986. Print.

Nesbit, Edith. *The House of Arden.* London: J. M. Dent & Sons Ltd., 1967. Print.

———. *Harding's Luck.* New York: Books of Wonder, 1998. Print.

———. *The Story of the Treasure Seekers.* London: Puffin Books, 1994. Print.

———. *The Phoenix and the Carpet.* London: Puffin Books, 1994. Print.

———. *Five Children and It.* London: Puffin Books, 1996. Print.

———. *The Story of the Amulet.* London: Puffin Books, 1996. Print.

———. *Wings and the Child or the Building of Magic Cities.* London: Hodder and Stoughton, 1913. Print.

Nikolajeva, Maria. *The Rhetoric of Character in Children's Literature.* Lanham, MD: Scarecrow Press Inc., 2002. Print.

Oliver Twist. Dir. Roman Polanski. Perf. Ben Kingsley, Barney Clark, and Jeremy Swift. Warner Brothers Pictures, 2005. Film.

Ostry, Elaine. *Social Dreaming: Dickens and the Fairy Tale.* New York: Routledge, 2002. Print.

Paul, Lissa. *Reading Otherways.* Portland, ME: Calendar Islands Pub., 1998. Print.

Pierce, Tamora. "Fantasy: Why Kids Read It, Why Kids Need It." *Only Connect: Readings on Children's Literature.* 3rd Ed. Eds. Shelia Egoff, Gordon Stubbs, Ralph Ashley, and Wendy Sutton. New York: Oxford UP, 1996. 179–83. Print.

Poovey, Mary. *Uneven Developments: The Ideological Work of Gender in Mid-Victorian England.* Chicago: U of Chicago P, 1988. Print.

Prickett, Stephen. *Victorian Fantasy.* Waco, TX: Baylor University Press, 2005. Print.

Rosenblatt, Louise. *Literature as Exploration.* New York: MLA, 1996. Print.

Rossetti, Christina G. *Sing-Song: A Nursery Rhyme Book.* London: George Routledge and Sons,1872. Print.

———. *Speaking Likenesses. Forbidden Journeys: Fairy Tales and Fantasies by Victorian Women Writers.* Eds. Nina Auerbach and U. C. Knoepflmacher. Chicago: U of Chicago P, 1991. 325–60. Print.

Rousseau, Jean-Jacques. *Emile or on Education.* Trans. Allan Bloom. New York: Basic Books, Inc., 1972. Print.

Rowling, J. K. *Harry Potter and the Sorcerer's Stone.* New York: Scholastic Press, 1998. Print.

Schor, Hilary M. *Dickens and the Daughter of the House.* Cambridge, UK: Cambridge UP, 1999. Print.

Silver, Carole G. *Strange and Secret Peoples: Fairies and Victorian Consciousness.* New York: Oxford UP, 1999. Print.

Snicket, Lemony. *A Series of Unfortunate Events; Book the First: The Bad Beginning.* New York: HarperCollins, 1999. Print.

———. *A Series of Unfortunate Events; Book the Thirteenth: The End.* New York: HarperCollins, 2006. Print.

—-. *The Basic Eight.* New York: Thomas Dunne Books, 1998. Print.

—-. *Why We Broke Up.* New York: Little, Brown Books for Young Readers, 2011. Print.

—-. *Watch Your Mouth: A Novel.* New York: Thomas Dunne Books, 2000. Print.

Sørensen, Knud. *Charles Dickens: Linguistic Innovator.* Arkona: Aarhus, 1985. Print.

Spellmeyer, Kurt. *Arts of Living: Reinventing the Humanities for the Twenty-First Century.* Albany: State University of New York Press, 2003. Print.

Springer, Nancy. Foreword. *At the Back of the North Wind.* By George MacDonald. New York: Tor, 1998. ix–xii. Print.

Stone, Harry. *Dickens and the Invisible World: Fairy Tales, Fantasy, and Novel Making.* London: Indiana UP, 1979. Print.

Stretton, Hesba. *Jessica's First Prayer and Jessica's Mother.* Philadelphia: Henry Altemus, 1897. Print.

Sucksmith, Harvey Peter. *The Narrative Art of Charles Dickens: The Rhetoric Sympathy and Irony of His Novels.* London: Oxford UP, 1970. Print.

Thiel, Elizabeth. *The Fantasy of Family: Nineteenth-Century Children's Literature and the Myth of the Domestic Ideal.* London: Routledge, 2008. Print.

Trilling, Lionel. "Little Dorrit." *Discussions of Charles Dickens.* Ed. William Ross Clark. Boston: D.C. Heath and Company, 1961. 93–100. Print.

Turner, Frank Miller. *Between Science and Religion: The Reaction to Scientific Naturalism in Late Victorian England.* London: Yale UP, 1974. Print.

Walder, Dennis. *Dickens and Religion.* London: Routledge, 2007. Print.

Walsh, Susan A. "Darling Mothers, Devilish Queens: The Divided Woman in Victorian Fantasy." *The Victorian Newsletter* 72 (1987): 32–36. Print.

Williams, Raymond. *The Country and The City.* New York: Oxford UP, 1973. Print.

———. *Writing in Society.* London: Verso, 1983. Print.

———. *Culture & Society: 1780–1950.* New York: Columbia UP, 1983. Print.

Wood, Naomi. "A (Sea) Green Victorian: Charles Kingsley and *The Water-Babies.*" *The Lion and The Unicorn* 19.2 (1995): 233–52. Print.

Wullschäger, Jackie. *Inventing Wonderland: The Lives and Fantasies of Lewis Carroll, Edward Lear, J. M. Barrie, Kenneth Grahme and A. A. Milne.* New York: The Free Press, 1995. Print.

Zelizer, Viviana. *Pricing the Priceless Child: The Changing Social Value of Children.* Princeton, NJ: Princeton UP, 1994. Print.

Zipes, Jack. *Sticks and Stones: The Troublesome Success of Children's Literature from Slovenly Peter to Harry Potter.* New York: Routledge, 2001. Print.

Index

51; Little Dorrit as heroine, 68, 76, 78, 79–81; Little Dorrit and identity, 77, 79–81; Little Dorrit and illness, 112–113; Little Dorrit and naming, 75, 77, 79–80; Little Dorrit's roles, 80; William Dorrit and education, 75; William Dorrit and neglect, 78; William Dorrit and speech, 76
Little Red Riding Hood, 27, 59
Little Women, 15–16
Locke, John, 10
Love You Forever (Munsch), 126
Lowry, Lois, 117
Lurie, Alison, 126

M

MacDonald, George, 1, 22–23, 27, 53, 81, 113, 131; and audience, 2, 8, 15, 131; and the imperfect child, 24–25, 34, 55, 82, 113; and "other," 6; and naming, 7; *At the Back of The North Wind*, 3, 22–25, 124, 135; Diamond and death, 81, 113; Diamond and education, 22, 82; Diamond's character, 22, 53–54; Diamond's death, 113; Diamond as "God's Baby," 23; Diamond's economic value, 54, 81–82; Diamond and the fairy world 54; and the fairy tale, 53; Diamond and illness, 113; Diamond as the imperfect child, 54, 81, 113–114; Diamond's journey, 53; Diamond as the Romantic child, 113; Diamond as the sentimental child, 81; Diamond's speech, 81; Nanny as a crossing sweep, 113; Nanny and education, 22; "The Fantastic Imagination," 54; *The Princess and Curdie*, 3, 53, 114, 135; fantasy world in, 82; and Victorian marriage plot, 54; Curdie's character, 56; Curdie as the imperfect child, 55–56; Princess Irene as the imperfect child, 55; *The Princess and the Goblin*, 3, 53, 114, 135; fantasy world in, 82; gender roles, 82–83; socioeconomic status, 55; and Victorian marriage plot; 54; Curdie's character, 55; Curdie as the imperfect child, 55; Princess Irene as the imperfect child, 55; Princess Irene's half-existence, 55
Magic Fishbone, The (Dickens), 44

Makman, Lisa Hermine, 53–54, 113
Manning, Sylvia Bank, 76, 79
Manson, Charles, 43
Marr, Melissa, 32
Mary Poppins (Travers), 65
Mayher, John, 15–16
Mayhew, Henry, 42–44, 143n7
McCann, Jim, 14
Mickey's Christmas Carol (Disney), 14, 17
Midsummer Night's Dream, A (Shakespeare) 5, 56
Midwinter Nightingale, (Aiken) 125
monsters, 6, 48, 59; and grotesque, 6, 50
Munsch, Robert, 126; *Love You Forever*, 126

N

naming, 6–7, 64–65, 84; in *Oliver Twist*, 66
Nesbit, E., 1, 27, 85, 109; and audience, 2, 8, 15, 86; on education, 28; and the imperfect child, 34; and "other," 6; and marketing, 28; and naming, 7; *Harding's Luck*, 3, 14, 27–28, 57, 135; and child value, 85; and the imperfect child character, 60, 85; Dickie and crippling, 63, 109; *The House of Arden*, 3, 14, 27, 57, 124, 135; and child value, 85; and education, 27–28; and fairy tales, 60; imperfect child characters, 60, 85; Dickie and crippling, 63, 109; Elfrida's name, 60–62; *Wings and the Child or the Building of Magic Cities*, 27
Newgate Calendar, The, 42–43, 102, 144n9, 145n6
Nikolajeva, Maria, 82–84

O

occultism, 5
Old Curiosity Shop, The (Dickens), 3, 16, 44, 92, 102, 124, 130, 139; and disease, 109; and death, 109; and fairy tales, 44; and fairy worlds, 39, 44–45; and Mary Hogarth, 98, 109; Kit as heroic prince, 44; and imperfect child, 45; Little Nell and character, 44, 48, 102; Little Nell and death, 57, 74, 91, 103–109, 113, 116, 134; Little Nell and education, 21; Little Nell as heroine, 68, 102; Little Nell as the imperfect child, 103–104, 107; Little Nell and innocence, 105;